Information Literacy and Social Justice

Radical Professional Praxis

Information Literacy and Social Justice

Radical Professional Praxis

Lua Gregory and Shana Higgins, Editors

Foreword by Toni Samek

Library Juice Press
Sacramento, CA

Published by Library Juice Press

PO Box 188784

Sacramento, CA 95818

http://libraryjuicepress.com/

Layout by Christopher Hagen.

This book is printed on acid-free, sustainably-sourced paper.

Library of Congress Cataloging-in-Publication Data

Information literacy and social justice : radical professional praxis / Lua Gregory and Shana Higgins, editors ; foreword by Toni Samek.
    pages cm
Includes bibliographical references and index.
    Summary: "Discusses information literacy and its social justice aspects, through a selection of chapters addressing the values of intellectual freedom, social responsibility, and democracy in relation to the sociopolitical context of library work"--Provided by publisher.
    ISBN 978-1-936117-56-7
1. Information literacy--Social aspects. 2. Information literacy--Political aspects. 3. Information literacy--Study and teaching. 4. Social justice. 5. Library science--Social aspects. 6. Library science--Political aspects. 7. Libraries and society. 8. Intellectual freedom. I. Gregory, Lua. II. Higgins, Shana.
    ZA3075.I5328 2013
    028.7--dc23
                            2013014281

Contents

Community Engagement as Social Change

Foreword

This unmatched monograph about information literacy and social justice, with its activist imperative, is inspired by two world-class educators: Paulo Freire and Henry Giroux. That fact in itself is a recipe for admirable intention. Most importantly, though, the editors deliver an excellent book. This is a victory volume, a text I have been waiting to read for a very long time. In other words, *Information Literacy and Social Justice: Radical Professional Praxis* is long overdue. Co-editors and practitioners Lua Gregory and Shana Higgins are most modest in their introduction. Because they have actually produced a genius four-part orientation to how information literacy that significantly improves upon the way it has been defined and even confined by the many normative information literacy model makers, functionalists and minders to date.

Our deliberate instruction in this work comes in four challenging lessons: (1) Information Literacy in the Service of Neoliberalism, (2) Challenging Authority, (3) Liberatory Praxis, and (4) Community Engagement. These are cumbersome and contested topics. However, Gregory and Higgins successfully attracted and recruited a stellar set of contributors to skillfully address them – not an easy task. We should not underestimate the collective will of projects like this one. Each contributor should be thanked for the risk they take on the page. I have, on a number of occasions, said publicly that information literacy is far too often realized in service of the state. This is rarely a popular observation. (And so I have been told.) But for almost twenty full years I have worked under the protection of my right and responsibility of academic freedom. The same cannot be said for all of the seventeen chapter contributors to this work. I admire them for their conviction. They also stand for compassion. And they are notably serious students of their own craft. If you look closely at their references (whom they cite), another level of understanding unfolds. These writers are readers and they have read well. The influential authors and activists cited are some of the very best commentators on information society today, including Noam Chomsky, James Elmborg, Kathleen de la Peña McCook, Christine Pawley, Peter McLaren, and Sam Trosow.

This book is a new staple for people who are interested in persuasion and consensus building with respect to literacy in all of its forms and its relationships with freedom, access, capital, and power. In an era of austerity, this is ever more important to unpack, tell and retell. Keywords used in the chapter titles are just one indicator of what is addressed in this book. For example: violence, neoliberal library, citizenship, crusade, tyranny, liberatory, hip-hop, and teflon. This is not your average information literacy text; thank goodness for that. It is high time we acknowledged openly how information literacy has been co-opted by corporatist efficiencies and risk management. What are we going to do about it? Look to this book for starters.

Information Literacy and Social Justice opens with an introduction that grounds us in core library values, such as intellectual freedom and lifelong learning, questions the possibility of library neutrality, and argues for an activist library labor orientation blended with social justice. In the context of this project, this simply means information literacy librarians' conscious acknowledgment of the human condition (which inherently brings with it tensions between individual and community values) in their work, both inside and outside of the classroom. As Henry Giroux would phrase it, we are asked to connect classroom to public life. This is a simple condition, but one not often found. Indeed, the editors pose a gut question: how does the "concept of information literacy and the work of instruction librarians come to be treated as ahistorical, as well as atomistic and mechanistic?" It is a good question, indeed one worth editing a book about. In so doing Gregory and Higgins intentionally introduce a new generation of critical literacy intellectuals who serve up a winning critique of the traditional "static construction of information literacy." As the editors explain, the chapters serve to illustrate how "critical information literacy differs from standard definitions of information literacy (ex: the ability to find, use, and analyze information) in that it takes into consideration the social, political, economic and corporate systems that have power and influence over information production, dissemination, access, and consumption."

The first chapter, The Violence of Information Literacy: Neoliberalism and the Human as Capital, by Nathaniel F. Enright, clearly mints the intellectual rigor found in this book. Those authors that follow uphold the gold standard. This work immerses the reader in ideology and theory and then brings it to street-level literacy application, including struggle. None of the authors let librarians off the hook, as they force us into the circle of complicity. But they also show us how to re-open this closed circuit and re-route our energies into resistance to complacency, as well as how to work alongside our fellow lifelong learners, not teach to them or for them. We are also guided to think about the importance of the broader education that sits underneath information literacy instruction. We can imagine the long-term value to the citizen that goes hand-in-hand with the short-term lesson in library language. This uncovers veiled vocation as education; it adds culture and context to the concrete.

The co-editors suggest the following four purposes of this book: to apply critical librarianship to classroom practice "in a concerted effort to further critical information literacy praxis," to provide concrete examples of our labor as social justice work, to expose "library/librarian neutrality in relation to the context of information production, dissemination, and manipulation and to recognize the social, economic, political and corporate forces and ideologies at play in information flows," and to recognize our *being* in our *doing*. The latter purpose is the meta message that has the potential to impact the reader at the personal-professional level. If we read this book flatly, we won't see how we are in it, as the "information literate," constructed neoliberal subject that Enright describes. If we read this book inside out and upside down, we can see how carefully it crafts a picture of the true price of that loss. Those who engage with this text won't get smarter (most of us don't). But they just might see information literacy more clearly for what it has been, what it has the potential to be, and how and what they, as people, might be while performing it. Perhaps the next project for Gregory and Higgins to tackle, in a critical series, is decision theory. Acknowledging the place and influence of certainty and uncertainty in information work is a connecting piece in the information society puzzle.

Toni Samek
Professor, School of Library and Information Studies, University of Alberta
St. Albert, Alberta, Canada
1 December 2012

Acknowledgments

Many hands helped to shape this book. We would like to thank those who made this project possible. You would not be holding this book in your hands today if it weren't for the contributors to this book, who worked hard to write, revise, and generate new ways of thinking about information literacy and social justice in their chapters. It has been a pleasure working with all of them this year, and without them, this project would still be a dream. We are indebted to Toni Samek, both for inspiring us and for her foreword to this volume. Additionally, we must thank Rory Litwin for accepting this project for Library Juice Press, a step that allowed many ideas to come to fruition. Alison Lewis deserves praise for her guidance through the somewhat hectic editing process. We are grateful for the interactions with Joanne Doucette, Sarah McCord, and Gabriela Sonntag, whose willingness to listen and valuable insights were refreshing when alternative perspectives were needed. And finally, we must thank our students, for sharing who they are and engaging in the process of learning and teaching, teaching and learning.

Lua wishes to acknowledge her colleagues at the University of Redlands and at the Massachusetts College of Pharmacy and Health Sciences whose support and encouragement made the adventure of this project so enjoyable. I would also like to recognize the support of friends and family over this busy year. My father Arthur, mother Linda, and brothers Tim, Braden and Ian were willing to endure my single-mindedness. In addition, Salem has earned an acknowledgement for her refreshing mischievousness. And last, Craig Carpenter, I am grateful for you, for your appreciation of critical thinking, and for your talent in locating obscure sci-fi films when I needed a break.

Shana wishes to express gratitude to her colleagues and administrators at the University of Redlands for support, encouragement, and opportunity that made this project possible. I owe a debt to the many librarians of Southern California Instruction Librarians (SCIL) Interest Group for informing and shaping my practice over the past six years, and to Jennifer Nutefall for her much needed mentorship over the past year. I'm not sure that my parents understand what it is that I do, but I thank them for their encouragement and love. And finally, I am most grateful to my best friend and partner, Willem Pennings, for his constant support and cheerleading, for making recess mandatory, and for his adventurous spirit.

"...one of the fundamental tasks of educators is to make sure that the future points the way to a more socially just world, a world in which critique and possibility–in conjunction with the values of reason, freedom, and equality–function to alter the grounds upon which life is lived."

Henry Giroux (2010) on the critical pedagogy of Paulo Freire in *Chronicle of Higher Education*, volume 57, issue 9.

Introduction

Lua Gregory and Shana Higgins

> Imagine a world where everything you see, hear, and touch has passed
> through a filter. Music, literature, art, motion pictures, and news media
> have all been stripped of ideas, images, or words that are objectionable
> or offensive to the status quo. This is your world.

Thus begins the course description for "Bleep! Censorship and Free
Speech in the U. S.," a first-year seminar that we, Lua Gregory and Shana
Higgins, taught in the Fall Term of 2010 at the University of Redlands. Our
goal was for students in our class to begin to reflect on their interaction with
various modes of communication in daily life, on their understanding of
the ideals of democracy and "freedom" circulating in the culture in which
they are immersed, and on the ways in which the limits of free speech are
reached in the name of national security, protection of youth, trademark,
profanity, corporate sovereignty, and market value. Our traditional-age
students (18-19 years of age) were experiencing the freedom of exceeding
the boundaries of their parents' worldviews, yet were surprisingly adherent
and uncritical of mainstream cultural norms in relation to information
and media consumption and production.

In preparation for, in the teaching of, and in reflecting afterwards on
this freshman seminar we found ourselves thinking more deeply about
the values of librarianship as developed in the *Intellectual Freedom Manual*
(2008) and the *ALA Policy Manual* as well as in the goals and outcomes of
ACRL's *Information Literacy Competency Standards for Higher Education* (2000).
We found correspondence with our own understandings of the theory and
practice of critical librarianship in the work of Sanford Berman, James
Elmborg, Barbara Fister, Heidi L.M. Jacobs, Cushla Kapitzke and Toni
Samek among others. Berman and Samek examine concepts of neutrality,
intellectual freedom, and social responsibility as articulated and practiced
by librarians and by our flagship professional organization the American
Library Association. Like them we consider librarianship a fundamentally
activist profession, thus rendering the notion of *neutrality* an "impossible

construct" (Samek, 2001, p. 1). Indeed, we think the work of Berman, Samek, and others before them have led to a generation—not a generation based on age—of librarians that see their profession as not neutral but as politically charged and activist in nature.

The Values of Librarianship

For Michael Gorman (2005) most of our professional "values and ideas are democratic values and ideas—intellectual freedom, the common good, service to all, the transmission of the human record to future generations, free access to knowledge and information non-discrimination" (p. 61). We believe that "[t]hose aspects of librarianship that commit librarians to serve democracy and human rights are what make the discipline essential to the survival of the human spirit. We assert that this commitment does not permit the librarian to be neutral" (McCook & Phenix, 2008, p. 25). Therefore, as Samek (2007) suggests, "core library values such as intellectual freedom need to be continuously revisited by individuals, institutions, and societies as a whole" (p. 10). Likewise, as Jacobs and Berg (2011) assert, "librarians can use the ALA Core Values as a way to reengage with the possibilities and potentials within information literacy to meet larger social goals" (p. 385) and that informed critical information literacy in practice exists, "especially between the connections with democracy, diversity, education, lifelong learning, the public good, and social responsibility" (p. 391). These voices help to illustrate the nature of the conversations we had in conceiving this project: the values of our professional organizations articulate an activist perspective inclined toward social justice. How then has the concept of information literacy and the work of instruction librarians come to be treated as ahistorical, as well as atomistic and mechanistic?

Critical Information Literacy

It is exactly this static construction of information literacy that a new generation of librarians from whom we've found inspiration specifically speak. They have adopted various critical theories to create a nascent practice of *critical information literacy*. Critical information literacy draws from *critical theory*, which "refers to a specific scholarly approach that explores the historical, cultural, and ideological lines of authority that underlie social conditions" (Sensoy & DiAngelo, p. 3, 2012) and also developing from *critical literacy*, the four dimensions of which include, "(1) disrupting the commonplace, (2) interrogating multiple viewpoints, (3) focusing on sociopolitical issues, and (4) taking action and promoting social justice" (Lewison, Flint, & Sluys, p. 382, 2002). Therefore, when we apply critical theoretical approaches to our work as librarians, we consider the historical, cultural, social, economic, political and other forces that affect information[1] so that we may explore ways to critique our understandings of reality and disrupt the commonplace; interrogate multiple viewpoints to identify the status quo and marginalized voices; and focus on sociopolitical issues that shape and suppress information in order to take informed action in the world. Furthermore when we apply critical theory to our teaching practices, we are working to create a critical pedagogy that "helps the learner become aware of the forces that have hitherto ruled their lives and especially shaped their consciousness" (Aronowitz, p. ix, 2009).

According to Henry Giroux (2009), critical pedagogy

> works to shift how students think about the issues affecting their lives and the world at large, potentially energizing them to seize such moments as possibilities for acting on the world and for engaging it as a matter of politics, power, and social justice. The appeal here is not merely to an individuals' sense of ethics; it is also an appeal to collectively address material inequities involving resources, accessibility, and power in both education and the broader global society while viewing the struggle for power as generative and crucial to any viable notion of individual and social agency. (p. 14)

Many educators have built their critical pedagogical perspectives on the theory of Paulo Freire. His *Pedagogy of the Oppressed* pivots on a com-

---

1 We do not wish to reify "information" and yet we cannot help doing so. For a recent and very thoughtful study of the manner in which "information" has been and is constructed read Ronald Day's *The Modern Invention of Information: Discourse, History, and Power* (2008).

munal praxis, in which reflection coupled with action (theory + practice) transforms the world. Definitions and descriptions of the practice of critical information literacy echo Freire's theoretical perspective of teaching and learning in *Pedagogy of the Oppressed*: teaching and learning require reflexivity, a shared experience such that we learn from and with each other, and a focus on process toward transformative understanding. Furthermore, Freire urged for a problem-posing pedagogy as an alternative to the "banking" model of education and its resultant student passivity in order to lead learners and teachers to consciousness-raising (transformative) experiences. For Freire the content, or program, of instruction must be developed in dialog with "the people," rather than be predetermined.

Critical information literacy differs from standard definitions of information literacy (ex: the ability to find, use, and analyze information) in that it takes into consideration the social, political, economic, and corporate systems that have power and influence over information production, dissemination, access, and consumption. The authors in this edited volume understand that when we limit the potential of information "to outcomes and standards, we run the risk of minimizing the complex situatedness of information literacy and diminishing – if not negating – its inherent political nature" (Jacobs, 2008, p. 258). Thus, critical information literacy embraces analyses of "sociopolitical ideologies embedded within economies of ideas and information" (Kapitzke, 2003, p. 7), a "collective questioning of how information is constructed, disseminated, and understood" (Cope, 2010, p. 25), and involves the development of a critical consciousness about information through which learning "becomes the essentially humanistic process of engaging and solving significant problems in the world" (Elmborg, 2006, p. 198).

Why Social Justice?

Social justice is a contested term, but in its simplest sense, it "is commonly understood as the principles of "fairness" and "equality" for all people and respect for their basic human rights" (Sensoy & DiAngelo, 2012, p. xvii). Social justice in political and economic thought is often aligned with "distributive justice" as in the "equal distribution of basic liberties and political rights" (Merkel, 2009, p. 42). However one of the fundamental areas of contestation is that "the demands of social justice might require that people are treated differently according to the diversity of human needs and capabilities" (Cramme & Diamond, 2009, p. 8). Equality may not be achieved merely by equal distribution. The concept of social justice in educational scholarship centers on race, class, and gender. Sonia Nieto (2010) argues "that it is impossible to be a teacher without taking into account such issues as gender, sexuality, language, race, social class, ability, and other individual and group differences" (p. x). When we consider these definitions of social justice in light of core principles and inherent democratizing values of librarianship and the aims of information literacy, we see the undercurrents of social justice that lie at the heart of the library profession.

Recent scholarship reflects a search for social justice in information literacy, for example the United Nations Educational, Scientific and Cultural Organization (UNESCO) and the International Federation of Library Associations and Institutions' (IFLA) "Beacons of the Information Society: The Alexandria Proclamation on Information Literacy and Lifelong Learning," as Heidi L. M. Jacobs (2008) limns, "underscores information literacy's connections with broader social justice ideas and initiatives" (p. 258). The Alexandria Proclamation claims that information literacy "lies at the core of lifelong learning," and it "enables individuals, communities and nations to attain their goals and to take advantage of emerging opportunities in the evolving global environment for shared benefit...to meet technological, economic and social challenges, to redress disadvantage and to advance the well being of all" (UNESCO & IFLA, 2005). More recently IFLA (2011) endorsed a statement in which they declared media and information literacy

> a basic human right in an increasingly digital, interdependent, and global world, and promotes greater social inclusion. It can bridge the gap between the information rich and the information poor. Media and Information Literacy empowers and endows individuals with knowledge of the functions of the media and information systems and the conditions under which these functions are performed.

Indeed the impulse to connect social justice with librarianship isn't a new phenomenon. A concern for the human condition and human rights has been an international movement for information and library workers for decades. Toni Samek has defined this progressive movement as *critical librarianship* (Robertson, 2007).

Social justice is also the aim of critical pedagogy, including Freire's conception of critical pedagogy. The chapters in this book explore what social justice means to information literacy and in particular, to librarians experimenting with critical information literacy inside and outside of the classroom. How can we as a profession engage students with the material inequities in information access, production, and dissemination? How do librarians present power structures within information economies and the effect this has on an informed citizenry and democracy? How might we highlight how information has shaped our consciousness, and on the other hand, how information is constructed by societal, cultural, political and other forces? What can we do to empower students to raise their critical consciousness of information and how can we inspire them to apply this outlook for fairness and the equality of all people? That we are concerned with these kinds of questions in our research and practice means that critical information literacy instruction begins to look very much like social justice pedagogy, despite its narrower focus. In Chapman and Hobbel's (2010) *Social Justice Pedagogy Across the Curriculum: The Practice of Freedom* they reference the work of Nieto and Bode (2008) who outline four outcomes of social justice education, which we have borrowed to shape this edited volume. Social justice education should:

> 1. Challenge, confront, and disrupt 'misconceptions, untruths, and stereotypes that lead to structural inequality and discrimination based on race, social class, gender, and other social and human differences,'
> 2. Provide 'all students with the resources necessary to learn to their full potential,'
> 3. Draw on the 'talents and strengths that students bring to their education,' and
> 4. Create a 'learning environment that promotes critical thinking and supports agency for social change' (p. 2)

This edited volume is divided into several sections that reflect some of the shared goals of critical information literacy and social justice pedagogy. Many of the contributions consider various democratizing values of the profession such as intellectual freedom, information access, and democracy, issues clearly linked to social justice initiatives.

In the first section, *Information Literacy in the Service of Neoliberalism*, authors discuss dominant political and economic ideologies that frame our personal, social, and work life. By confronting our own complicity in the workings of neoliberalism, the contributions in this section will inspire reflexivity in relation to our information literacy instruction and programs. Nathaniel Enright unpacks the discourse of information literacy to reveal the "information literate" as the ideal type of neoliberal subject, and implores us, as educators and librarians, to study the complex social and political construction of information literacy; otherwise we have no hope of aligning such a notion with social justice. Likewise Maura Seale argues that the current framing of information literacy reinforces and reproduces a neoliberal ideology that is fundamentally anti-democratic and antithetical to social justice imperatives; critical theory may be the intervention to find an authentically critical information literacy practice. And Jeff Lilburn illustrates the intertwined discourses on information literacy, 21st Century or global citizenship, and the neoliberal subject through the lens of the fictional work of Kazuo Ishiguro's *Never Let Me Go*.

The second section, *Challenging Authority*, offers a space for contributors to confront "misconceptions, untruths, and stereotypes" (Nieto & Bode, 2008, p. 11) apparent in the teaching of authoritative information sources in the classroom and the resultant inequitable consumption and/or discrimination of marginalized voices and information products. Andrew Battista suggests that engaging students in the act of curation via social media platforms, and enabling the instruction librarian to destabilize reified notions of academic authority, encourages the acquisition of critical evaluative habits of mind. Carrie Donovan and Sara O'Donnell ask us to empower students to embody scholarship as equal and active participants in ongoing conversations in their disciplines, thus challenging instruction librarians to subvert the status quo in relation to teaching scholarly communication practices and processes. And Andrea Baer presents the burgeoning field of Digital Humanities as a space in which to engage students in debates regarding current, and perhaps reified scholarly practices.

In section three, *Liberatory Praxis: Students and Teachers as Co-Learners* contributors draw on the "talents and strengths that students bring" (Nieto & Bode, 2008, p. 12) to the classroom in order to collectively dialogue on transforming the social order, or the status quo. Anne Leonard and Maura Smale describe a semester-long course in which they engage in what Elmborg called "a critical practice of librarianship" (Elmborg, 2006, p. 198) by examining and interrogating the lifecycle of information alongside their students. By drawing out the conceptual connections between hip-hop and information literacy skills, Dave Ellenwood engages students in critical dialogs centered on cultural knowledge, social justice and critical perspectives. Lua Gregory and Shana Higgins discuss how capitalism and neoliberalism reinforce inequalities and therefore endanger student welfare and forestall liberation. Assignments and dialogue in their first year seminar encouraged students to identify power structures in the U.S. media in order to develop awareness and critical consciousness in relation to information production and dissemination. Comparing critical information literacy to legal information literacy, Yasmin Sokkar Harker suggests the former will inform the latter in order for law students to begin to understand information as a social construct and to examine power structures that shape the creation, organization and dissemination of legal information. Demonstrating the use of problem-posing pedagogy to expand students' understanding of the role librarians play in social justice and democratizing efforts Amanda Swygart-Hobaugh provides an informative content analysis of students' usage of critical theories to analyze intellectual freedom issues in their lives.

The last section, *Community Engagement as Radical Professional Praxis* offers examples of critical information literacy beyond the classroom. Christopher Sweet offers a model for linking information literacy to service learning courses, highlighting how such collaborations can lead to students becoming "agents of change" to address authentic social justice issues in their local communities. And finally, Patti Ryan and Lisa Sloniowski describe library outreach and programming that make critical sociopolitical interventions and act as radical pedagogical praxis, prioritizing democratic values and social responsibility, while providing a template for academic libraries as members of their communities.

We are in intellectual debt to scholars who have created a solid foundation on which discussions on critical pedagogies and critical information literacy may flourish. For example, James Elmborg, Paulo Freire, Henry Giroux, Heidi L. M. Jacobs, Peter McLaren, Toni Samek, Ira Shor and the editors and authors, Maria T. Accardi, Emily Drabinski, and Alana Kumbier, whose remarkable book, *Critical Library Instruction: Theories and Methods* (2010), has ignited a wider dialogue of critical information literacy in the profession. The contributions in this current volume continue discussions on critical information literacy by considering elements of librarianship that support social justice initiatives within the framework of library values and the landscape of information flows. We hope this book is a step toward "building librarianship in a solid foundation of human dignity, freedom, social justice and cultural diversity" by grappling with "social, political, cultural, legal, economic, technological and ideological issues" (Samek, 2007, p. 43) and by providing a space for librarians to "talk about actual classroom practices and activities" for which others can engage and reflect upon (Jacobs, 2008, p. 260) in order to "find ways of being in the world and in our profession that are more rewarding and more humanizing" (Elmborg, 2012, p. 23).

As with any book, there are limitations to what can be achieved. Important perspectives are missing from this volume focused primarily on higher education. The intersection of information literacy and social justice in the K-12 setting and from the public library viewpoint would provide a broader dialog. We see this book as part of a discussion for librarians that is barely beginning, and look forward to future reflections on social justice, critical information literacy, and the ways in which teaching is a political act that can be a catalyst for progressive change in our communities and the world.

The purpose of this book, then, is:

To apply the lenses of democracy, social justice, and human rights discussed in library literature and policies to classroom practice in a concerted effort to further critical information literacy praxis.

To provide practical examples of librarians currently teaching the context of information production, dissemination, and consumption from a democratizing and social justice stance.

To dismantle the concept of library/librarian neutrality in relation to the context of information production, dissemination, and manipulation and to recognize the social, economic, political and corporate forces and ideologies at play in information flows.

To "find ways of being in the world and in our profession that are more rewarding and more humanizing" (Elmborg, 2012, p. 23).

References

Aronowitz, S. (2009). Foreword. In S. L. Macrine (Ed.), *Critical pedagogy in uncertain times: Hopes and possibilities* (pp. ix-xi). New York, NY: Palgrave Macmillan.

Chapman, T. K., & Hobbel, N. (2010). Introduction. In T. K. Chapman & N. Hobbel (Eds.), *Social justice pedagogy across the curriculum: The practice of freedom* (pp. 1-6). New York: Routledge.

Cope, J. (2010). Information literacy and social power. In E. Drabinski, A. Kumbier & M. Accardi (Eds.), *Critical library instruction: Theories and methods* (pp. 13-28). Duluth, Minnesota: Library Juice Press.

Cramme, O., & Diamond, P. (2009). Rethinking social justice in the global age. In O. Cramme & P. Diamond (Eds.), *Social justice in the global age* (pp. 3-20). Cambridge: Polity Press.

Day, R. E. (2008). *The modern invention of information: Discourse, history, and power.* Carbondale: Southern Illinois University Press

Darder, A., Baltodano, M., & Torres, R. D. (2003). *The critical pedagogy reader.* New York: Routledge.

Elmborg, J. (2006). Critical information literacy: Implications for instructional practice. *The Journal of Academic Librarianship*, 32(2), 192-199.

Elmborg, J. (2012). Critical information literacy: Definitions and challenges. In C. W. Wilkinson & C. Bruch (Eds.), *Transforming information literacy programs: Intersecting frontiers of self, library culture, and campus community* (pp. 75-95). Chicago, IL: Association of College and Research Libraries.

Freire, P. (2000). *Pedagogy of the oppressed* (30th ed.). New York: Continuum.

Giroux, H. (2009). The attack on higher education and the necessity of critical pedagogy. In S. L. Macrine (Ed.), *Critical pedagogy in uncertain times: Hopes and possibilities* (pp. 11-26). New York, NY: Palgrave Macmillan.

Giroux, H. (2010, October 17). Lessons from Paulo Freire. *The Chronicle Review.*

Retrieved from http://chronicle.com/article/Lessons-From-Paulo-Freire/124910/

Gorman, M. (2005). Library values in a changing world. In N. Horrocks (Ed.), *Perspectives, insights and priorities: 17 leaders speak freely of librarianship* (pp. 55-62). Lanham, Maryland: The Scarecrow Press.

Jacobs, H. L. M. (2008). Information literacy and reflective pedagogical praxis. *The Journal of Academic Librarianship, 34*(3), 256-262.

Jacobs, H. L. M., & Berg, S. (2011). Reconnecting information literacy policy with the core values of librarianship. *Library Trends 60*(2), 383-394.

Kapitzke, C. (2003). Information literacy: A review and poststructural critique. *Australian Journal of Language and Literacy, 26*(1), 53-66.

International Federation of Library Associations and Institutions (IFLA). (2011). IFLA mediaand information literacy recommendations. Retrieved from http://www.ifla.org/en/publications/ifla-media-and-information-literacy-recommendations

Lewison, M., Flint, A. S., & Sluys, K. V. (2002). Taking on critical literacy: The journey of newcomers and novices. *Language Arts, 79*(5), 382-392.

McCook, K. de la Peña, & Phenix, K. J., (2008). Human rights, democracy, and librarians. In K. Haycock & B. E. Sheldon (Eds.), *The portable MLIS: Insights from the experts* (pp. 23-34). Westport, CT: Libraries Unlimited.

McLaren, P., & Jaramillo, N. E. (2009). Critical pedagogy, Latino/a education, and the politics of class struggle. In S. L. Macrine (Ed.), *Critical pedagogy in uncertain times: Hopes and possibilities* (pp. 55-78). New York, NY: Palgrave Macmillan.

Merkel, W. (2009). Towards a renewed concept of social justice. In O. Cramme & P. Diamond (Eds.), *Social justice in the global age* (pp. 38-58). Cambridge: Polity Press.

Nieto, S. (2010). Foreword. In T. K. Chapman & N. Hobbel (Eds.), *Social justice pedagogy across the curriculum: The practice of freedom* (pp. ix-x). New York: Routledge.

Nieto, S., & Bode, P. (2008). *Affirming diversity: The sociopolitical context of multicultural education* (5th ed.). Boston, MA: Pearson.

Robertson, T. (2007, November 13). Critical librarianship: An interview with Toni Samek. [Web log post]. Retrieved from http://bclaifc.wordpress.com/2007/11/13/critical-librarianship-an-interview-with-toni-samek/

Samek, T. (2007). *Librarianship and human rights: A twenty-first century guide.* Oxford, England: Chandos Publishing.

Sensoy, Ö., & DiAngelo, R. (2012). *Is everyone really equal? An introduction to key concepts in social justice education.* New York, NY: Teachers College Press.

United Nations Educational, Scientific and Cultural Organization (UNESCO) & International Federation of Library Associations and Institutions (IFLA). (2005). *Beacons of the information society: The Alexandria Proclamation for information literacy and lifelong learning.* Retrieved from http://www.ifla.org/publications/beacons-of-the-information-society-the-alexandria-proclamation-on-information-literacy-

Information Literacy in the Service of Neoliberalism

The Violence of Information Literacy: Neoliberalism and the Human as Capital

Nathaniel F. Enright
Royal Melbourne Institute of Technology

The spectacular and the cataclysmic seem to have been the defining features of capitalism during the opening years of the 21st century. The financial crisis presently engulfing the planet, of course, is no exception. Although the further immiseration of vast sections of the world's population has been assured by a volatile combination of stock market depreciations, mortgage foreclosures, the bankruptcy of entire nations as well as vast state-sponsored corporate bailouts the flip-side to such calamitous events is that it provides us with the opportunity to think through some of the contradictions embedded within the very logic of capital. In fact, it is commonplace now to suggest that the present financial crisis represents a fundamental challenge to the basic organizing frame of neoliberal capitalism. From Tunisia to Wall Street people are questioning the long-term viability of capitalism. Paradoxically, an entire cottage-industry of critique has been spawned by the recent crisis—from hip-hop battles featuring fictionalized versions of Keynes and Hayek (Papola & Roberts, 2010; Papola & Roberts, 2011) as the primary combatants to articles like Philip Collins' (2008) *Karl Marx: did he get it all right?* in the Rupert Murdoch owned *Times* and Peter Gumbel's (2009) feature in *Time* entitled *Rethinking Marx*—everywhere the seeds of doubt have been sown.

Unsurprisingly, the current crisis has also generated much scholarly reflection pointing to, amongst other things, nostalgia for Keynesian economics, the expectant death of neoliberalism and a potential return to Marxism as a useful lens of socioeconomic analysis. In point of fact, 2011 not only bore witness to the publication of Eagleton's *Why Marx was Right* but also had Eric Hobsbawm (2011) insisting that in order to properly comprehend the nature of contemporary capitalism we "must ask Marx's questions" (p. 13). In the same year, global dissatisfaction over the distribution and concentration of wealth culminated in global revolt toppling regimes in

Northern Africa and the Persian Gulf. In the global North the discontent surrounding the all pervading phenomenon of capitalist expansion spilled onto the streets and spread across campuses emboldened by the slogan "we are the 99%"–a phrase that sought to directly problematize the material realities of wealth disparity under neoliberalism[1].

In the discipline of Library and Information Science (LIS) voices and ideas that have long been confined to the "critical margins" (Trosow, 2001, p. 362) have been given buoyancy as forms of critique have gained traction. Critical librarianship (Samek, 2007) is in ascendance and monograph titles like *Critical Theory for Library and Information Science* (2010) and *Foundations of Critical Media and Information Studies* (2011) which even a few years ago would have appeared misplaced now seem surprisingly euphonious. And yet despite the resurgence of critique, most critical research in LIS still tends to stop short at formulating any explicit critique of capitalist social relations thereby deemphasizing the relationship between 21st century librarianship, the expansion of capital and the resultant forms of discipline and control developing from capital's late modern augmentation. The failure to link LIS with a broader critique of capitalism has resulted in a research program that fails to connect with the real, "everyday life" constraints emerging from the "information society" and driven by capital and its social relations. Sadly, the failure to position LIS within a systematic critique of capitalism also gives rise to an insufficient form of critique that consistently fails to scrutinize the central tenets of LIS practice by dislocating its historical specificity from the socio-economic context in which they are necessarily embedded.

This chapter offers a socio-historical account of the development and ascendancy of information literacy practices and places it firmly within the context of an expanding neoliberalism. The convergence between information literacy and neoliberalism can be understood as an attempt by states to reconceptualize the relationship between education and training and

---

1 According to a UNDP Human Development report the "world's richest 500 individuals have a combined income greater than that of the poorest 416 million. Beyond these extremes, the 2.5 billion people living on less than $2 a day–40% of the world's population–account for 5% of global income. The richest 10%, almost all of whom live in high-income countries, account for 54%" (UNDP, 2005, p. 4).

education and participant. This chapter reveals that information literacy has been defined narrowly as a core function of the neoliberal attempt to individualize political, economic and social development. Further, I will attempt to show how information literacy has converged with the human capital approach to education and suggest that the "information literate" is constructed as an ideal type of neoliberal subject.

Heads Buried in the Sand: The Silence and Invisibility of Neoliberalism in LIS

In his 1985 paper *Literacy, Technology and Monopoly Capital* Richard Ohmann makes the assertion that the emergence of mass literacy coincided with the epoch of monopoly capital. Although we should be cautious of attempts to reduce literacy to an epiphenomenal effect of capitalism, Ohmann's (1985) insistence regarding the symbiosis between the expansion of mass literacy and the concomitant strengthening of capitalism at least "presumes that questions of literacy and technology are inextricable from political questions of domination and equality" (p. 675). It is this kind of perspective that seems entirely absent from the majority of LIS literature pertaining to the notion and practice of information literacy. This chapter, then, attempts to address these shortcomings by taking seriously the material realities of capitalist social life in which the development of information literacy is necessarily embedded. That is, I will suggest that information literacy arises at a specific socio-historical moment in the reconstitution of capitalist social relations. I will suggest that that moment of reconstitution is occurring on a planetary basis where social relations of exploitation and commodification are expanded into new areas of social life under the auspices of neoliberalism.

Despite the echolalic appeals to study information literacy *in context* it is hardly surprising that a discipline "trapped in its own discursive formations" (Radford, 2003) and plagued by a host of other serious academic maladies has barely acknowledged, let alone comprehended, the nature of the neoliberal project. This is baffling given that many scholars consider neoliberalism to be the "defining political economic paradigm of our time" (McChesney, 1999, p. 7). Curiously, LIS scholars have had very little to say

about this epoch defining paradigm. Significantly, the rest of the academic
and scholastic world seems to have taken the emergence and expansion
of neoliberalism very seriously indeed.

A recent humanities-wide study demonstrates that neoliberalism has
been the subject of "nearly 1,000 academic articles annually between 2002
and 2005" (Boas & Gans-Morse, 2009, p. 138). My own research found a
mere 6 papers in the Library and Information Science Abstract database
during the same time-span (16 papers from the period 1980-2011). Similarly,
I was able to locate only 16 papers where the keyword neoliberalism (or
any of its multiple variants: neoliberal, neo-liberal, neo-liberalism) was
utilized in the Library, Information Science & Technology Abstracts (29
from the period 1980-2011). The papers retrieved from the above databases
were most frequently book reviews and not original research as such.
In the two major Australian LIS journals—*Australian Library Journal* and
Australian Academic and Research Libraries—I retrieved a grand total of zero
citations for the keyword *neoliberalism* and all of its associated variants.
Of the handful of papers that were retrieved, only one—an editorial in
Library Review (McMenemy, 2009)—was engaged explicitly in unpacking
the assumptions and predilections of neoliberalism. Although I tend to be
rather circumspect of anything uttered by a politician, the former Prime
Minister of Australia Kevin Rudd has recently declared that we need "a
frank analysis of the central role of neo-liberalism." Indeed. This is where
this chapter fits in.

However, uncovering the central components at the core of the neoliberal
project is a complex assignment. According to some socio-political analysts
(Boas & Gans-Morse, 2009; Thorsen, 2010) the literature is characterized
by conceptual confusion with much of the work operating with multiple
and imprecise definitions. Rather than viewing such imprecision as a failure of scholastic cogency, it speaks directly to the multiple and dynamic
ways in which neoliberalism is taken up and utilized in different contexts
around the globe.

A Brief Review of Neoliberalism: Living in Capitalized Times

Neoliberalism is best understood as a constellation of ideas and practices which ensures the perpetual reorganization and intensification of capitalist social relations by deploying the state to construct market relations throughout everyday life. By asserting the primacy of capital, neoliberalism subverts political forms, social structures and economic arrangements by subordinating all areas of social life to the rule of capital. As such, neoliberalism has variously been described, amongst other things, as a "virulent and brutal form of market capitalism" (Giroux, 2005, p. 2), "radicalized capitalist imperialism" (Ong, 2006, p. 1), "disaster capitalism" (Klein, 2008), a "system of relentless domination" (Saad-Fijo, 2003, p. 10) and a mode of organization which decimates social bonds by "destroying collective structures" (Bourdieu, 1998). Consequently, David Harvey (2005) suggests that the world has witnessed "an emphatic turn towards neoliberalism in political-economic practices and thinking since the 1970s" (p. 2). And although neoliberalism has developed into an "unchallenged ideology; nothing short of an overwhelming, mind controlling ethic" (Conway & Heynen, 2006, p. 17) its uneven historical development and geographical spread has led a number of contemporary scholars to emphasize the differences *within* the neoliberal project (see for example Greenhouse (Ed.), 2010 and Saad-Filho & Johnston (Eds.), 2005). Nevertheless, there is some broad agreement about the historical emergence of the neoliberal project. Popular accounts of the genealogy of neoliberalism point to the economic downturn of the 1970s which annihilated the credibility of Keynesian political economy. Combined with ever diminishing economic growth, high inflation, massive unemployment, the collapse of the Bretton Woods Agreement in 1973, two "oil shocks", the bankruptcy of New York City, and the increasing flight of industrial and manufacturing capital to the developing economies of the so-called Third World, Keynesian orthodoxy appeared to be failing in precisely the areas it claimed for itself, namely: the need for state intervention in the economy in order to "redistribute risk so as to shield the inevitable losers in a capitalist market" (Dean, 2009, pp. 52-53). As such, the neoliberal turn aimed to "minimise the size of government, make space for competitive forces, enlarge the scope and reach of the private sector, (re)distribute wealth on the basis of market principles and break down labour unions and other 'anti-market' or 'anti-competitive' institutions" (Tickell & Peck, 2003, p. 13). According to Harvey– and broadly corroborated by most contemporary critics–the chief strategies in the neoliberal toolkit revolved around four key areas:

> 1) *Privatization,* especially of formerly public goods. This has accelerated as the form of the state has evolved from a Keynesian welfare state which, at least, partially de-commodified certain services and social relations including some housing, medical care, public transport, education, telecommunications etc, toward a neoliberal state which has systematically re-commodified such services and worked to extend the profit imperative and property rights to ever new resources and areas of social life. Harvey further suggests that the process of privatization has been frequently accompanied by violence which states routinely use to enforce private property.
>
> 2) *Financialization* which sought to turn any product or service into an instrument of economic speculation. This form of speculative capitalism was made easier by the de-linking of the American dollar from the gold standard which had the cumulative effect of converting all major currencies into speculative commodities.
>
> 3) *The Management and Manipulation of Crises,* which for Harvey (2005) is the active mechanism for "accumulation by dispossession" (pp. 160-165; see also Harvey, 2003, ch. 4.). The sudden interest rate rise in the US in 1979, for example, forced countries indebted to the US to declare bankruptcy which left local economies and resources free for the further exploitation and advancement of the US economy. According to Harvey, the debt crises that punctuated the developing economies of Latin America throughout the 1980s and 1990s were "orchestrated, managed and controlled both to rationalize the system and to redistribute assets" (p. 162) to the US and to ensure its continued global financial dominance and
>
> 4) *State Redistributions* in which the neoliberal state becomes the primary mechanism for the redistribution of wealth to the upper classes. This is precisely the sense in which critics suggest that neoliberalism is primarily concerned with the "restoration of class power" (Harvey, 2005; Duménil & Lévy, 2004).

As such, the description provided by Saad-Filho (2008) of the mechanics of neoliberalism is worth highlighting:

> Neoliberalism combines an accumulation strategy, a mode of social and economic reproduction and a mode of exploitation and social domination based on the systematic use of state power to impose, under the ideological veil of non-intervention, a hegemonic project of recomposition of the rule of capital in all areas of social life. (p. 34)

The marketization of daily life—what Saad Filho describes as the "recomposition of the rule of capital in all areas of social life"—is of particular concern. Neoliberalism cannot simply be conceived of as an economic doctrine. As such, the current chapter engages the critiques advanced by Ong (2006; 2007), Rose (1990; 1999) and others that posit neoliberalism as a "technology of governing" which harnesses the discourses of freedom, empowerment and autonomy for the regulation of everyday life. In this sense neoliberalism is implicated in the creation of new forms of identity and subjectivity having mobilized the market in an attempt to destroy collective forms of identity. The intensely individualized neoliberal subject is said to be empowered through market choices yet the corollary is that inequalities and other miscarriages of justice are defined away from the contradictions and deep structural embededdness of capital towards the suggestion that such maladies result from a deficiency in individual choice, action or conduct. As Leitner, Sheppard, Sziato, and Maringanti (2007) argue, "Under neoliberalism, individual freedom is redefined as the capacity for self-realization and freedom from bureaucracy rather than freedom from want, with human behaviour reconceptualised along economic lines" (pp. 5-6). The increasing incursion of the market into everyday life, which for many is the very crux of neoliberalism, restructures the values and relations of markets into a fully integrated model for the wider organization of politics and society. In fact, as Comaroff and Comaroff (2001) posit: "...neoliberalism aspires, in its ideology and practice, to intensify the abstractions inherent in capitalism itself: to separate labor power from its human context, to replace society with the market, to build a universe out of aggregated transactions" (p. 14).

Ties that Bind: Neoliberal Theory and Information

Although barely acknowledged in LIS, the conceptualization of information within the economic sciences has had a profound impact on the way we currently understand information (Mattessich, 1993). Indeed, our understanding of the contemporary notion of information—its commodification and centrality to the social organization of capitalism—can be enriched by a serious engagement with some of the fundamental precepts of neoliberalism which have reconfigured the material organization of society over the last few decades. Long before pundits began pontificating about the novelty of the post-industrial society and the importance of information for economic growth, a group of libertarian intellectuals and economists gathered around Friedrich August von Hayek's Mont Pelerin Society began to take seriously the decisive role of information in economic development. Hayek, "probably the single most influential individual economist or political philosopher to shape what is now understood as neoliberalism" (Peters, 2001, p. 13), was instrumental in this regard. In a series of papers produced in the 1930s and 1940s, Hayek introduced what is now known as the *knowledge problem* where he challenged the traditional assumption of complete and objective knowledge. For Hayek, knowledge was necessarily social because it invariably consisted of "...dispersed bits of incomplete and frequently contradictory knowledge which all the separate individuals possess" (Hayek, 1945, p. 519). This leads Hayek (1945) to convey:

> The economic problem of society is thus not merely a problem of how to allocate "given" resources—if "given" is taken to mean given to a single mind which deliberately solves the problem set by these "data." It is rather a problem of how to secure the best use of resources known to any of the members of society, for ends whose relative importance only these individuals know. Or, to put it briefly, it is a problem of the utilization of knowledge not given to anyone in its totality. (pp. 519–20)

From the very beginning then the neoliberal understanding of information was one that was inextricably linked to the phenomenon of marketization, a process characterized by the "dominance and scope of markets in social life" (Fisher, 2010, p. 45). Indeed for Hayek, the relationship between information and market was unproblematic because for him the market not only guaranteed individual freedom but would allow for the continued creation of new knowledge. The market then, transformed as it was by the superabundance of subjective knowledge, became *the* institution for the coordination, exchange and application of the sum of knowledge of individuals such that Hayek could declare that "the price system is a mechanism for communicating information" (Hayek, 1945, p. 526). In many ways, Hayek's market-oriented understanding of the subjective nature of knowledge prefigures the logic of post-industrialism where the imperative to incorporate and subsume all subjective potential–the ability to create and innovate–belongs both to the realm of freedom and the productive powers of capital.

Further, Hayek's understanding of knowledge formed the backbone of his critique of planned or socialist economies. Although complete, total or perfect knowledge can never exist, the free market provides a kind of spontaneous social order through which incomplete, subjective knowledge is mediated. By acting with complete self-interest, individuals within a market nevertheless develop a perfect system–both rational and benevolent–for the satisfaction of individual needs and desires through the interaction and exchange of knowledge. This kind of market order is preferred by and considered optimal by neoliberals as it is conceptualized as a self-regulating system. It is precisely within this context that neoliberalism attempts to dissuade the state from interference with or the overregulation of the market lest it damage the self-regulating, spontaneous mechanisms of market order. It should be noted however that during its early gestation, "neoliberalism remained a marginal economic movement" and could barely challenge the dominance of the Keynesian commitment to "regulatory policies designed to stabilise capitalism and protect citizens from its worst excesses" (Dean, 2009, p. 52). Indeed, Hayek's thinking remained obscure until the development of digital networking technologies which made the theory technologically possible. Referring to the convergence of this kind of radical liberal economics with technology as the "cybernetic hypothesis," Tiqqun (2001) proposes that neoliberalism merges with and takes over from the technological discourses by taking liberal economic theory and:

> ...grafting it onto the cybernetic promise of a balancing of systems.
> The hybrid discourse that resulted from this, later called "neo-liberal,"
> considered as a virtue the optimal market allocation of information -
> and no longer that of wealth - in society. In this sense, the market is but
> the instrument of a perfect coordination of players thanks to which the
> social totality can find a durable equilibrium. Capitalism thus becomes
> unquestionable, insofar as it is presented as a simple means - the best
> possible means - of producing social self-regulation. (p. 24)

Eventually, the prominent role assigned to information by neoliberals would intersect with the claims and promises of socio-political and economic reorganization based around the widespread diffusion of information and its associated technologies. Everywhere it seems, the two doctrines merge, intertwine and mutate so as to become one. Consider, for example, the enthusiastic promotion of the information society where the disintegration of the centralized institutions of Keynesianism would give rise to a radically decentralized society in which everybody would be able to exercise power through the system of information technologies spread throughout society. Such a society would, argued some, alleviate the aberrations of government and pave the way for a "friction-free capitalism" (Gates, 1996, p. 180) which would guarantee the end of antagonism and ideological conflict between labor and capital. In this way, the information society discourse does not simply reassert the ideas of neoliberalism but renders them technologically. The confluence is clear. If neoliberalism aimed at radically restructuring the relations between capital, labor, and the state by both "freeing" the market from governmental regulation and enforcing market relations throughout everyday life, the model of social organization enabled by network technology made possible this emancipation as well as legitimized the market vis-à-vis network technology as ideal instruments for the regulation and administration of social reproduction. It is in this sense that Harvey (2005) suggests: Information technology is the privileged technology of neoliberalism (p. 159).

In this way, capital—forever attempting its own reproduction and expansion—could merge the discourses of neoliberalism and the information society. Certainly, by constructing markets for information, neoliberalism activates those abstractions inherent in capitalism and tends towards making individuals compete for information. This apparent autonomization of the political from the economic, the public from the private, can be seen in terms of commodity fetishism, that is, the tendency of social relations under capitalism to be reproduced in a "'fantastic form' which conceals their reality as relations of class domination" (Holloway & Picciotto, 1991, p. 114). These illusions are necessary for the continual reproduction of capitalist social relations, and hence the survival of capital, "by channelling the conflicts arising from the real nature of capitalist society into the fetishised forms of the bourgeois political processes" (Holloway & Picciotto, 1991, p. 114). Thus, this fetishized autonomization of workers into individuals-citizens is a *reality* that depends on the success of reproducing the extensive relations that form the *illusion* of freedom/autonomy.

Another founding member of the Mont Pelerin Society, Fritz Machlup, provided significant legitimation for the primary role of knowledge for economic growth. Indeed, the current interest in the production and use of knowledge has an intellectual heritage that dates back to Machlup's seminal work *The Production and Distribution of Knowledge in the United States* (1962). Already in 1958 Machlup suggested that total knowledge production for the US was a staggering $136,436 million accounting for 29% GDP. Significantly, Machlup also identified education as contributing almost 61 million to the national economy. As Machlup's influence consolidated, scholars and social commentators alike began to consider seriously how a global expansion of the knowledge based economy might ensure increased flexibility of production and, rather crucially, might provide for the most efficient means through which to capture the massive amount of dispersed, tacit and subjective knowledge. The answer, in part, lay in the promotion of human capital theory which will be discussed in the next section.

Neoliberalism's Highly Prized Achievements: The Profanity of Human as Capital

> The mere thought of investment in human beings is offensive to some among us. Our values and beliefs inhibit us from looking upon human beings as capital goods, except in slavery, and this we abhor. We are not

unaffected by the long struggle to rid society of indentured service and to evolve political and legal institutions to keep men free from bondage. These are achievements that we prize highly. Hence, to treat human beings as wealth that can be augmented by investment runs counter to deeply held values. It seems to reduce man once again to a mere material component, to something akin to property. And for man to look upon himself as a capital good, even if it did not impair his freedom, may seem to debase him. (Schultz, 1961, p. 2)

And debase humanity, it has. Human capital theory profanes human existence by surrendering all aspects of life to the unremitting logic of capital. The idea of human capital was introduced by Mincer in 1958 in *Investment in Human Capital and Personal Income Distribution*, and was developed by subsequent scholars from the Chicago School of Economics including most notably Gary Becker (1964, 1976), T.W. Schultz (1961, 1963), Fritz Machlup (1962, 1980, 1982a,1982b,1984) and Milton Friedman (2002). Broadly speaking, human capital refers to investment in skills development and education and conceives human capital as "a form of investment… precisely analogous to investment in machinery, buildings, or other forms of non human capital" (Friedman, 2002, p. 94). In theory, an individual can invest in human capital – through things like education and training – and economic rewards should accrue proportionate to how much human capital one owns. It is this idea that permits Schultz (1961) to assert that "Laborers have become capitalists…from the acquisition of knowledge and skill that have economic value" (p. 3). This idea dovetails precisely with the neoliberal claim that the market eliminates social antagonism between labor and capital by transforming the position of labor–and indeed every aspect of human life–by making it "an investment in a future of potential access to greater social wealth" (Vishmidt, 2010). This is the sense in which Foucault (2008) claimed, in his lectures on neoliberalism, that as a result of the compunction to continue training and retraining individuals were increasingly becoming "entrepreneurs of the self."

Interestingly, Ursula Huws (2003) provides an alternative definition of human capital as "the reproduction of the knowledge workforce itself" (p. 134). Huws comprehends human capital theory as a constitutive element in the neoliberal attempt to expand the social reproduction of labor power through education and training. Although the discourse surrounding human capital formation is seductive insofar as it positions every individual as a potential capitalist, what it fails to mention is that the majority of workers still depend on wage labor for survival. As such, any aggregate improvement in the skills and knowledge of the workforce—that is, the increased capacity of labor power—functions primarily to enhance the production and reproduction of capital itself. On this point, Machlup (1962) was strikingly clear:

> We need an educational system that will significantly raise the intellectual capacity of our people. There is at present a great scarcity of brainpower in our labor force…Unless our labor force changes its composition so as to include a much higher share of well-trained brainpower, the economic growth of the nation will be stunted and even more serious problems of employability will arise. (p. 135)

In this manner, systems of education become privileged sites for the reproduction of capital and the subordination of labor. It is important to note that human capital theory has significantly transformed government approaches to the funding and provision of education. Friedman's famous and influential essay, "The Role of the Government in Education", prioritizes the centrality of the "rational, utility-maximizing individual" who invests in education and training until "the marginal utility…is equal to the marginal cost…" (Romano, 2005, pp. 27-28) thereby transforming education into one of the primary mechanisms for human capital investment. In this way, individuals are asked to participate in expanded systems of education where the primary goal is not self-improvement or empowerment but rather "to raise the economic productivity of the human being" (Friedman, 2002, p. 94).

The Subsumption of Information Literacy to Capital: An Australian Case Study[2]

Up to this point I have demonstrated the ways in which neoliberal strate-

---

2 While much of the detail will focus on distinctly Australian approaches to information literacy, the general suggestion is that many of the basic trends have a wider applicability and resonate with much of what is going on elsewhere in the world. Nevertheless, the reason for focusing on

gies of government involve a more-or-less constant expansion of the areas
of social life which are commodified and determined by market relations
and as such "education"–reconstructed as human capital development–has
been a major focus for the neoliberal processes of privatization, commodification and commercialization. In the realm of education, neoliberal
doctrine has continued to privilege the market over the state attempting
to position the necessity of competition and individual responsibility as
core determinants for success in an increasingly flexible, global knowledge economy. In this way education–and universities in particular–have
been increasingly reconstituted as profit oriented institutions whose major
purpose is the functional training of the labor force in line with the needs
of capital. In Australia, the emergence of information literacy takes place
precisely within the context of the progressive alignment of skill formation
with the logic of capital and is often disguised behind a discourse about
the power of learning.

In the late 1980s, the Australian government began restructuring tertiary education based on the belief that "our education and training
systems should play an active role in responding to the major economic
challenges facing Australia" (Dawkins & Holding, 1987, p. iii). Ever since,
economic imperatives have guided the widespread reform of education
often conflating learning with employment skills and elevating economic
competitiveness as the chief object of education. In this way, education is
frequently mobilized as the primary vehicle for the maintenance of Australia's strategic advantage in the knowledge economy. In this context, the
ideology of lifelong learning is deployed so as to ensure the widespread
and perpetual re-training of the labor force so as to continue to compete
in a global economy characterized by the rapid emergence of new information technologies. This kind of logic has been emphasized time and
again in government policy. Consider for example, the assertion made
by the former Minister for Employment, Education, Training and Youth

the Australian context is not because it is somehow typical but rather that it is exceptional. The
progressive subsumption of information literacy to the dictates of the state and capital is as Mutch
(2008) says "a process that went furthest in Australia" (p. 17) and is evidenced by the production
of significant government reports, namely: the Mayer Key Competencies (1992) and the Candy
Report (1994). This paper then will serve as a warning to all those who tend to downplay the obvious interconnections between the state, capital and information literacy.

Affairs that there is:

> ...little doubt that the nations which will succeed in the 21st century will
> be 'knowledge societies' – societies rich in human capital, effective in
> their capacity to utilise and deploy their human resources productively
> and successful in the creation and commercialisation of new knowledge.
> In such a world there will need to be greater opportunities than ever
> before for lifelong learning – for preparation not just for the first job but
> for succeeding jobs. (Kemp, 1999)

Similarly, the Departmental position on Lifelong Learning makes explicit
the connections between education, skill formation and the knowledge
economy, finding that:

> ...the lifelong learning policy agenda is built on assumptions about the
> importance of skills in the New Economy. Almost all industrial sectors
> are increasingly knowledge-based and economic returns are obtained
> from a range of intangible inputs, one of which is workers' skills. Par-
> ticipation in education and training is increasing and economic rewards
> are flowing to people with high skills. (Watson, 2003, p. 14-15)

Underpinning all of this discourse is the assumption of a link between
education and strengthened economic performance.

A slew of Australian ministerial documents, government reports, and
library association documents have reinforced the strength of this discourse by proposing a series of reforms based around the development
of key competencies designed to increase competitiveness in the global
economy. Unsurprisingly, information literacy has constituted the center-
piece of these reforms. It is impossible to give a detailed account here of
how information literacy has converged with competence based education
within the Australian policy context. Instead I will highlight a number
of influential policies and papers that prioritize a generic knowledge and
skills framework built around information literacy.

In Australia, the desired generic skills or "key competencies" as they
were to be called, were enumerated in the Mayer Committee's *Putting
general education to work: the Key Competencies report* (1992). Of the seven key
competencies proposed by the committee, two were directly related to the
use and distribution of information. Although never directly employing

the term "information literacy," this report has routinely been identified as a milestone in the promotion of information literacy in Australia (Victoria University, n.d.). Significantly, this report positioned "collecting, analysing and organising" (pp. 16-17) and "communicating ideas and information" (pp. 18-19) as "essential for effective participation in the emerging patterns of work and work organisation" (p. 5). From the very beginning it seems information literacy was conceptualized narrowly as an instrument for economic prosperity and not as a mechanism of social transformation. In a similar vein, the *Candy Report* (1994), which amongst other things, aimed at expanding "learning after graduation" (p. 33) and promoted lifelong learning as a way to facilitate "an internationally competitive workforce" (p. xi) suggested that all graduates from Australian universities should be information literate. Already, we should be able to perceive the ways in which "information literacy" is subsumed within the discourse of competency. Information literacy is increasingly shaped to fit labor market demand and redesigned to produce adequate responses to the specific demands of business such that these key competencies become credentialized as an expression of value in the marketplace. Finally, in 2000 librarians from Australia and New Zealand drafted the first edition of the *Australia and New Zealand Information Literacy Framework* (Bundy, 2004). Significantly, the framework positioned information literacy as a *prerequisite* for social inclusion, participative citizenship and the like. This informational limiting of citizenship and social participation emanates from the unquestioning acceptance of the post-industrialism thesis (Bell, 1973) such that the qualities and the attributes of the information literate identified here are coterminous with the features of post-industrial work identified by Bell, so long ago.

Homo economicus: The Information Literate as Neoliberal Subject

In a rare discussion of neoliberalism from within the boundaries of LIS, John Budd (2007) notes that:

> Neoliberalism operates most effectively through rhetoric. If an idea can be stated in a way that is attractive to a reader or listener, it is more likely

to be accepted. Further, if an idea that inherently contains elements that are damaging to polity, the public good, and the public sphere, it is more likely to be accepted if it paints the opposite picture. The rhetoric of neoliberalism relies on insinuating the ideas of markets and transactions into common usage, so that practices that are not market and transaction driven adopt the language as presenting truth. (p. 175)

And although it should be fairly evident by now that the promotion of information literacy has served as instrument to reproduce the capitalist social form, what is less clear is how such a debased version of information literacy has come to be hegemonic to the point of becoming truth. The key to comprehending this development is an understanding of the ways in which, to borrow from Foucault (1982), "human beings are made subjects" (p. 208) under neoliberal conditions. As a mode of governing, neoliberalism sets in motion the individual as a free subject and attempts to secure the conditions under which people participate in their own self-governance. In this sense, the ideal neoliberal subject is one who is conceived as being free in multiple senses: free to choose but also free in the sense of being liberated from external governmental coercion. As such, the ideal neoliberal subject is one who governs themselves. This freedom allows the retreat of the state from service provision—evident in the classic formulation from the *Review of Higher Education Financing and Policy* where "primary responsibility for learning and choosing when to learn rests with the individual" (West, 1998, p. 44)—whilst simultaneously implementing a logic of ruthless individualism which forces individuals to be primarily responsible for their own well being. By forcing those who would become information literate to constantly respond to the need and will of the labor market, the neoliberal articulation of information literacy redefines citizens as consumers and investors competing in a marketplace of ideas. Indeed, the precariousness and competitiveness of the labor market tends to reinforce and reflect the ideal neoliberal subject. The flexibilization associated with neoliberalism encourages "workers to see themselves not as "workers" in a political sense, who have something to gain through solidarity and collective organization, but as "companies of one" (Read, 2009, p. 30) who need to endlessly compete to secure the highly specialized, short-term labor that is on offer. As such, every process associated with becoming and maintaining information literacy becomes an investment in human capital.

In an earlier paper (Enright, 2011) I discussed the strategies which capital employs to separate subjective knowledge from the worker and to immediately absorb and integrate that knowledge back into the circuit of production and profit. Under conditions of neoliberalism, the creation of wealth increasingly depends on the organization and production of this knowledge. It is precisely in this sense that information literacy practices arise so as to contain and control the creation of subjective and diffuse knowledges. Of course, information literacy most frequently takes place in spheres that are typically thought of being outside production; yet intrinsic to it. The common critique of contemporary capitalism is that it expands to make all areas of social life an active articulation of production. But as Read (2009) demonstrates:

> ...at the exact moment in which all of social existence becomes labor, or potential labor, neoliberalism constructs the image of a society of capitalists, of entrepreneurs. As production moves from the closed space of the factory to become distributed across all of social space, encompassing all spheres of cultural and social existence, neoliberalism presents an image of society as a market, effacing production altogether. (pp. 33-34)

As such the constant imposition of work—or literacy practices—manifests itself not as work but as conscious investment strategies designed to maximize human capital in the marketplace. The material everyday practices of information literacy then help to construct and reinforce the dominant position of the neoliberal subject.

The argument that I wish to finally advance here is not only that the information literate is the neoliberal subject *par excellence,* but is structured around the notion of human as *homo economicus.* Indeed, in all of the policy the information literate is always conceptualized as a rational, self-interested individual who can recognize "the need for information" and continually "re-evaluates the nature and extent of the information need." It really is as if Becker's calculation that "all human behaviour can be viewed as involving participants who maximize their utility from a stable set of preferences and accumulate an optimal amount of information and other inputs in a variety of markets" (Becker, 1976, p. 14) has come to pass.

The Defeat of Social Justice and the Violence of Information Literacy

I have thus far characterized neoliberalism as a system which permits the unending expansion and construction of market relations through everyday life. I have further argued that neoliberalism produces new subject formations and in the specific context of information literacy are built around notions of entrepreneurship and individualization. And I have also observed that neoliberalism understands human behavior from the perspective of the market. In all of these senses and more, neoliberalism and its construction of information literacy run counter to any notion of social justice. Of course, Hayek (1979) once famously argued that social justice "with reference to a society of free men, the phrase has no meaning whatever"(p. 3). He would eventually come to characterize social justice as a "mirage" (Hayek, 1976). And I must agree. It seems unlikely that there will be any social justice so long as neoliberalism continues to subordinate all aspects of human endeavor to the calculus of profit. What there will be is violence. And lots of it. This is precisely the critique leveled by Frederici (2001) who argued that neoliberalism "requires the destruction of any economic activity not subordinated to the logic of accumulation, and this is necessarily a violent process" (p. 133). In a similar manner, Bourdieu (1998) located the essence of neoliberalism in fire and blood: "The ultimate foundation of this entire economic order placed under the sign of freedom is in effect the *structural violence* of unemployment, of the insecurity of job tenure and the menace of layoff it implies." Indeed, this violence is precisely what motivates many to participate in developing their information literacy skills. These were exactly the themes that J. Elspeth Stuckey (1991) picked up on in her book *The Violence of Literacy* where she argued that literacy had become a mechanism of oppression rather than liberation. In fact, Stuckey makes a point that is co-extensive with the current chapter, finding that:

...the usual speculations about the nature and need for literacy are misguided. These speculations are wrong because the assumptions about economic and social forces on which they are based are faulty. Literacy itself can be understood only in its social and political context, and that context, once the mythology has been stripped away, can be seen as one of entrenched class structure in which those who have power have a vested interest in keeping it...Far from engineering freedom, our current approaches to literacy corroborate other social practices that prevent freedom and limit opportunity. (p. viii)

Hopefully I have been able to demonstrate that the same is true of information literacy and that our approach will encourage others to study the information literacy in its complex social and political totality. Because this is the only hope information literacy has to be allied to the notion of social justice.

References

Australian Education Council Mayer Committee. (1992). *Putting general education to work: The key competencies report.* Canberra: Australian Education Council and Ministers of Vocational Education, Employment and Training.

Becker, G. S. (1964). *Human capital: A theoretical and empirical analysis, with special reference to education.* New York: National Bureau of Economic Research.

Becker, G. S. (1976). *The economic approach to human behaviour.* Chicago: University of Chicago Press.

Bell, D. (1973). *The coming of post-industrial society: A venture in social forecasting.* New York: Basic Books.

Boas, T. C., & Gans-Morse, J. (2009). Neoliberalism: From new liberal philosophy to anti-liberal slogan. *Studies in Comparative International Development, 44,* 137-161.

Bourdieu, P. (1998). Utopia of endless exploitation: The essence of neoliberalism. *Le Monde Diplomatique: English Edition.* Retrieved from http://mondediplo. com/1998/12/08bourdieu

Budd, J. (2007). *Self-examination: The present and future of librarianship.* Westport, CT: Libraries Unlimited.

Bundy, A. (Ed). (2004). *Australian and New Zealand information literacy framework: Principles, standards and practice* (2nd ed). Adelaide: Australian and New Zealand Institute for Information Literacy. Retrieved from http://www.literacyhub.org/ documents/InfoLiteracyFramework.pdf

Candy, P., Crebert, G., & O'Leary, J. (1994). *Developing lifelong learners through undergraduate education.* Canberra: Australian Government Publishing Service.

Collins, P. (2008, October 21). Karl Marx: did he get it all right? *The Times.* Retrieved from http://www.metamute.org/editorial/articles/karl-marx-did-he-get-it-all-right

Comaroff, J., & Comaroff, J. (2001). *Millennial capitalism and the culture of neoliberalism*. Durham, NC: Duke University Press.

Conway, D & Heynen, N. (2006). The ascendency of neoliberalism and the emergence of contemporary globalisation. In D. Conway & N. Heynen (Eds.), *Globalization's contradictions: Geographies of discipline, destruction and transformation* (pp. 17-34). London: Routledge.

Dawkins, J. S., & Holding, A. C. (1987). *Skills for Australia*. Canberra: Australian Government Publishing Service.

Dean, J. (2009). *Democracy and other neoliberal fantasies: Communicative capitalism and left politics*. Durham, NC: Duke University Press.

Duménil, G., & Lévy, D. (2004). *Capital resurgent: Roots of the neoliberal revolution*. Cambridge, MA: Harvard University Press.

Duménil, G., & Lévy, D. (2011). *The crisis of neoliberalism*. Cambridge, MA: Harvard University Press.

Eagleton, T. (2011). *Why Marx was right*. London: Yale University Press.

Enright, N. F. (2011). You can't polish a pumpkin: Scattered speculations on the development of information ethics. *Journal of Information Ethics, 20*(2), 103-126.

Fisher, E. (2010). *Media and new capitalism in the digital age: The spirit of networks*. New York: Palgrave.

Frederici, S. (2001). War, globalization, reproduction. In V. Bennholdt-Thomsen, N.G. Faraclas & C. von Werlhof (Eds.), *There is an alternative: Subsistence and worldwide resistance to corporate globalization* (pp. 133-145). Melbourne, Australia: Spinifex Books.

Friedman. M. (2002). *Capitalism and freedom* (40th ed.). Chicago, IL: University of Chicago Press.

Foucault, M. (1982). The subject and power. In H. Dreyfuss and P. Rabinow (Eds.), *Beyond structuralism and hermeneutics*. Brighton, England: Harvester Books.

Foucault, M. (2008). *The birth of biopolitics: Lectures at the collège de France 1978-1979*. (G. Burchell, Trans.). New York: Picador Press.

Fuchs, C. (2011). *Foundations of critical media and information studies*. London: Routledge.

Gates, B. (1996). *The road ahead*. New York: Penguin.

Giroux, H. (2005). The terror of neoliberalism: Rethinking the significance of cultural politics. *College Literature, 32*(1), 1-19.

Greenhouse, C.J. (Ed.). (2010). *Ethnographies of neoliberalism*. Philadelphia, PA: University of Pennsylvania Press.

Gumbel, P. (2009, January 29). Rethinking Marx. *Time*. Retrieved from http://www.time.com/time/specials/packages/article/0,28804,1873191_1873190_1873188,00.html

Harvey, D. (2003). *The new imperialism*. Oxford: Oxford University Press.

Harvey, D. (2005). *A brief history of neoliberalism*. Oxford: Oxford University Press.

Hayek, F. A. (1937). Economics and knowledge. *Economica, 4*(13), 33-54.

Hayek, F. A. (1945). The use of knowledge in society. *American Economic Review,* *35*(4), 519–530.

Hayek, F. A. (1976). *Law, legislation and liberty, volume 2: The mirage of social justice.* London: Routledge & Kegan Paul Ltd.

Hayek, F. A. (1979). *Social justice, socialism & democracy: Three Australian lectures.* Turramurra, Australia: Centre for Independent Studies

Hobsbawm, E. J. (2011). *How to change the world: Marx and Marxism, 1840-2011.* London: Little, Brown and Company.

Holloway, J., & Picciotto, S. (1991). Capital, crisis and the state. In S. Clarke (Ed.), *The state debate.* London: Macmillan.

Huws, U. (2003). *The making of a cybertariat: Virtual work in a real world.* New York: Monthly Review Press.

Kemp, D. (1999). "An Australian perspective." *OECD Conference, Preparing youth for the 21st century: The policy lessons from the past two decades.* Paper presented in Washington D.C. 23-24 February 1999.

Klein, N. (2007). *The shock doctrine: The rise of disaster capitalism.* London: Allen Lane.

Leckie, J., Given, L. M., & Buschmann, J. E. (Eds.). (2010). *Critical theory for library and information science.* Santa Barbara, CA: Libraries Unlimited.

Leitner, H., Sheppard, E. S., Sziarto, K., & Maringanti, A. (2007). Contesting urban futures: Decentering neoliberalism. In H. Leitner, J. Peck & E. Sheppard (Eds.), *Contesting neoliberalism: The urban frontier* (pp. 1-25). New York: Guilford Press.

Mattessich, R. (1993). On the nature of information and knowledge and the interpretation in the economic sciences. *Library Trends, 41*(4), 567-594.

Machlup, F. (1962). *The production and distribution of knowledge in the United States.* Princeton, NJ: Princeton University Press.

Machlup, F. (1980). *Knowledge and knowledge production: Vol. 1. Knowledge: Its creation, distribution, and economic significance.* Princeton, NJ: Princeton University Press.

Machlup, F. (1982a). *The branches of learning: Vol. 2. Knowledge: Its creation, distribution, and economic significance.* Princeton, NJ: Princeton University Press.

Machlup, F. (1982b). *Lecture on theory of human capital.* Islamabad: Pakistan Institute of Development Economics.

Machlup, F. (1984). *The economics of information and human capital: Vol. 3. Knowledge: Its creation, distribution, and economic significance.* Princeton, NJ: Princeton University Press.

Mayer, E. (1992). *Key competencies: Report of the committee to advise the Australian education council and ministers of vocational education, employment and training on employment-related key competencies for postcompulsory education and training [Mayer report].* Canberra: Australian Education Council and Ministers of Vocational Education, Employment and Training.

McChesney, R. W. (1999). Introduction. In N. Chomsky, *Profit over people: Neoliberalism and global order* (pp. 7-16). New York: Seven Stories Press.

McMenemy, D. (2009). Rise and demise of neoliberalism: Time to reassess the impact on public libraries. *Library Review, 58*(6), 400-404.

Mincer, J. (1958). Investment in human capital and personal income distribution. *The Journal of Political Economy, 66*(4), 281-302.

Mutch, A. (2008). *Managing information and knowledge in organizations: A literacy approach.* New York: Routledge.

Ohmann, R. (1985). Literacy, technology and monopoly capital. *College English, 47*(7), 675-689.

Ong, A. (2006). *Neoliberalism as exception: Mutations in citizenship and sovereignty.* Durham, NC: Duke University Press.

Ong, A. (2007). Neoliberalism as a mobile technology. *Transactions of the Institute of British Geographers, 32*(1), 3-8.

Papola, J., & Roberts, R. (2010, January 23). Fear the boom and bust: A Hayek vs. Keynes rap anthem [Video file]. Retrieved from http://www.youtube.com/watch?v=d0nERTFo-Sk

Papola, J., & Roberts, R. (2011, April 27). Fight of the century: Keynes vs. Hayek round two [Video file]. Retrieved from http://www.youtube.com/watch?v=G TQnarzmTOc&feature=channel&list=UL

Peters, M. (2001). *Poststructuralism, Marxism and neoliberalism: Between theory and politics.* New York: Rowan & Littlefield.

Radford, G. P. (2003). Trapped in our own discursive formations: Toward an archaeology of library and information science. *Library Quarterly, 73*(1), 1-18.

Read, J. (2009). A genealogy of homo-economicus: Neoliberalism and the production of subjectivity. *Foucault Studies, 6*, 25-36.

Romano, F. (2005). *Clinton and Blair: The political economy of the third way.* London: Routledge.

Rose, N. (1990). *Governing the soul: The shaping of the private self.* London: Routledge.

Rose, N. (1999). *Powers of freedom: Reframing political thought.* Cambridge: Cambridge University Press.

Saad-Filho, A. (2003). Introduction. In A. Saad-Filho (Ed.), *Anti-capitalism: A Marxist introduction* (pp. 1-26). London, England: Pluto Press.

Saad-Filho, A., & Johnston, D. (Eds.). (2005). *Neoliberalism: A critical reader.* London: Pluto Press.

Saad-Filho, A. (2008). Marxian and Keynesian critiques of neoliberalism. *Socialist Register, 44*, 28-37.

Samek, T. (2007). *Librarianship and human rights: A twenty-first century guide.* London, England: Chandos Publishing.

Schultz, T. W. (1961). Investment in human capital. *The American Economic Review, 51*(1), 1-17.

Schultz, T. W. (1963). *The economic value of education.* New York: Columbia University Press.

Stuckey, J. Elspeth. (1991). *The violence of literacy.* Portsmouth, NH: Heinemann Educational Books, Inc.

Thorsen, D. E. (2010). The neoliberal challenge: What is neoliberalism? *Contemporary Readings in Law and Social Justice, 2*(2), 188–214.

Tiqqun. (2001). The cybernetic hypothesis. *Tiqqun, 2*, 1-83. Retrieved from http://cybernet.jottit.com/

Trosow, S. (2001). Standpoint epistemology as an alternative methodology for library and information science. *Library Quarterly, 71*(3), 360-382.

United Nations Development Programme. (2005). *Human development report 2005.* New York, NY: Hoechstetter Printing Company. Retrieved from http://hdr.undp.org/en/media/HDR05_complete.pdf

Victoria University. (n.d.). Information literacy initiatives in Australia. Retrieved from http://w2.vu.edu.au/library/InfoLit/il_initiatives.htm#mayer

Vishmidt, M. (2010). Human capital or toxic asset: After the wage, part 1. *Reartikulacija.* Retrieved from http://www.reartikulacija.org/?p=1487

Watson, L .(2003). *Lifelong learning in Australia.* Canberra: Department of Education, Science and Training. Commonwealth of Australia.

West, R. (1998). *Learning for life. Final report review of higher education financing and policy.* Canberra: Australian Government Publishing Service.

The Neoliberal Library

Maura Seale
Georgetown University

"There really is no alternative" (Thatcher, 1980).

In 1989, the American Library Association Presidential Committee on Information Literacy, which was created in 1987 with the charge of defining information literacy and developing ways to integrate information literacy into learning environments and educator training, issued its Final Report (American Library Association Presidential Committee, 1989). Although the term "information literacy" had been used by library science scholars in the 1960s and 1970s, it was not formally codified until this moment (Tuominen, Savolainen, & Talja, 2005). This strongly worded report, which argued "Information literacy is a survival skill in the Information Age," thus began the process of institutionalizing information literacy within librarianship and defining it as a core function and mission of the profession. This process continued with the development of the Big Six Skills model of information seeking and use in 1990 and the creation of information literacy programs and standards by educational institutions and professional associations such as the American Association of School Librarians and the Association of College and Research Libraries since the 1990s (Tuominen, et al., 2005).[1] Information literacy has become the predominant way to frame the educational role of libraries and librarians; it has become "common sense" and is often uncritically and unthinkingly used by both library scholars and practitioners. Pawley (2003) articulates this general definition as "the skills to use and locate information in a variety of formats, and the intellectual ability to evaluate such information" (p. 423). There are, of course, exceptions to this; for example, advocates

---

1 Hall (2010) notes that the Public Library Association has done very little with information literacy, despite public libraries' investment in providing instruction and training. This essay thus focuses primarily on academic and school librarianship, which have engaged with information literacy to a much greater degree.

of critical information literacy such as Accardi, Drabinski, and Kumbier (2010), Elmborg (2006), Simmons (2005), Jacobs (2008), Doherty (2007), Swanson (2004) and Kapitzke (2003a, 2003b, 2001), and other scholars such as Lloyd (2007, 2009), Tuominen, et al. (2005), and Pawley (2003) both critique this understanding of information literacy and work to revise and reframe it. However, this work tends to be on the fringes of librarianship, rather than at the heart of it.

What is striking about this dominant understanding of information literacy is how little it engages with other disciplines, including critical theory and education, despite the clear connection to those disciplines and the claims of library and information science to interdisciplinarity. Librarianship generally fails to engage with the critical and theoretical traditions of related disciplines in a consistent way; this is particularly strange given librarianship and information literacy's ongoing concern with knowledge and information production and educational practices and systems. This essay will argue that librarianship must employ the interventions of scholars in other disciplines around power and politics in order to understand and critique its framing of information literacy specifically and education more generally. This is crucial, because dominant notions of information literacy reinforce and reproduce neoliberal ideology, which is invested in consolidating wealth and power within the upper class through the dispossession and oppression of non-elites. Neoliberalism is fundamentally anti-democratic and uninterested in social justice; an engagement with critiques of knowledge production and neoliberalism by critical theorists and education scholars is the first step in developing a notion of information literacy that is critically engaged, contextualized, and promotes social justice.

Rethinking Knowledge and Information Production through Critical Theory

In *The History of Sexuality*, Michel Foucault (1978) argues that during the nineteenth century, rather than repressing sex and sexuality, Western society

Put into operation an entire machinery for producing true discourses concerning [sex]. Not only did it speak of sex and compel everyone to do so; it also set out to formulate the uniform truth of sex. As if it suspected sex of harboring a fundamental secret. As if it needed this production of truth. As if it was essential that sex be inscribed not only in an economy of pleasure but in an ordered system of knowledge. (p. 69)

The creation of discourses around sex allowed the production of knowledge about sex that could then be known. It allowed the "incorporation of perversions" and a "specification of individuals" (p. 42-43); perversion could be identified and it was no longer a behavior, but rather inhered to an individual. This individual could then be identified and subjugated, as power operates through discourse. In Foucault's theorization, power "is produced from one moment to the next, at every point, or rather in every relation from one point to another. Power is everywhere; not because it embraces everything, but because it comes from everywhere" (p. 93). Discursive formations are the systems through which power operates and through which it is contested or supported; power relations are embodied in the state, the law, and in social hegemonies (p. 92-93). Power works not only by prohibiting certain forms of discourse but also through the production of discourses. In essence, power operates through knowledge production.

Edward Said, in *Orientalism* (1994), uses Foucault's articulation of the nexus of discourse, knowledge, and power to trace the formation of Oriental Studies as a discipline. Orientalism, Said argues, is a discursive formation, the essence of which is the "ineradicable distinction between Western superiority and Oriental inferiority" (p. 42). It is "a Western style for dominating, restructuring, and having authority over the Orient" (p. 3) through the production of knowledge about the Orient, but only specific forms of knowledge, for it is also a "set of constraints upon and limitations of thought" (p. 42). Orientalism is not invested in "empirical data" about the Orient, but rather "representing institutionalized Western knowledge of the Orient" (p. 67-69); it is a "closed system, in which objects are what they are because they are what they are, for once, for all time, for ontological reasons that no empirical material can either dislodge or alter" (p. 70). The discourse of Orientalism cannot be removed from relations of power:

"it is, above all, a discourse that is by no means in direct corresponding relationship with political power in the raw, but rather is produced and exists in an uneven exchange with various kinds of power, shaped to a degree by the exchange with power political...power intellectual...power cultural...power moral" (p. 12). Orientalism cannot be separated from the historical and political contexts in which it was produced, but it is also not reducible to those contexts; colonialism did not cause Orientalism, but reinforced it and was reinforced by it. Despite the disappearance of the formal colonialism of the nineteenth and early twentieth centuries, Orientalism has continued to pervade contemporary discursive practices, attitudes, and policies.

The implications of these theories for librarianship are numerous, but the most basic is that discursive practices matter, that the ways in which material realities are represented in language have effects beyond the linguistic. Pawley (2003) argues that the term "information literacy" embeds two contradictory ideals – "a promethean vision of citizen empowerment and democracy, and, on the other, a desire to control 'quality' of information" (p. 425) – and that ultimately, this tension can be productive and should be explored. The constructed nature of disciplines, such as Oriental Studies, and discourses, such as psychology, can offer librarianship a framework for developing a more critical version of information literacy. This version of information literacy would highlight the way discursive practices act to regulate the questions that can be asked and the conclusions that can be drawn, as well as emphasize that knowledge production is also historically situated and embedded in power relations. This can help learners recognize their own positionality and the ways in which different epistemologies and knowledges are valued due to power relations. The production of knowledge never occurs outside power relations—whether capital, colonial relations, or social hierarchies such as race, class, gender, and sexuality—and knowledge contributes to the maintenance of these hierarchies.

Moreover, the work of these theorists allows library scholars and practitioners to interrogate their own discipline and discursive formations. Similar to Orientalism, discourse around teaching and learning within librarianship functions as what Said calls a "closed system." These topics are generally framed in terms of information literacy, which in turn encapsulates and contains these discussions due to its institutionalization and consequent ability to function as a "natural" – and unquestioned – category (Pawley, 2003, p. 445). Despite the obvious linkages between library instruction and research and practice in education, pedagogy, and composition, library practitioners and scholars do not tend to engage with these fields and very few interrogate or challenge the dominant notion of information literacy. Scholars that do, such as Lloyd (2007, 2009), Tuominen et al. (2005), and the critical information literacy movement generally accept the frame of information literacy and focus their efforts on complicating and expanding on the basic premise. Lloyd, for example, describes information literacy as it is currently envisioned as "reduced, over-simplified, and focused turned towards describing information skills" (2009, p. 245), while Tuominen et al. call attention to its almost exclusive focus on "binary logic" (2005, p. 337). This is not necessarily bad; as Pawley (2003) and Tuominen et al. (2005) point out, this rhetorical strategy has allowed librarians to articulate and claim a space in the educational process. However, in the current closed discursive system around library instruction, learning, and literacy, the notion of information literacy has acted to close off critique and render other discursive moves irrelevant, insignificant, and unimportant even prior to their articulation. Concepts in this discursive space only refer back to themselves. For example, the Association of College and Research Libraries' Visual Literacy Competency Standards for Higher Education, which were recently revised, essentially duplicate ACRL's Information Literacy Standards for Higher Education, despite the stated goal of "address[ing] some of the unique issues presented by visual materials" (Association of College and Research Libraries Visual Literacy Task Force, 2011). This is also true of ACRL's Information Literacy Standards for Anthropology and Sociology Students, as a comparison of Standard One, Performance Indicator 1 across all three sets of standards reveals (Table 1).

Table 1: Comparison of Information Literacy Standards and Performance Indicators

Type of Information Literacy	Standard One	Performance Indicators
Information Literacy (Association of College and Research Libraries, 2000)	The information literate student determines the nature and extent of the information needed.	The information literate student defines and articulates the need for information.

Outcomes

Confers with instructors and participates in class discussions, peer workgroups, and electronic discussions to identify a research topic, or other information need

Develops a thesis statement and formulates questions based on the information need

Explores general information sources to increase familiarity with the topic

Defines or modifies the information need to achieve a manageable focus

Identifies key concepts and terms that describe the information need

Recognizes that existing information can be combined with original thought, experimentation, and/or analysis to produce new information.

Visual Literacy (ACRL Visual Literacy Task Force, 2011)	The visually literate student determines the nature and extent of the visual materials needed.	The visually literate student defines and articulates the need for an image.

Outcomes

Defines the purpose of the image within the project (e.g., illustration, evidence, primary source, focus of analysis, critique, commentary)

Defines the scope (e.g., reach, audience) and environment (e.g., academic environment, open web) of the planned image use Articulates criteria that need to be met by the image (e.g., subject, pictorial content, color, resolution, specific item) Identifies key concepts and terms that describe the needed image

Identifies discipline-specific conventions for image use.

Information Literacy for Anthropology and Sociology Students (ALA/ACRL/ Anthropology and Sociology Section Instruction and Information Literacy Committee Task Force on IL Standards, 2008)	Define and articulate the information need. *(Note: this is not described as a "standard" but rather as "What the student needs to do.")*	

Outcomes

Identifies and describes a manageable research topic or other information need appropriate to the scope of research questions in anthropology and sociology, using discipline-specific terminology, methods, and contexts.

Reads background sources in anthropology and sociology to increase familiarity with the topic. Examples: *Encyclopedia of Social Issues; Encyclopedia of Cultural Anthropology; Sage Encyclopedia of Social Science Research Methods.*

Identifies and lists key concepts, terms, social theories, culture groups, places, and names related to the topic in preparation for searching for information on it. Examples: uses the discipline-focused encyclopedias, *Thesaurus of Sociological Indexing Terms,* and *Outline of Cultural Materials* of the Human Relations Area Files (HRAF). Reevaluates the nature and extent of the information need to clarify, revise, or refine the question after some initial research, reading, interviews, and work with data and/or a population have taken place. *(Note: These are not described as "outcomes" but rather as "Key behaviors for success.")*

These do not differ in any substantive way. The Visual Literacy and Anthropology/Sociology Information Literacy standards simply accept and reproduce the original Information Literacy standards. This is not to argue that they necessarily need to differ from the original standards, but rather that there seems to have been no effort to contest or critically examine the original Information Literacy standards in the creation of these documents. These standards were, of course, all produced within the same professional organization, but even newer concepts, such as transliteracy, look remarkably similar in library discourse:

> "Transliteracy is the ability to read, write and interact across a range of platforms, tools and media from signing and orality through handwriting, print, TV, radio and film, to digital social networks" ("Beginner's Guide to Transliteracy," 2010); and
> "Information literacy is a set of abilities requiring individuals to 'recognize when information is needed and have the ability to locate, evaluate, and use effectively the needed information'" (ACRL, 2000).

Transliteracy, in contrast to information literacy, highlights communication modes, but again, both essentially hinge on the individual's capacity to read and write within a specific context or community; the same website even notes:

> Because transliteracy has its origins outside of libraries, the original thinkers in no way intended it to challenge nor replace information literacy. Transliteracy began as a descriptive concept, designed to understand how people navigate their way across various media. Transliteracy can help inform and supplement a successful information literacy program. The two concepts are not mutually exclusive and share quite a bit of common ground. ("Beginner's Guide to Transliteracy," 2010)

Information literacy and transliteracy also share quite a bit of common ground with literacy, which Cook-Gumperz describes as "a complex of communicative language practices and historically influenced attitudes to these practices that unite or divide a community" (2006, p. 17). The notion of transliteracy not only essentially reproduces the fundamental ideas of information literacy, with the addition of new and social media to make it particularly relevant to twenty-first century librarians, but duplicates its disavowal of any commonalities with the ways literacy is understood outside of the closed system of information literacy discourse. These discursive practices around information literacy reproduce themselves and act to constrain alternative discourses that might critique, contest, and challenge their hegemony; they deploy power and define the truth of teaching and learning within librarianship. The production of this discourse has been built around particular power relations and specific motivations – the goal of professional organizations to claim territory – and this discourse works to maintain power relations, rather than question them. This discursive regime is not dehumanizing in the same ways as those described by Foucault and Said, but it is neither innocent nor the only possible discourse, and, as such must be dismantled to create space for alternative and minority views.

The power relations embedded in discursive practices are, like Oriental-ism, tied to the historical and political contexts in which they are produced and subsequently operate. Scholars of library history have charted the roles played by gender and class in the formation of the public library (Garrison, 2003) and the work of public libraries in promoting the assimilation of immigrants (Pawley, 2010). Librarianship's interest and investment in clas-sifying and ordering knowledge, in ascribing order to the world, too, are an enactment of power that often reproduces contemporary social, economic, and political inequities as Berman (1971) and Olson (2001) have argued. Although information literacy appears in scholarship prior to 1989, it was only formally codified by the American Library Association Presidential Committee on Information Literacy in its Final Report issued that year. The report begins by asserting "No other change in American society has offered greater challenges than the emergence of the Information Age" (ALA Presidential Committee, 1989) and goes on to say:

> Out of the super-abundance of available information, people need to be able to obtain specific information to meet a wide range of personal and business needs. These needs are largely driven either by the desire for personal growth and advancement or by the rapidly changing social, political, and economic environments of American society. What is true today is often outdated tomorrow. A good job may be obsolete next year. To promote economic independence and quality of existence, there is

a lifelong need for being informed and up-to-date.

How our country deals with the realities of the Information Age will have enormous impact on our democratic way of life and on our nation's ability to compete internationally. Within America's information society, there also exists the potential of addressing many long-standing social and economic inequities. To reap such benefits, people--as individuals and as a nation--must be information literate." (ALA Presidential Committee, 1989, para. 2)

The report outlines the ways in which information literacy can benefit individuals, business, and citizenship. Access to information can "improve [the] situations" of "minority and at-risk students, illiterate adults, people with English as a second language, and economically disadvantaged people." In terms of business, information is "now our most important, and pervasive resource," while "Information workers now compose more than half the U.S. labor force" (ALA Presidential Committee, 1989). Moreover

there is ample evidence that those who learn now to achieve access to the bath of knowledge that already envelops the world will be the future's aristocrats of achievement, and that they will be far more numerous than any aristocracy in history. (ALA Presidential Committee, 1989)

Perhaps it is somewhat unsurprising then that the report has somewhat less to say about citizenship than it does about individuals and business; it notes that "Any society committed to individual freedom and democratic government must ensure the free flow of information to all its citizens" (ALA Presidential Committee, 1989). The report goes on to call for a "Coalition for Information Literacy," with an advisory committee comprised of "nationally prominent public figures from librarianship, education, business, and government" (ALA Presidential Committee, 1989).

The most striking aspect of this report is how completely and uncritically it embraces neoliberalism, which Harvey (2005) summarizes as "a theory of political economic practices that proposes that human well-being can best be advanced by liberating individual entrepreneurial freedoms and skills within an institutional framework characterized by strong private property rights, free markets, and free trade" (p. 2). This is signaled in numerous ways. The report's continual invocation of the "Information Age," its contention that employment in information-related fields predominates and that empowerment lies in information indicate a deep interest in information technologies, which is key to neoliberal discourse, as is the rhetoric of individual freedom that pervades this report (Harvey, 2005, p. 3-4; p. 36-37). The report's investment in neoliberalism truly emerges, however, through its pervasive appeal to the economic sphere. Information literacy is tied to "business needs," "advancement," "the economic environment," "a good job," and "our nation's ability to compete internationally." It can address "economic inequities" and thereby create an "aristocracy of achievement" (ALA Presidential Committee, 1989). The freedom and well-being of individuals and societies is thus repeatedly framed using the vocabulary of economics and business and is thus reduced to a "freedom of the market," in which individual workers must compete by becoming more and more flexible (Harvey, 2005, p. 38, 75-76). The implications of this redefinition of freedom are that "each person is held responsible and accountable for his or her own actions and well-being," as fewer social protections and services are provided by employers and the state (Harvey, 2005, p. 65, 75-76; Saunders, 2010). The core logic of this report, then, is that because individuals can choose to become information literate and because information literacy can resolve social and economic inequities, those inequities are ultimately the fault of those individuals (Saunders, 2010); in contrast, by embracing information literacy, individuals can become "aristocrats." As Harvey (2005) describes it, "(p)ersonal failure is generally attributed to personal failings, and the victim is all too often blamed" (p. 76).

The codification and institutionalization of information literacy occurred during and immediately following Ronald Reagan's presidency and Margaret Thatcher's tenure as Prime Minister, during which the welfare state was dismantled, labor was disempowered, industry and banking were deregulated, inequalities in wealth and power intensified, and deindustrialization sped up, as neoliberalism ideology was embraced and implemented by governments in both the United States and United Kingdom (Harvey, 2005; Saunders, 2010). As May (2002) argues, the notion of the "Information Age" or "Information Society" is a rhetorical strategy used to obscure the actual "new" economy, which is dominated by low-wage and unstable service work rather than well-paying information work requiring higher education (Stevenson, 2009). The ALA Presidential Committee's Final Report duplicates this move and shifts the blame for social and economic inequities onto the very individuals disempowered by those inequities; if an individual cannot find a well-paying job, it is because she or he has not actively pursued information literacy. The report wholeheartedly rationalizes and supports the adoption of neoliberalism that occurred during the 1980s.

Rethinking Political Economy through Educational Theory

Educational scholars have recently begun to investigate the impact of neoliberalism on education. Hursh (2007) demonstrates the embeddedness of No Child Left Behind and similar educational reforms in neoliberal ideology. Saunders (2010) interrogates higher education and argues that neoliberal ideology "strengthens and extends some of the nefarious purposes of our colleges and universities" through "the infiltration of economic rationality with higher education, which has resulted in the prioritization of revenue generation and efficiency, corporate governance replacing shared and collegial models of decision making, faculty acting like entrepreneurs, and students being treated and identifying themselves as customers" (p. 66). Brancaleone and O'Brien (2011) theorize learning outcomes and argue that "learning outcomes, through their bureaucratisation and marketisation, imply the adjustment of one's social relations, mode of work/ learning and hence, of consciousness, to an economic empirical base" (p. 507); they "constitute an illusory promise, which is set within the very real context of a neoliberal drive towards educational commodification" (p. 514). Learning outcomes, as developed and deployed within a neoliberal context, are not flexible or open, and do not theorize learning as a complex, recursive, and unpredictable system of processes. Instead, learning is presumed to be quantifiable and is justified and valued economically, as leading to greater earnings and thus a high return on investment. Henry Giroux, a prominent theorist of critical pedagogy, explicitly places critical pedagogy linked to an ongoing project of democratization in opposition to neoliberalism, for it

> offers the possibility of resistance to the increasing depoliticization of
> the citizenry, provides a language to challenge the politics of accom-
> modation that connects education to the logic of privatization, refuses
> to define the citizen as simply a consuming subject, and actively opposes
> the view of teaching as market-driven practice and learning as a form
> of training. (2004, p. 38)

Educators, he argues, must contest "the increasingly dominant view
propagated by neoliberal gurus such as Milton Friedman, that profit
making is the essence of democracy and accumulating material goods
the essence of the good life" by employing this vision of critical pedagogy
(2004, p. 39).

As with critical theorizations of knowledge production and discursive practices, the analyses of neoliberalism by educational theorists and
scholars are applicable to librarianship in two different registers. Most
straightforwardly, this work can offer librarianship a way to complicate
current formulations of information literacy by foregrounding information economics; for example, Saunders (2010) explicitly discusses the
"redefinition of research results, discoveries, and creations" from more or
less public goods intended to be shared in order to promote knowledge
creation to "'intellectual property' that should be sold on the open market"
under neoliberalism (p. 57). This can help learners more fully grasp the
contemporary information ecosystem, appreciate the results of the commodification of information and knowledge, and apply those insights to
their own research practices. More specifically and in line with recent
trends within librarianship, this work can also help librarians and learners articulate the goals of the Open Access movement. The perspective
gained from applying the critiques of educational scholars and theorists
to discursive practices around information literacy within librarianship,
however, is significant and troubling.

In 1998, the American Library Association issued "A Progress Report
on Information Literacy," which tracked progress on the recommendations made in the 1989 Final Report. The Progress Report also included
several new recommendations:

Recommendation 1: Forum members should encourage and champion the growing support of accrediting agencies...Recommendation 2: Teacher education and performance expectations need to include information literacy skills...Recommendation 3: Librarian education and performance expectations need to include information literacy...Recommendation 4: Forum members need to identify ways to illustrate to business leaders the benefits of fostering an information literate workforce. (American Library Association, 1998)

What is revealed in the Progress Report is an intensification and expansion of neoliberal ideology. The focus on accreditation and performance expectations and therefore accountability in the first three recommendations exemplify the neoliberal commodification of education: these concepts "stand for educational product" (Brancaleone & O'Brien, 2011, p. 513). In framing education as a standardized and measurable product, "the question of *who* gets access to educational opportunities" is obscured; that is, economic, political, and social inequities are erased and notions of power and social justice are ignored (Brancaleone & O'Brien, 2011, p 512). Recommendation four, in a different move, redefines learning in neoliberal terms as mere "job training" (Giroux, 2004, p. 45) and individuals become "a mere factor of production," who are flexible and easily exploitable due to power inequities, and ultimately disposable (Harvey, 2005, p. 167-169). This formulation of workers goes unchallenged in an *American Libraries* article about information literacy published that same year: "[T]he average 21st-century worker may need the skills to cope with as many as seven major employment changes in his or her lifetime" (quoted in Pawley, 2003, p. 422).

The neoliberal turn within information literacy discourse is apparent in numerous documents and publications. The ACRL Information Literacy Standards (2000) and the American Association of School Librarians' Standards for the 21st-Century Learner (2007), with their reliance on measurable learning outcomes, embody the commodification of education and the obscuring of inequities (Brancaleone & O'Brien, 2011). These standards also rely on what Saunders (2010) refers to as the "homo oeconomicus," the individual who consumes, is rational and autonomous, and who "no longer [needs] to rely on a larger society or to work together to attend to their common issues, problems, and needs nor do they belong to any particular class" (p. 47-48). This is particularly obvious in the Information Literacy Standards, which take as their subject "the information literate student," who exists outside of social, political, and economic contexts (ACRL, 2000). The lack of context in both sets of standards, as well as in practitioner guidelines such as the CRAAP test ("Evaluating Information," 2010), and the perceived neutrality of information embody Saunders's (2010) description of faculty teaching in the neoliberal university. Faculty (and according to these standards, librarians) "now should be neutral disseminators of ideological content" and the classroom should be a "space of sterile learning" (p. 61). The appeal to "authoritative" sources of information in the ACRL Standards and CRAAP test – usually defined as that produced by for-profit publishers and thus only available through library subscriptions and purchases – reinforces the notion that students are consumers and that information and learning are commodities (Saunders, 2010). Finally, the ACRL Standards only gesture towards the connection between information literacy and employment that is made explicit in the ALA's Final Report (1989) and Progress Report (1998), but the AASL Standards do note that "Technology skills are crucial for future employment needs" (American Association of School Librarians, 2007). As Giroux (2004) and Saunders (2010) point out, education under neoliberalism is primarily job training for disposable workers. The invocation of technology in the AASL Standards is also part of neoliberal discourse, which holds that "there is a technological fix for each and every problem" (Harvey, 2005, p. 68). As Stevenson (2009) notes, the focus on technological fixes closes off alternate explanations, such as longstanding social and economic inequities exacerbated by neoliberal policies, and renders market forces as the sole solutions to those problems.

The institutionalization of neoliberal ideology within librarianship is even more evident in the work of Megan Oakleaf, whose most recent project was *The Value of Academic Libraries: A Comprehensive Research Review and Report* (2010). It begins:

> Government officials see higher education as a national resource. Employers view higher education institutions as producers of a commod-

ity—student learning. Top academic faculty expect higher education institutions to support and promote cutting-edge research. Parents and students expect higher education to enhance students' collegiate experience, as well as propel their career placement and earning potential. Not only do stakeholders count on higher education institutions to achieve these goals, they also require them to demonstrate evidence that they have achieved them. The same is true for academic libraries; they too can provide evidence of their value. Community college, college, and university librarians no longer can rely on their stakeholders' belief in their importance. Rather, they must demonstrate their value. (p. 4)

The logic of the market pervades this paragraph, from education as a commodity, to students and parents as customers, to the importance of measurable evidence and economic value. The report goes on to list recommendations, such as:

"Record and increase library impact on student enrollment"
"Link libraries to improved student retention and graduation rates"
"Enhance library contribution to student job success"
"Track library influences on increased student achievement"
"Demonstrate and develop library impact on student learning"
"Document and augment library advancement of student experiences, attitudes, and perceptions of quality" (Oakleaf, 2010)

Each of these recommendations requires the development of measurable outcomes, the creation of assessment tools, and the gathering of quantitative and qualitative data in order to establish "value," which Oakleaf defines primarily in economic terms: "Value can be defined in a variety of ways and viewed from numerous perspectives...including use, return-on-investment, commodity production, impact, and alternative comparison" (2010, p. 19). The view of library instruction in Oakleaf's work is embedded in a "view of teaching as market-driven practice and learning as a form of training" and completely antithetical to Giroux's articulation of critical pedagogy (2004, p. 38) and yet Oakleaf's work is heavily lauded and embraced by library scholars and practitioners. *The Value of Academic Libraries* was commissioned by ACRL and in 2011, Oakleaf received the Ilene F. Rockman Instruction Publication of the Year Award. She is frequently invited to speak at library conferences, has received numerous grants, and has been hired by eleven university libraries as a consultant (Oakleaf, 2012a; Oakleaf, 2012b). For many libraries and librarians, it might make strategic sense to adopt Oakleaf's approach to defining and measuring value, as external administrators pressure them to demonstrate the work they perform, in an era of austerity. However, this sort of strategic use of Oakleaf's work does not require that libraries and librarians accept its underlying neoliberal ideology as true and the only valid way to describe and justify the work of academic libraries and librarians. There is no sense that Oakleaf is maintaining any sort of critical distance in her work on the value of libraries, and this lack is repeated in the reuse of her work within librarianship more broadly; the closed discursive system undoubtedly promotes the uncritical adoption of ideas that seem authoritative and obvious.

Steven Bell, like Oakleaf, is also widely regarded as a leader within librarianship, although he identifies more as a practitioner and less as a scholar. He is a regular columnist for *Library Journal*, publishes a popular blog, "The Kept-Up Academic Librarian," and is currently the vice president/president-elect of ACRL. And as with Oakleaf, neoliberal ideology is at the heart of much of his work. One of his columns, for example, focuses on business practices and publications:

> As an ex-business librarian, I developed a great appreciation for business, but there's more to it than that. I want to continuously improve as a "leadager," a leader who also manages. Keeping up with the world of business is a real boon-a constant source of inspiration and ideation. If you think there's no place for business in libraries, think again. Does your library provide chat reference? Guess where that service originated–business call centers. Do you offer self-check technology? That idea evolved from the ATM.
>
> Paying more attention to business isn't selling out. It's about discovering new possibilities to improve the library experience. (Bell, 2011)

Bell not only uncritically ventriloquates business rhetoric but elides the differences between the purposes of chat reference and business call centers, between checking out materials and using an ATM, between learners and customers. However, the economic realm is not just a source of meaningless words for Bell – what he is most interested and invested in is promoting a vision of higher education as completely subject to neoliberalism. In a column on what he refers to as the "unbundling" of higher education, Bell (2012c) writes approvingly of "start-up firms that see an industry ripe for disruption" and seek to monetize it by offering free or low-cost educational content in response to an "affordability crisis." In another column, he celebrates the increasing popularity of certificates by misreading a study and claiming that "compared to those enrolled in regular degree programs, certificates holders are the ones actually getting jobs" (Bell, 2012b). It is not just the possibility that certificates might improve employment prospects that make them so attractive to Bell; it is also that education for any other reason is not actually important:

> We can certainly debate the merits of having our citizens obtain a well-rounded, liberal arts grounded education that prepares them well to be smart, engaged citizens. The supporters of alternate forms of higher education might agree, but would argue that it's just too darn expensive for most of those good-citizens-to-be. (Bell, 2012b)

Bell's contempt for education that is not completely subject to market imperatives is even more obvious in another column, purportedly about library service:

> If you want to rile up faculty and academic librarians, just refer to higher education as a business. It can be incredibly off putting to many higher education personnel to suggest their work is in any way connected to profit making or any form of consumer-oriented exploitation that comes along with commerce. A new report is recommending that higher education might achieve transformative improvements by finally admitting the need to focus on functioning like any other business by shifting to a more customer-oriented operation...

> The other thing you can do to agitate your colleagues is to consistently refer to students as customers. They dislike this because it suggests we are salespeople who now operate under the principle that the customer is always right. It also cheapens the noble causes and lofty values of the delivery of higher education. Customer service representatives and enlightenment don't mix. What if that thinking is plain wrong?...

> I can already hear the negative reactions. "Looks like another business fad is being sold to us as the way to save higher education." "Let's see how quickly the administrators can lose interest in this waste of time."

Unlike the naysayers, this report strongly resonates with me because I've been arguing for years that academic librarians need to pay closer attention to the library experience received by every community member. (Bell, 2012a)

Bell summarily dismisses any sort of education that attempts to function outside of the market system as a hodgepodge of "noble causes" and "lofty values" that are outdated and irrelevant. Instead, higher education must act like a business – not because institutions are under pressure due to a decrease in public funding – but because, in a particularly insidious move by Bell, this will somehow, in an unspecified way, help students. What Bell envisions for higher education, then, is an educational product of uncertain quality, produced by a de-professionalized and low-wage workforce of adjunct professors (and librarians) employed by wealthy for-profit institutions, most likely delivered online to customer-students, who consume it in order to compete for similar sorts of low-wage service positions in the neoliberal economy. These customer-students do not attempt to critically engage with already existing knowledge, nor do they create new knowledge; they learn to earn, and take on debt to do so, due to the systematic defunding of education under neoliberal policies (Harvey, 2005, p. 76). This is the "disruptive and transformative change" that Bell is so eagerly anticipating and that those "naysayers" are so strongly resisting and challenging. Bell repeatedly casts himself as the voice in the wilderness, but his ideas dominate discourse within librarianship. The neoliberal subtext of his work is often cloaked by his emphasis on serving users, often through instruction. The "unbundling" of courses and degrees, the growth in vocational certificates, and the application of business goals and practices are portrayed by Bell as fundamentally positive, as they obviously empower users by offering them both a wider range of choices and the freedom to choose. These ideas of better service, increased access, more choices, and greater freedom are powerful, and strongly resonate with the core values of librarianship (ALA, 2004), and it is undoubtedly due to this resonance that they have become a key part of the dominant discourse within librarianship. But as Harvey (2005), drawing on the work of Karl Polanyi, points out, within a neoliberal framework,

The idea of freedom 'thus degenerates into a mere advocacy of free enterprise,' which means 'the fullness of freedom for those whose income,
leisure and security need no enhancing, and a mere pittance of liberty
for the people, who may in vain attempt to make use of their democratic
rights to gain shelter from the power of the owners of property.' [...] The
good freedoms are lost, the bad ones take over. (p. 37)

Notions of choice and freedom have become tied to "differentiated con-
sumerism and individual libertarianism," and, as such, are guaranteed
only in the marketplace and are disconnected from any sort of social
justice (Harvey, 2005, p. 42, 65). Harvey (2005, p. 69) also argues that
neoliberal states are generally hostile towards and have consistently acted
to limit democratic governance, despite their constant invocation of ideas
like freedom that would seem to be bound up with the idea of democracy,
particularly in an American context. The ALA, in its articulation of the
core values of librarianship, carefully unpacks ideas of democracy, freedom,
service, and social responsibility and subverts neoliberal ideology by framing these values as "public goods" and as existing outside of the market
system (ALA, 2004). However, dominant discourse within librarianship,
as well as in broader society, tends to elide distinctions between different
varieties of freedom and so consumer choice becomes synonymous with
democratic choice, and freedom in the market becomes democracy. It is
in this context that the work of Bell and Oakleaf have become so persua-
sive to so many library scholars and practitioners, who fail to realize the
implications of neoliberal ideology, and who fail to realize that the futures
envisioned by dominant discourses within librarianship are not the only
futures available. A re-envisioned or perhaps even a critical information
literacy could begin to work towards this sort of parsing and contestation
of ideology, but it cannot do this work in its current formulation, which
ignores power and context. Neoliberal discourse is at the center of the
closed system of library discursive practices, including those around information literacy and by and large, it remains unchallenged. Neoliberalism,
as Harvey (2005) argues, is fundamentally anti-democratic and actively
works against social justice; it consolidates wealth and power among a
few and works to disempower the great majority of people, particularly
those who are already oppressed due to hierarchies of race, class, gender,

nationality, and sexuality, and information literacy discourse uncritically participates in this.

Innocence and Alternatives

As Henry Giroux (2004) contends, "pedagogy is never innocent," and information literacy, from its emergence to its recent formulation, has and continues to uncritically adopt and reproduce neoliberalism within a closed discursive system that works to deny alternative conceptions of library pedagogy and instruction (p. 38). The knowledge produced by librarianship and information literacy discursive practices is an enactment of power that naturalizes and authorizes neoliberalism and constrains the questioning of inequalities. The dominance of neoliberal discourse within librarianship results in a movement away from social justice, as neoliberalism is characterized by the dismantling of social services and programs, the degradation of the environment, the creation of the disposable worker, greater income inequality, the consolidation of economic and political power among elites, and the subversion of democracy, accomplished through "accumulation by dispossession" (Harvey, 2005, p. 199). To Giroux (2004), "critical pedagogy at its best attempt to provoke students to deliberate, resist, and cultivate a range of capacities that enable them to move beyond the world they already know without insisting on a fixed set of meanings" (p. 39). Information literacy, if theorized differently, could work to challenge neoliberal discourse rather than eagerly adopting it; it could truly become a form of critical pedagogy and subject neoliberalism to critical analysis and thereby work to derive alternatives (Harvey, 2005, p. 198). This would entail an almost complete rethinking of the concept, but it is crucial at this historical moment, as education continues to be reshaped to fit market imperatives, as librarianship struggles to define its role in late capitalism, as librarians and scholars become disposable workers due to market forces. Library instruction and pedagogy specifically and librarianship more generally needs to begin promoting an awareness of the field's embeddedness within a neoliberal political and economic context, and engaging critically with that context in order to open up a discursive space in which alternatives to neoliberalism can be conceptualized and implemented. For there are alternatives, even following three decades of the neoliberal policies and practices that began with Thatcher and Reagan.

References

Accardi, M. T., Drabinski, E., & Kumbier, A. (2010). *Critical library instruction: Theories and methods*. Duluth, Minn.: Library Juice Press.

American Association of School Librarians. (2007). *Standards for the 21ˢᵗ-century*. Retrieved from http://www.ala.org/aasl/sites/ala.org.aasl/files/content/guidelinesandstandards/learningstandards/AASL_LearningStandards.pdf

American Library Association (1998). *A progress report on information literacy: An update on the American Library Association Presidential Committee on Information Literacy: Final report*. Retrieved from http://www.ala.org/acrl/publications/whitepapers/progressreport

American Library Association (2004). *Core values of librarianship*. Retrieved from http://www.ala.org/offices/oif/statementspols/corevaluesstatement/corevalues

American Library Association/Association of College and Research Libraries/Anthropology and Sociology Section Instruction and Information Literacy Committee Task Force on IL Standards. (2008). *Information literacy standards for anthropology and sociology students*. Retrieved from http://www.ala.org/acrl/standards/anthro_soc_standards

American Library Association Presidential Committee on Information Literacy. (1989). *Final report*. Retrieved from http://www.ala.org/acrl/publications/whitepapers/presidential

Association of College and Research Libraries (2000). *Information literacy competency standards for higher education*. Retrieved from http://www.ala.org/acrl/standards/informationliteracycompetency

Association of College and Research Libraries Visual Literacy Task Force. (2010). *ACRL visual literacy competency standards for higher education*. Retrieved from http://www.ala.org/acrl/standards/visualliteracy

Beginner's guide to transliteracy « libraries and transliteracy. Retrieved from http://librariesandtransliteracy.wordpress.com/beginner's-guide-to-transliteracy/

Bell, S. (2011). A little business won't hurt—and it may help. *From the Bell Tower*. Retrieved from http://lj.libraryjournal.com/2011/12/opinion/steven-bell/a-little-business-wont-hurt-and-it-may-help-from-the-bell-tower/

Bell, S. (2012a). Blueprinting for better library customer service. *From the Bell Tower*. Retrieved from http://lj.libraryjournal.com/2012/06/opinion/steven-bell/blueprinting-for-better-library-customer-service-from-the-bell-tower/

Bell, S. (2012b). More certificates – less research. *From the Bell Tower*. Retrieved from http://lj.libraryjournal.com/2012/06/opinion/steven-bell/more-certificates-less-research-from-the-bell-tower/

Bell, S. (2012c). Unbundling higher education. *From the Bell Tower*. Retrieved from http://lj.libraryjournal.com/2012/02/opinion/unbundling-higher-education-from-the-bell-tower/

Berman, S. (1971). *Prejudices and antipathies: A tract on LC subject headings concerning people*. Scarecrow Press, Metuchen, New Jersey.

Brancaleone, D., & O'Brien, S. (2011). Educational commodification and the (economic) sign value of learning outcomes. *British Journal of Sociology of Education, 32*(4), 501-519. doi 10.1080/01425692.2011.578435

Cook-Gumperz, J. (2006). *The social construction of literacy*. Cambridge, UK; New York: Cambridge University Press.

Doherty, J. J. (2007). No shhing: Giving voice to the silenced: An essay in support of critical information literacy. *Library Philosophy and Practice, 9*(2). Retrieved from http://digitalcommons.unl.edu/libphilprac/

Doherty, J. J., & Ketchner, K. (2005). Empowering the intentional learner: A critical theory for information literacy instruction. *Library Philosophy and Practice, 8*(1). Retrieved from http://digitalcommons.unl.edu/libphilprac/

Elmborg, J. (2006). Critical information literacy: Implications for instructional practice. *The Journal of Academic Librarianship, 32*(2), 192-199.

Evaluating Information: Applying the CRAAP Test. Retrieved from http://www.csuchico.edu/lins/handouts/eval_websites.pdf

Foucault, M. (1978). *The history of sexuality*. New York: Pantheon Books.

Garrison, D. (2003). *Apostles of culture: The public librarian and American society, 1876-1920*. Madison: University of Wisconsin Press.

Giroux, H. A. (2004). Critical pedagogy and the postmodern/modern divide: Towards a pedagogy of democratization. *Teacher Education Quarterly, 31*(1).

Giroux, H. A. (2010). Bare pedagogy and the scourge of neoliberalism: Rethinking higher education as a democratic public sphere. *Educational Forum, 74*(3), 184-196. doi 10.1080/00131725.2010.483897

Hall, R. (2010). Public praxis: A vision for critical information literacy in public libraries. *Public Library Quarterly, 29*(2), 162-175.

Harvey, D. (2005). *A brief history of neoliberalism*. Oxford; New York: Oxford University Press.

Hursh, D. (2007). Assessing 'No Child Left Behind' and the rise of neoliberal education policies. *American Educational Research Journal, 44*(3), 493-518.

Jacobs, H. L. M. (2008). Information literacy and reflective pedagogical praxis. *The Journal of Academic Librarianship, 34*(3), 256-262.

Kapitzke, C. (2001). Information literacy: The changing library. *Journal of Adolescent and Adult Literacy, 44*(5), 450-456.

Kapitzke, C. (2003a). Information literacy: A review and poststructural critique. *Australian Journal of Language and Literacy, 26*(1), 53-66.

Kapitzke, C. (2003b). Information literacy: A positivist epistemology and a politics of outformation. *Educational Theory, 53*(1), 37-53/

Lloyd, A. (2007). Learning to put out the red stuff: Becoming information literate through discursive practice. *Library Quarterly, 77*(2), 181-198.

Lloyd, A. (2010). Framing information literacy as information practice: Site ontology and practice theory. *Journal of Documentation, 66*(2), 245-258.

Luke, A., & Kapitzke, C. (1999). Literacies and libraries: Archives and cybrarics. *Pedagogy, Culture and Society, 7*(3), 467-491.

May, C. (2002). *The information society: A sceptical view.* Malden, MA: Polity Press..

Oakleaf, M.J. (2012a). Consulting. Retrieved from Retrieved from http://meganoakleaf.info/consulting.html.

Oakleaf, M.J. (2012b). CV. Retrieved from http://meganoakleaf.info/oakleaf-cv-feb2012.pdf.

Oakleaf, M. J., Association of College and Research Libraries, & American Library Association. (2010). *The value of academic libraries: A comprehensive research review and report.* Chicago, IL: Association of College and Research Libraries, American Library Association.

Olson, H. A. (2001). The power to name: Representation in library catalogs. *Signs: Journal of Women in Culture & Society, 26*(3), 639-668.

Pawley, C. (2003). Information literacy: A contradictory coupling. *Library Quarterly, 73*(4), 422-452.

Pawley, C. (2010). *Reading places: Literacy, democracy, and the public library in cold war America.* Amherst: University of Massachusetts Press.

Said, E. W. (1994). *Orientalism.* New York: Vintage Books.

Saunders, D. B. (2010). Neoliberal ideology and public higher education in the United States. *Journal for Critical Education Policy Studies, 8*(1), 41-77.

Simmons, M. H. (2005). Librarians as disciplinary discourse mediators: Using genre theory to move toward critical information literacy. *portal: Libraries and the Academy, 5*(3), 297-311.

Stevenson, S. (2009). Digital divide: A discursive move away from the real inequities. *Information Society, 25*(1), 1-22. doi:10.1080/01972240802587539

Swanson, T. (2004a). A radical step: Implementing a critical information literacy model. *portal: Libraries and the Academy, 4*(2), 259-273.

Swanson, T. (2004b). Applying a critical pedagogical perspective to information literacy standards. *Community & Junior College Libraries, 12*(4), 65–78.

Thatcher, M. (1980). *Press conference for American correspondents in London | Margaret Thatcher Foundation.* Retrieved 3/5/2012, 2012, from http://www.margaretthatcher.org/document/104389

Tuominen, K., Savolainen, R., & Talja, S. (2005). Information literacy as a sociotechnical practice. *Library Quarterly, 75*(3), 329-345.

"You've Got to Know and Know Properly": Citizenship in Kazuo Ishiguro's *Never Let Me Go* and the Aims of Information Literacy Instruction

Jeff Lilburn
Mount Allison University

It has become commonplace to state that information literacy helps to produce an informed and engaged citizenry. Along with its contributions to student success in academic pursuits, information literacy is regularly credited with providing individuals with the foundation and skills necessary for their roles as citizens and members of their communities. Less common in Library and Information Studies (LIS) discourse celebrating the benefits of an informed citizenry is critical examination of what it actually means to be a citizen. As Christy Stevens and Patricia Campbell (2006) observe, "global citizenship" and "lifelong learning" have become "hooray words" used in mission statements and planning documents, but their meaning is often obscured by uncritical acceptance that these concepts are "inherently good" (pp. 536-537). LIS champions the development of informed citizens, or of global citizens, but little consideration is given to what an informed citizen might actually aspire to do, change or contribute to society. It is the premise of this chapter that an information literacy practice that fails to examine critically the meaning of a key concept used to justify its importance risks espousing a limited and impoverished form of citizenship.

Citizenship, like democracy, is a contested term. Definitions of citizenship generally include references to membership in a community or nation state entailing protections and rights as well as duties and responsibilities. Citizenship can be active and critical, or it can simply mean allegiance to an existing way of life, what Henry Giroux (2006) calls "patriotic correctness" (p. 111). Darin Barney's recent work considers the need for more active forms of citizenship in contemporary democratic societies. For Barney (2007b), citizenship is at its core a "way of knowing and acting, a way of being in the world, a practice" (p. 38); it is the practice of political judgment – judgment "brought to bear on claims about justice and... a life lived well in common with others" (p. 44). One outcome of Barney's move to define citizenship through political judgment is that citizenship can be enacted in ways that may not be immediately identifiable as such, or in ways that are not always understood to be acts of citizenship (pp. 43-44). Barney points to the examples of public displays of mourning by the Madres de Plaza de Mayo in Argentina and the development of technologies intended to circumvent authoritarian state censorship or surveillance, each of which is part of a struggle for justice and an act carried out by persons practicing citizenship (p. 43). Barney's research focuses largely on questions around technology and demonstrates how citizens are routinely excluded from decisions concerning the development and implementation of new technologies. Citizens, Barney (2007a) argues, should have the right to exercise political judgment on new technologies since technologies, and the manner in which they are used and regulated can have "dramatic consequences for human social, economic, and cultural relationships and practices" (p. 23). Barney's more general contention, most pertinent here, is that democratic societies deny individuals opportunities to exercise political judgment when some questions are simply not treated as questions at all, when certain questions are not understood to be within the realm of political judgment of citizens.[1] In North American society, for instance, citizens may be asked to make judgments on issues of taxation, but the capitalist ideology that provides a foundation to society's regulation is almost never offered as a question (Barney, 2007b, p. 44). The extent to which citizens can be said to be informed, critical and engaged hinges on the extent to which they are aware not just of the questions they are permitted to ask but of the full scope of the range of questions they might ask.

With Barney's ideas about citizenship serving as springboard, I turn to a work of fiction, Kazuo Ishiguro's novel, *Never Let Me Go*, to investigate the representation of acts of citizenship and apply that inquiry to the aims

---

1 Barney's more specific arguments with regards to technology could also be brought to bear on Ishiguro's novel as a means of discussing LIS's relationship to technology, but this is not my primary concern here.

of information literacy instruction. Although Ishiguro's novel is not about libraries or librarians, it offers a thoughtful consideration of the social, political, and cultural contexts that influence acts of teaching. It also explores different ways in which individuals enact political judgment and practice citizenship and the consequences of those alternative acts of judgment. Set in England, *Never Let Me Go* imagines a world where decisions made during a time of rapid technological change lead to the development of an organ donation program that uses human clones as donors. The program, the reader is told, developed quickly, with no time "to take stock, to ask the sensible questions" (Ishiguro, 2010, p. 262). Questions about how, or even whether, the organ donation program should proceed were not publically discussed or debated; they were, it would seem, outside the realm of political judgment of citizens.[2] In a world where there were suddenly new ways to cure previously incurable conditions, the desirability of that cure means there was little incentive to delve too deeply into the program's full implications. People preferred to believe the organs "appeared from nowhere" and "did their best not to think about" the cloned children created to be donors (pp. 262-263). The action of the novel takes place many years after the program is launched and is, to a large degree, concerned with the upbringing and education of the clones, or students, as they are called, a group that is not offered nominal English citizenship and whose humanity is debated.[3] Ishiguro also explores how those who are ostensibly English citizens but were denied meaningful opportunities to exercise their political judgment when the program was being developed nevertheless seek and find other means to respond to a program – and a society – that regularizes and condones exploitation and murder.

Ishiguro depicts two principal challenges to the organ donation program, and it is here that I wish to focus my discussion. One is an activist movement that aims to change the way the organ donation program is run. The other is an act of resistance by a teacher who attempts to subvert the dominant ideology at Hailsham, the school where the cloned students are

---

2 The organ donation program did lead to "arguments" but these, according to Miss Emily, occurred after the program was already in place (pp. 262-263).

3 People "tried to convince themselves [that the cloned children] weren't really like us; that [they] were less than human" (p. 263). They also question whether the students have souls (p. 260).

raised and educated.[4] Both of these oppositional efforts involve decisions and actions that have an impact on the education of the students. With these attempts to challenge the organ donation program, Ishiguro explores two engaged forms of citizenship that seek to bring about positive change in the lives of students. However, one ultimately supports and sustains existing social hierarchies, while the other is open to the possibility that things could be fundamentally different from the way they happen to be at the moment;[5] one accepts that certain matters are not the object of political judgment of citizens, while the other refutes the basis on which certain questions are excluded from public inquiry.

Consideration of the two forms of citizenship represented in Ishiguro's novel can help develop a clearer articulation of the forms of citizenship promoted by librarians teaching information literacy. Recent studies of information literacy instruction have called for a more interdisciplinary and theoretically informed understanding and expression of information literacy pedagogy.[6] Some LIS scholars have been particularly critical of information literacy instruction that is based on standards and the acquisition of applied skills. Such an approach is often viewed as offering an instrumental approach to teaching that supports the societal status quo without adopting a critical stance towards it.[7] In response to these criticisms have come suggestions that LIS engage more closely with critical theory and with research on critical pedagogy.[8] For its part, *Never Let Me*

---

4 Keith McDonald (2007) suggests that Kathy's narrative might also be considered a form of resistance. In his discussion of the "autobiographical trope" Ishiguro employs to construct the novel, McDonald describes Kathy's passivity and acceptance of her lot as "enraging" (pp. 80-81). He also concedes that some readers "will undoubtedly find heroism in her ability to recount her experiences in a world that goes so far as to disenfranchise her from the human mass, where she is reduced to a cog in a bioconsumerist culture" (p. 81).

5 To be a citizen practicing political judgment, Barney (2007a) contends, we must be open to the possibility that the good life, a life lived well in common with others, "might entail something different from the way things just happen to be at the moment" (pp. 15, 38-39).

6 See, for example, Pawley (2003), Swanson (2004), Elmborg (2006), and Jacobs (2008).

7 Jacobs (2008) contends that when we limit the potentials of information literacy to "outcomes and standards, we run the risk of minimizing the complex situatedness of information literacy and diminishing – if not negating – its inherent political nature" (p. 258). Pankl and Coleman (2010) contend that IL standards are "predicated upon the idea of using information to achieve purposes, rather than highlighting the purposiveness of the researcher" (p. 8). A reliance on standards has also been faulted for essentially taking the place of pedagogy in library instruction (Harris, 2010, p. 279).

8 Recent examples include Jabobs (2008), Pankl and Coleman (2010) and Cope (2010).

Go has been described by one literary scholar as "critical science fiction" that functions to comment critically on, and to intervene in, the history of the present (Griffin, 2009, p. 653).[9] Ishiguro's novel is deeply invested in pedagogy and uses characters who are teachers to raise questions about teaching, about the meaning of citizenship, and about teaching's place in creating a just society. With this in mind, Ishiguro's fictional representation of teaching and citizenship will be used as a lens through which to consider the implications of librarian teaching practice.

Acts of Citizenship

Narrated by Kathy H., a thirty-one year-old "graduate" of Hailsham, an institution resembling a traditional English boarding school, *Never Let Me Go* imagines an alternative history of the recent past. The novel is set in England in the late 1990s and presents a world that is, in many ways, "disturbingly similar to our own" (McDonald, 2007, p. 76). However, the England Ishiguro portrays differs from the one we know in at least one significant respect: in the England of the novel, scientific breakthroughs in the post-war period made it possible to clone human beings by as early as the 1950s. The clones, or students, are created for the specific purpose of supplying medical science with organs used to treat non-clone patients. Kathy H. is one of these students. Much of the novel takes place at Hailsham, where the students are raised and educated until their mid- to late-teens when they are then sent off to various locations across the country. Kathy and her two closest friends, Ruth and Tommy, are sent to the Cottages, rural farmhouses in a secluded setting where students stay for a year or two, after which time they will either begin training to become "carers" or begin making their "donations." Kathy is a carer and travels the country visiting various institutions, or "centres," as they are called, to look after students who have started to "donate" their organs. Students make up to four donations, after which they "complete," or die. By

---

9 Griffin (2009) suggests that, intertextually, the novel belongs to the same critical tradition as the work of Frederic Jameson and Donna Haraway in that it "challenges conceptions of difference as absolute categories and contests the ethical imperatives underlying the insistence on such absolute difference (p. 653).

the end of the novel, Kathy has acted as carer for both Ruth and Tommy and is set to make her first "donation" within the next year.

At no point in Kathy's narrative is there an indication that the students contemplate any sort of organized resistance to their plight.[10] Instead of imagining ways to rebel or escape, a few students latch on to rumors of possible deferrals for couples able to demonstrate that they are in love and deserving of additional time together. Acting on those rumors, Kathy and Tommy pursue a deferral and, towards the end of the novel, inquire about their eligibility in a meeting with Miss Emily, Hailsham's former head guardian, and Marie-Claude (Madame), the mysterious visitor who occasionally appeared to select and take away the students' best artwork. It is here that Kathy and Tommy learn that there are, in fact, no deferrals. It is also here that readers learn more about the origin and purpose of Hailsham – that it came into being as a result of a progressive activist movement hoping to improve the living conditions of those created to be donors. Miss Emily explains that around the country, students were being reared in "deplorable conditions," but at Hailsham, guardians were able to keep students "away from the worst of those horrors" (p. 261). Miss Emily and Marie-Claude were a part of this movement. Along with a couple of other schools, Hailsham "challenged the entire way the donations programme was being run" (p. 261) and, for a time, was considered an "example of how we might move to a more humane and better way of doing things" (p. 258). However, a variety of factors converge to undermine the efforts of the movement and it eventually loses its political power and influence. Afterwards, Miss Emily tells Kathy and Tommy, "no one wanted to be seen supporting us any more" (p. 263), and the world "wanted you back in the shadows" (p. 265).

Compared with the compliant, condoning response of the general public, the actions of the individuals associated with the movement suggest a form of citizenship that is active, critical and engaged. Yet, in the character of Miss Emily, Ishiguro explores a form of citizenship that seeks to bring about positive change but instead merely succeeds in sustaining

---

10 Much of the critical reception to the novel has focused, at least in part, on the students' unquestioning acquiescence to their fate. See for example Black (2009), Mullan (2009) and Toker and Chertoff (2008).

the existing order of things. At Hailsham, students are not encouraged to interrogate the world or their place in it. On the contrary, their lessons, or "culture briefings" (p. 110), as they are called, are often nothing more than role-playing exercises where students practice at fitting in with the various types of people they will encounter in the outside world. It is an approach to education more concerned with conformity than with inquisitive inquiry. What's more, the guardians mislead the students and shield them from many of the details about their situation and identities. "We fooled you," Miss Emily acknowledges to Kathy and Tommy towards the end of the novel: "we had a sense of what could work, what was best for the students in the long run" (pp. 267-68). Similarly, students' art and writing, and in particular the art and writing projects that enable their participation in the "exchanges,"[11] serve in large part as distractions that encourage "an instrumental philosophy of individual worth" and work "to repress the students' possible resistance" (Black, 2009, p. 795).[12] Miss Emily's apprehension about possible student resistance is further suggested in her explanation of why Miss Lucy, a guardian who attempts to give students a fuller picture of who they are and of their place in the eyes of the outside world, had to be let go. Why would you have devoted time and effort to your lessons, art and writing, Miss Emily asks Kathy and Tommy, had you known what lay in store for you? She answers the question herself, saying: "you would have told us it was all pointless, and how could we have argued with you?" (p. 268). With these words, Miss Emily acknowledges that the efforts of her movement did not serve the interests of students, but rather indoctrinated them into the very system she and her movement set out to change.

Miss Emily's investment in the existing social order, as opposed to a commitment to radical change, is especially apparent in her attitude towards the rumors about deferrals. She fails to see the harm in the rumors and describes them as something for students "to dream about, a little fantasy," which at worse will lead to the disappointment of a few (p. 258).

---

11 The exchanges are a kind of "exhibition-cum-sale" of students' drawings, paintings, writings and other creative activity permitting students to purchase each other's works (Ishiguro, 2010, p. 16).
12 Black (2009) also argues that the students' art-making, the "handing over of their 'inner selves' to figures of authority," prefigures the exploitative process of organ donation (pp. 794, 798).

Of course, it could be argued that the rumors serve another purpose: to discourage students from pursuing more radical ways of taking control of their own lives and fates. When Miss Emily tells Kathy and Tommy that "you wouldn't be who you are today if we'd not protected you" (p. 268), she betrays a troubling refusal to acknowledge the immediately dire circumstances of their lives and the role she and her Hailsham colleagues played in shaping the unquestioning compliance necessary to ensure that students submitted to their circumstances. Missing from Miss Emily's account is consideration of the alternative paths students' lives might have taken had they not been prevented from knowing more about who they are and about the political decisions that led to their subordinate position in society. Also missing is consideration of the alternative paths Miss Emily and others involved in the movement could have taken to make a more meaningful difference in students' lives. Miss Emily may have acted with good intentions, she may have challenged the way the organ donation program is run, but at Hailsham, where certain questions simply are not asked, she offers students an education that instead trains them to live in accordance with the dominant ideology that constrains them.

Ishiguro offers a more radical form of citizenship, one that questions rather than upholds Hailsham's ideological foundations, in the character of Miss Lucy. In one pivotal scene, she overhears a group of students talking about their futures. Deciding that she can remain silent no longer, Miss Lucy intervenes and tells students what all of the other guardians keep concealed. "You've been told and not told," she says, "but none of you really understand, and… some people are quite happy to leave it that way" (p. 81). Miss Lucy makes clear that she is not content to leave things as they are. She tells the students about the donations and how each of them was brought into the world for the same specific purpose. She tells them that none of them is intended to have the kinds of futures she overheard them talking about: "none of you will go to America, none of you will be film stars," she says, "your lives are set out for you" (p. 81). Miss Lucy explains to the students that they will become adults but that before they are old, before they are even middle-aged, they will start to "donate" their vital organs. That, she says, is what "each of you was created to do" (p.

81). Kathy claims that she and other students know all of this already, but Miss Lucy's intervention does more than simply explain to students who they are. Her assertion that some people would be happier if students remained uninformed about their situation alludes to the attitudes held by those outside of Hailsham who benefit from the organ donation program and prefer not to know too much about it. Miss Lucy's explanation also serves as a rebuke of her fellow guardians. Most importantly, her intervention is an act of resistance against the dominant ideology at Hailsham, as well as a call for students to resist the fates that have been set out for them. "If you're going to have decent lives," she says, "then you've got to know and know properly" (p. 81). Miss Lucy twice uses this phrase – "if you're going to have decent lives" – seemingly signaling to students that a decent life is a reasonable and obtainable goal for them to pursue. While Miss Emily, after explaining how the political climate supportive of her movement suddenly disappeared, tells Kathy and Tommy that "you have to accept that sometimes that's how things happen in this world" (p. 266), Miss Lucy refuses to accept such a claim. She refuses the position of powerlessness ascribed to the students and attempts to do what Miss Emily's movement does not: empower students by making it known that they can question and challenge the system into which they were "born." They must know and know properly. They can seek out information and create knowledge about their circumstances. By suggesting that another path is, in fact, possible, Miss Lucy begins to signal to students that the future which, they are told, is already set out for them is not the only option. Although she is removed from her position shortly after the events described in this scene and is therefore unable to build on the work she begins, Miss Lucy's subversive action and her repeated refrain, "if you're going to have decent lives," model for students the sort of resistance that is required for them to change their situation. Miss Lucy performs an act of teaching that recognizes as its ultimate purpose the realization of social change. Her intervention is also an act of political judgment by a person practicing citizenship in its more radical form.

The Activist Nature of Librarian Work

It is Miss Lucy's example that needs to be brought to bear on information literacy pedagogy. Recent work on information literacy has directed greater attention to the influence that political power and dominant ideologies have on education. Teaching, including the teaching of information literacy, occurs, as Heidi Jacobs (2008) explains, within a sociopolitical context. Jacobs points to information literacy's connection to social justice ideas and initiatives and argues that information literacy is "not only educational but also inherently political, cultural and social" (p. 258). James Elmborg (2006) also describes education as a political activity and cites the work of Paulo Freire, Henry Giroux and others to explain how schools often enact the dominant ideology of their society. For this reason, Elmborg argues, educators must either accept this dominant ideology or "intentionally resist it and posit alternative models" (2006, p. 193). Neutrality, he insists, is "not an option" (p. 193). A position of neutrality works merely to uphold the societal status quo and leaves imbalances of power and privilege unexamined. As Jonathan Cope (2010) argues, the failure to "foster students' capacity to question the dominant values and beliefs of a given society is akin to an endorsement of those concepts" (p. 19). In other words, adopting a position of neutrality means accepting that certain questions can be excluded from the realm of political judgment of citizens. Neutrality is not a sign of impartiality but rather a failure or a refusal to recognize that teaching does, in fact, take place within a specific sociopolitical context. Miss Lucy clearly recognizes the dominant ideology at work at Hailsham and chooses to resist it. She also recognizes the need to move beyond critique – to not only recognize, acknowledge and examine injustice and oppression, but also to act in a manner that can achieve change.

According to literary scholar Elizabeth Ammons (2010), the move beyond critique in literary analysis is a necessary one. She describes how educators in the humanities often focus on helping students recognize and understand oppressive systems of human power with the apparent goal of teaching them critical thinking (pp. 12-13). Educators "expose injustices and the ideologies driving them" (p. 12) and explain how, very often, "we are all implicated in these systems of oppression" (pp. 33-34). But there, Ammons contends, is where the teaching generally stops: "we leave our students enlightened... but we fail to give them workable theory or tools" for translating "progressive analysis into positive social action" (p. 34). Ammons' analysis of this pedagogical practice begs the question: to what end do we teach critical thinking? The same question must be asked of information literacy: to what end do we teach it, and to what end do we help students become informed and engaged citizens?[13] Ammons responds to her question by advocating for what she describes as a "literary analysis for activist social change" (p. 4). She argues that "activist literary texts," by which she means works such as Harriet Beecher Stowe's *Uncle Tom's Cabin* and Marilynne Robinson's *Housekeeping* which themselves advocate social transformation, require that we "go beyond critique to the concrete issue of change and how to achieve it" (p. 35). Moreover, Ammons' argues that educators need to go a step further and assume – as Miss Lucy does – an explicitly activist position in their teaching. Recognizing the activist elements in literary texts, Ammons argues for an activist pedagogy (p. 35).

A similar argument can be made for information literacy and the work of librarians. A reading of librarian practice that takes into account the sociopolitical context in which that practice occurs suggests that the work of librarians often places them in opposition to dominant political influence, rhetoric and ideology. Librarians regularly position themselves as promoters and defenders of the public interest. They encourage and provide space and support for free and independent inquiry and scholarship, defend user rights and user privacy, and work to develop new models for scholarly publishing that maximize public access to publically funded research. ALA's Core Values of Librarianship (2004), for example, emphasize equitable access for all library users, resistance to censorship and a commitment to the public good and user privacy. Similarly, libraries are very often represented as spaces offering an alternative to the consumerist ethic that dominates much of society beyond library walls. As author and

---

13 The question posed a decade ago by Christine Pawley (2003) in her examination of the discourse used in IL scholarship–"what is information literacy for and who is it for?"–remains an important question in need of further consideration (p. 445). How LIS understands and defines the purpose of an informed citizenry is crucial to the development of an answer to this question.

activist Naomi Klein (2003) asserted at the joint ALA/CLA conference in Toronto, librarians have chosen to represent values that are "distinctly different from the ones that currently govern the globe:" they choose to represent and defend "knowledge (as opposed to mere information gathering), public space (as opposed to commercial or private space) and sharing (as opposed to buying and selling)." These choices are political. The commonly shared values of librarians are not neutral, but resistant. Librarians' refusal to remain neutral is what makes them relevant. It is what ensures that they continue to provide individuals and communities with spaces for learning, discussion and the exchange of ideas that are open, accessible, supportive and safe. In the current political and economic climate of austerity measures, cuts to education, and moves to privatize or eliminate public services, the values librarians have traditionally advanced and defended are being challenged. These values are under threat, yet librarians continue to defend them. They continue to intervene. This reading of librarian practice, like Ammons' reading of activist literary texts, arguably leads to the conclusion that the work of librarians *already* places them in the position of being activists, and that a critical theory of information literacy for activist social change is merely consistent with much of their current professional practice.

To be sure, the reading of librarian practice offered in the preceding paragraph is incomplete. Consideration of other aspects of library work could lead to very different, less laudable conclusions. For example, according to Ajit Pyati (2010), the information society of the internet age represents not, as some have argued, a radical newness or break from the past, but a continuation and intensification of capitalist practices (p. 245). The information age has, Pyati contends, been "highly beneficial to capitalism's increasing global reach and spread, ushering in an era of informational and techno-capitalism" that is closely associated with increasing global inequities (p. 245). In many cases, libraries have been quick to adopt new commercially distributed information technologies, thereby increasing their dependence on commercial products and services. Often, new technologies are adopted without first adopting a critical stance towards them. As John Buschman (2003) argues, LIS tends to "celebrate rather than evaluate" new technologies and often remains disconnected from scholarship raising critical questions about technologies (pp. 149-50). By uncritically adopting, promoting and legitimizing commercial online information discovery and retrieval tools, commercial social networking platforms and other commercially-owned and controlled information and communication technologies, an argument could be made that libraries have helped to uphold and advance exploitative capitalist practices.[14] It could also be argued that by entering into partnerships and restrictive license agreements with commercial IT developers and "content" providers, libraries have accelerated the incorporation of capitalist practices in libraries. By so doing, it could further be suggested that librarians – not unlike Miss Emily who, despite her good intentions, manages only to preserve (for a while) Hailsham's system of oppression – have helped to uphold the dominant ethic to which they claim to offer an alternative.

The differences and discrepancies between these two readings of librarian practice offer what is perhaps the strongest argument for the need of a critical theory of information literacy that provides a clear articulation of its meanings and purposes. As Ajit Pyati argues, librarians need a critical theory that allows them to differentiate between aspects of information society that further domination and aspects that promote greater human freedom (p. 245). As discussed above, information literacy, like any form of literacy, is "always an embedded or situated cultural practice conditioned by ideology, power and social context" (Jacobs, p. 259). The reading of acts of citizenship represented in Ishiguro's novel offered here provides a glimpse at what is possible when educators move beyond critique of that context. It is, admittedly, only a glimpse of what is possible. Ishiguro's novel offers no happy endings. Nevertheless, the novel illustrates, in dramatic fashion, how teaching is a political activity with a range of possible consequences and outcomes. It illustrates what can happen when those responsible for a system of education accept (and enact) the dominant ideology of their society. It also explores the possibility of alternative models. While not a part of the same American literary tradition discussed by Ammons, *Never Let Me Go*, a novel described by one critic as a "metaphor for the inequali-

---

14 I discuss these issues at more length elsewhere (Lilburn, 2012).

ties and predations of national and global economic systems" (Black, p. 796), can also be read as literature that urges readers to take action and to question what it is that makes action unthinkable (Robbins, 2007, p. 294). Miss Lucy's decision to resist the dominant ideology of Hailsham arguably points the way to the development of a clearer articulation of the goals of information literacy instruction. Unlike Miss Emily and the Hailsham guardians who fail to enable students' active participation in a movement ostensibly created for their benefit, Miss Lucy seeks to open new possibilities for students by encouraging them to question the causes of their subordinate position in society. To do so, they must know and know properly. Both Miss Emily and Miss Lucy exercise political judgment, but only Miss Lucy is willing to defy the logic of a system designed to preserve students' subservient position within a system that exploits them. When considering the meaning and purpose of information literacy, librarians must decide on the form of citizenship promoted through their teaching. They must decide whether the citizenship they help to produce is one that works to strengthen and uphold existing social, economic and political structures or whether it is one that dares to question and, if necessary, challenge the ideological foundations on which inequitable or oppressive distributions of social, economic and political power are based. As Ishiguro shows, the decisions educators make about the form of citizenship they bring to their teaching can have very meaningful implications for the lives of their students and for the ways we live together.

References

American Library Association. (2004). Core values of librarianship. Retrieved from: http://www.ala.org/offices/oif/statementspols/corevaluesstatement/co-revalues

Ammons, E. (2010). *Brave new words: How literature will save the planet.* Iowa City, University of Iowa Press.

Barney, D. (2007a). One nation under Google: Citizenship in the technological republic. The Hart House Lecture, 6 . University of Toronto, 22 March 2007. http://darinbarneyresearch.mcgill.ca/Work/One_Nation_Under_Google.pdf

Barney, D. (2007b). Radical citizenship in the republic of technology: A sketch. In L. Dahlberg & E. Siapera (Eds), *Radical democracy and the Internet* (pp. 37-54). New York: Palgrave.

Black, S. (2009). Ishiguro's inhuman aesthetics. *Modern Fiction Studies, 55*(4), 785-807.

Buschman, J. E. (2003). *Dismantling the public sphere: Situating and sustaining librarianship in the age of the new public philosophy.* Westport, CT: Libraries Unlimited.

Cope, J. (2010). Information literacy as social power. In M. T. Accardi, E. Drabinski & A. Kubier (Eds.), *Critical library instruction: Theories and methods* (pp. 13-28). Duluth, MN: Library Juice Press.

Elmborg, J. (2006). Critical information literacy: Implications for instructional practice. *The Journal of Academic Librarianship, 32*(2), 192-199.

Giroux, H. A. (2006). *America on the edge: Henry Giroux on politics, culture, and education.* New York: Palgrave.

Griffin, G. (2009). Science and the cultural imaginary: The case of Kazuo Ishiguro's *Never Let Me Go. Textual Practice, 23*(4), 645-663.

Harris, B. (2010). Encountering values: The place of critical consciousness in the competency standards. In M.T. Accardi, E. Drabinski & A. Kubier (Eds.), *Critical library instruction: Theories and methods* (pp. 279-292). Duluth, MN: Library Juice Press.

Ishiguro, K. (2010). *Never let me go.* Toronto, ON: Vintage Canada.

Jacobs, H. L. M. (2008). Information literacy and reflective pedagogical praxis. *The Journal of Academic Librarianship, 34*(3), 256-262.

Klein, N. (2003). Why being a librarian is a radical choice. Speech at the Joint American Library Association / Canadian Library Association Conference, 23 June. Retrieved from http://dissidentvoice.org/Articles7/Klein_Librarian.htm

Lilburn, J. (2012). Commercial social media and the erosion of the commons: Implications for academic libraries. *portal: Libraries and the Academy, 12*(2), 139-153.

McDonald, K. (2007). Days of past futures: Kazuo Ishiguro's *Never Let Me Go* as 'speculative memoir.' *Biography, 30*(1), 74-83.

Mullan, J. (2009). On first reading Kazuo Ishiguro's *Never Let Me Go.* In S. Matthews & S. Groes (Eds.), *Kazuo Ishiguro: Contemporary critical perspectives* (pp. 104-113). London: Continuum.

Pankl, E., & Coleman, J. (2010). "There's nothing on my topic!" Using the theories of Oscar Wilde and Henry Giroux to develop critical pedagogy for library instruction. In M.T. Accardi, E. Drabinski & A. Kubier (Eds.), *Critical library instruction: Theories and methods* (pp. 3-12). Duluth, MN: Library Juice Press.

Pawley, C. (2003). Information literacy: A contradictory coupling. *Library Quarterly, 73*(4), 422-452.

Pyati, A. (2010). Herbert Marcuse: Liberation, utopia, and revolution. In G. J. Leckie, L. M. Given & J. E. Buschman (Eds.), *Critical theory for library and information science: Exploring the social from across the disciplines* (pp. 237-48). Santa Barbara, CA: Libraries Unlimited.

Robbins, B. (2007). Cruelty is bad: Banality and proximity in *Never Let Me Go. Novel: A Forum on Fiction, 40*(3), 289-302.

Stevens, C. R., & Campbell, P. J. (2006). Collaborating to connect global citizenship, information literacy, and lifelong learning in the global studies classroom. *Reference Services Review, 34*(4), 536-556.

Swanson, T. (2004). A radical step: Implementing a critical information literacy model. *portal: Libraries and the Academy, 4*(2), 259-273.

Toker, L., & Chertoff, D. (2008). Reader response and the recycling of Topoi in Kazuo Ishiguro's *Never Let Me Go. Partial Answers: Journal of Literature and the History of Ideas, 6*(1), 163-180.

Challenging Authority

From "A Crusade against Ignorance" to a "Crisis of Authenticity": Curating Information for a Participatory Democracy

Andrew Battista
University of Montevallo

There is a social justice imperative to information literacy instruction. Librarians are responsible in helping students become sustainable learners, citizens who cultivate networks of information that compel them to pursue fairness, equality, and basic human rights. It follows that the tools and organization methods librarians emphasize can ultimately affect the makeup of society. A contingent of information literacy scholarship has interpreted library instruction to be, like all pedagogy, a process with political and social consequences. Accardi, Dabrinski and Kumbier (2010) outline "critical information literacy praxis" in a volume of essays drawn from the frameworks of Paulo Freire, Henry Giroux, bell hooks, and others (p. xii). Their collection follows Pawley (2003), Durrani (2008), and Jacobs (2008), who describe how information literacy is implicated in the process of democracy.

More recently, Rioux (2010) has posited a "metatheory" of social justice that, according to him, undergirds library and information science. Rioux suggests that librarians should promote a society "in which individuals and groups are treated fairly and enjoy equal share in that society's benefits" (p. 10-11). Jacobs (2010) also recognizes the implicit social justice underpinnings of information literacy, and she regards the International Federation of Library Associations' (IFLA) "Alexandria Proclamation on Information Literacy" as an exemplary statement on the relationship between knowledge and social justice. According to IFLA (2005), the ability to find, evaluate, and appropriate information to further one's agenda is "a basic human right" (para. 2). . Each of these definitions recognize that people who exhibit information literacy can, in turn, use their critical faculties to promote fair distribution of resources for all people.

This chapter explores student use of social media platforms, specifically those that encourage the curation of existing internet content (e.g., Facebook, Twitter, Google RSS, and Storify), to build the information literacy skills that are intrinsic to engaged citizens. Social media platforms disrupt knowledge hierarchies and thus are ideal tools with which to practice the critical thinking and information management skills that lead to activism. Information literacy scholarship is replete with discussions of how social media can be useful in the classroom (Farkas, 2007; Click & Petit, 2010; Mackey & Jacobson, 2011; Bobish, 2011). However, the literature often stops short of making explicit connections between social media tools and the potential they hold to shape a just society. In this chapter, I argue that information literacy instruction which invites students to curate content on social media platforms is an essential component of a democracy-centered education in the 21st century. Rather than treating information-seeking as a task-oriented process—a vestige of an academy that has too long served unjust industrial economies—librarians should instead stress curation, a skill that invites students to envision knowledge-seeking and information organization as an ongoing, perpetually-evolving process that will guide their professional and public lives.

Education, Citizenship, and the Social Justice Orientation of Information Literacy

Information literacy is grounded in theories of justice and democracy. Indeed, the most relevant definitions call attention to the fundamental expectation of a citizen: that he or she knows what is happening, senses what is important, and understands what issues rightly or wrongly occupy public attention.[1] Information literacy as construed today emerges from the Greco-Roman concept of the capable citizen who pursues an education to prepare for public life in a democracy. In this vein, Shapiro and Hughes (1996) argue that information literacy should be understood as "a

---

1 The Association of College and Research Libraries (ACRL) implies in its definition that the goal of information literacy is to "create a more informed citizenry" (par. 1). See also Pawley (2003) for an interpretation of information literacy as "a promethean vision of citizen empowerment and democracy" (p. 425).

new liberal art [...] as essential to the mental framework of the educated information-age citizen as the trivium of basic liberal arts (grammar, logic and rhetoric) was to the educated person in medieval society" (Information Literacy as a New Liberal Art section, para. 1). Like liberal arts inquiry, information literacy inflects every aspect of a person's living and learning experience. It is the cornerstone of a curriculum that incubates what Reece (2011) calls "the citizen-self," a public identity that emerges from "serious critical inquiry in the service of citizenship" (para. 26). Although the category of citizenship as an identity is ratified by the state and thus fraught with contradictions, it can be a useful way to frame the purpose of a college education. Andrew Delbanco (2012) explores this very question in his meditation on the university. He writes that a college education should help students "develop certain qualities of mind and heart requisite for reflective citizenship," which include:

1. A skeptical discontent with the present, informed by a sense of the past.
2. The ability to make connections among seemingly disparate phenomena.
3. Appreciation of the natural world, enhanced by knowledge of science and the arts.
4. A willingness to imagine experience from perspectives other than one's own.
5. A sense of ethical responsibility. (p. 3)

Delbanco's list is a good definition of an engaged citizen, yet it can easily double as a description of people who pursue social justice. Education for the sake of democracy is the primary way citizens learn to "organize to take control of the powerful institutions of society, or create new social institutions through which to build social justice, fairness, equality, economic opportunity—in short, the conditions necessary for the self-development of all members of society" (Sehr, 1997, p. 17). A curriculum that understands the social importance of information literacy recognizes that all democratic citizens owe a debt of responsibility to the state. Information literacy learning makes it possible for integrated service and reflection to continue after students complete their formal education.

In addition to being influenced by Greco-Roman political philosophy, contemporary attitudes toward information literacy borrow from the Enlightenment-era ideologies espoused by Thomas Jefferson (Bivens-Tatum, 2012). Jefferson, the founder of the University of Virginia and a shepherd of the land-grant university model in America, championed a publically-funded education system that encouraged "the diffusion of knowledge among the people" (p. 99). One of Jefferson's most famous statements on the role of education in a democracy occurs in his letter to George Wythe. Jefferson writes that America should wage "a crusade against ignorance; establish and improve the law for educating the common people" so that the young democracy would

> know that the people alone can protect us against these evils, and that the tax which will be paid for this purpose is not more than the thousandth part of what will be paid to kings, priests and nobles who will rise up among us if we leave the people in ignorance. (p. 100)

The Jeffersonian program hinged on a learned citizenry passionate about shaping society for the betterment of all people. Benjamin Barber (1998) quickly reminds us that many would dismiss Jefferson, a slave owner and a racist, as a hypocrite. It is valid to wonder if Jefferson really did advocate for the betterment of all people in his lifetime. Nevertheless, Barber maintains it is the very spirit of free inquiry and the felt sense of responsibility to the polity within Jefferson's vision that enabled positive social change. Jefferson may not have used the term "information literacy," but it is clear that his conception of an educated American resembles the kind of citizen-scholar librarians hope to shape through critical informa-tion literacy instruction.

A "Crisis of Authenticity": The Shortcomings of Information Literacy Instruction in 21st Century Democracy

Jefferson's ideal of a democracy sustained by informed citizens has been re-inaugurated in a 21st century context. On October 1, 2009, Barack Obama recognized the United States' first National Information Literacy Awareness month by naming a "crisis of authenticity" that affects "a world where anyone can publish an opinion or perspective, whether true or not, and have that opinion amplified within the information marketplace" (para. 2). Obama's recognition of National Information Literacy Awareness can be interpreted as an articulation of the central challenge faced by digital age citizens: the fact that technology floods us with chances to absorb information. Because of the liberties preserved by the Constitution, especially freedom of the press, a so-called "crisis of authenticity" has always been a condition of information in the United States. However, the ease with which people can produce and circulate ideas today makes the difficulty of critical evaluation all the more acute. Nevertheless, Obama understands that in the digital age, our ability to evaluate what we read and watch is just one barrier to consuming information responsibly. Time and human attention are finite, and today's citizens need not only be able to discern, but also be able to organize massive amounts of information to learn about and then intervene in civic affairs. By calling attention to our information abundance, Obama reconstitutes information literacy as a core principle of a participatory democracy.[2] He argues that our digital age demands "a new type of literacy [that] also requires competency with communication technologies, including computers and mobile devices that can help in our day-to-day decisionmaking" (Obama, 2009, para. 1). Obama's acknowledgement of National Information Literacy Awareness month is a direct response to the proliferation of social media platforms and the learning opportunities they present, yet it is also an implicit critique of a democracy that has underprepared its citizens to be conscientious custodians of information.

The "crisis of authenticity" of which Barack Obama speaks presents a crossroads for information literacy librarians. Librarians must decide what kind of literacy skills are needed to promote a just democracy in the age of social media, and they must determine if these literacy skills are actually cultivated through a curriculum that reinforces repetition and rote learning. As it stands, information literacy pedagogy has trended toward mechanistic education models that date back to the early 20th century. As

---

2 Johnson (2012) advances the concept of "information abundance" as an alternative to "information overload." He argues that "information overload" is an inadequate term because "as much as we'd like to equate our brains with iPods or hard drives, human beings are biological creatures, not mechanical ones... Instead of the lens of efficiency and productivity, maybe we should start looking at [information consumption] through the lens we use to view everything else we consume: health" (p. 5).

education became professionalized in the wake of the World War II G.I. bill, "it was increasingly decoupled from the life and practice of democracy" (Barber, 1998, p. 161). Public institutions lost sight of education as preparation for public service, and instead gravitated toward heuristics that reinforce repeatable actions, efficient labor, and other skills valued by manufacturing and production industries. Today, many pedagogical systems have continued to jettison the ideal of education for democracy in favor of education that benefits private enterprise. Take, for example, the standards-based No Child Left Behind Act of 2001, which reinforces rote learning in compulsory education. Because it makes funding contingent on test performance, the No Child Left Behind Act establishes patterns of teaching and learning that carry over into our colleges and universities. Subsequently, individual institutions and national accrediting bodies alike tend to privilege learning believed to be empirically measurable over process-oriented, provisional inquiry.[3]

In the end, curricula that emerge from No Child Left Behind fail to prepare citizens to be public members of a state who are compelled to pursue an egalitarian society. Instead, students today see education merely as a precursor to a professional career, a necessary rung on the ladder that leads to private wealth.[4] Still, it's doubtful that task-based pedagogy is even adequate training for today's jobs. In her recent book *Now You See It*, Cathy Davidson (2011) argues that many models of learning on which we rely "not only bore kids but prepare them for jobs that no longer exist as they once did" (p. 81). Existing measures of knowledge, especially multiple-choice tests, often do not correspond with the complexity information seekers experience in today's digital landscapes, but instead reinforce rote learning and decision making in a context where there is an ostensible "correct choice." Creating tests with illusion of definite knowledge does not coalesce with how most people teaching in humanistic disciplines

---

3 Perhaps the corollaries to the No Child Left Behind paradigm in higher education are standardized tests, which act as gate-keeping instruments, and rubrics like the College Learning Assessment, a test designed to assess "core outcomes espoused by all of higher education—critical thinking, analytical reasoning, problem solving and writing," but reduce these skills to various "real-world tasks that are holistic and drawn from life situations" (Arum & Roksa, 2011, p. 21-23).

4 There has been a spate of books that outline problems of learning in higher education. In addition to Arum and Roksa (2011), see Taylor (2010) and Delbanco (2012).

understand epistemology, nor does multiple choice assessments set up students to be engaged citizens in a world where information is exchanged on social media platforms dynamically. In the digital age, Davidson (2011) says, "kids have to make choices among seemingly infinite possibilities," and thus she believes that there is a mismatch "between our national standards of testing and the way students are tested every time they sit by themselves in front of a computer screen" (p. 124). Davidson's point is particularly salient for information literacy instruction. The more complex our digital networks of information become, the greater the distance grows between pedagogies that build mechanistic information gathering, and fluid contexts that demand open-ended information seeking. To be clear, task-oriented information seeking undermines the education of citizens who will pursue a just society, and it perpetuates a vision of education that ignores the collective health of a democracy.

Information literacy can be task-oriented because it emerged in the context of a 20th century educational system designed to train industrial workers. This is at least how several critics in the community have pointed out the problematic parallels between task-based learning and informa-tion literacy pedagogy.[5] As Kopp and Olson-Kopp (2010) point out, the ACRL Information Literacy Competency Standards for Higher Education seem to imagine research as a task to be fulfilled only to meet the needs of specific occasions or to complete an assignment.[6] They argue this perception causes instructors to reduce the information-seeking process to a series of repeatable steps:

> when they [students] complete a hands-on task such as using truncation in a search, they are for the most part developing technical expertise– learning how to operate machines, as it were, without considering their purposes, functions, or effects on others. (Kopp & Olson-Kopp, 2010, p. 58)

---

5 For a concise history of information literacy pedagogy and its place within the academy, see Grassian and Kaplowitz (2009, p. 3-23).
6 The ACRL says that people who are information literate "[d]etermine the extent of information needed, [a]ccess the needed information effectively and efficiently, [e]valuate information and its sources critically, [i]ncorporate selected information into one's knowledge base, [u]se information effectively to accomplish a specific purpose, [and u]nderstand the economic, legal, and social is-sues surrounding the use of information, and access and use information ethically and legally" ("Information," para. 3).

Pawley is another vociferous critic of task-based information literacy pedagogy. She points to an internal contradiction between the ideological spirit of free thinking that shapes information literacy and the systems of evaluation we use to talk about measuring information literacy learning outcomes. According to Pawley (2003), since the ACRL Competency Standards refer, "in the techno-managerial tradition, to the need for 'effective and efficient' information access," they unwittingly reinforce "a hierarchical system wherein expert authorities determine what counts as 'knowledge'" (p. 426). While the ACRL Competency Standards have legitimized information literacy pedagogy in many important ways, they also unfortunately perpetuate a tendency for information seekers to "fit all contingencies to an 'iron bed,' the dimensions of which are predefined by a cultural, social, and economic elite" (p. 426-427). One of the major problems with the incongruity Pawley describes is that it assumes the process of seeking information begins only when one faces a particular problem, most typically generated by an assignment for college coursework. In fact, the process of finding information in the digital age is much more fluid than the process the ACRL standards describe. When students see the completion of an assignment as the chief goal of seeking information, they lose the ability to see themselves as participants in public discourse, and they fail to imagine ways that they can grow their information sources to serve them beyond a singular task that occupies them.

Social Media and Curation: New Possibilities

Because information literacy is a fluid ethic, we must depart from task-driven models of instruction and treat inquiry as a process that hinges on how well we build information networks. To redress the shortcomings of information literacy instruction that perpetuate rote learning, I suggest that teachers and information literacy librarians make social media curation tools an integral part of assignments and class projects. Given the goals of critical information literacy pedagogy, there are several important reasons why social media should be foregrounded.

First, social media places learning into the public sphere, thereby encouraging radical participation in the collective work of democracy. The greatest benefit of social media is that it is a public process, challenging mainstream media and other top-down hierarchies of information. As Jeff Jarvis (2011) explains, the publicness that drives social media platforms is "profoundly disruptive" and "threatens institutions whose power is invested in the control of information and audiences" (p. 11).[7] Social media should be integrated into our pedagogy because it offers an alternative to the mainstream media which, according to Giroux in an interview with *Truthout*, disenfranchises students by creating "subjectivities [...] identities [... and] desires" which are "at odds with their own possibilities for freedom" (Strauss, 2011, para. 24). Users contribute to information on social media networks, and they share in the collective process of advancing discourses to benefit a larger community. This attitude toward public involvement in society has helped people influence some profound social change in the past two years. Recent movements, such as the Egyptian revolution and the Occupy Wall Street demonstrations are good instances of how social media can bring people and information together to affect meaningful change.[8] Even more isolated events demonstrate how information discovery on social media platforms can lead to action. When the Susan G. Komen Fund announced that it would no longer support Planned Parenthood, a massive social media campaign pushed the nonprofit to rescind its decision and restore its support of reproductive rights for all women. Lynch (2012) sees this public backlash as almost entirely the result of information sharing and activism that occurred on Facebook, Twitter, and other social media networks. These recent events remind us that people who learn and contribute to knowledge on social media networks can have a tangible impact on society. Yet this impact begins with individual acts of evaluation and consumption of information on social media platforms.

Secondly, we should teach students to use social media platforms as

---

7 The word "publicness" is Jarvis's invention. He admits in a footnote that "publicness" is "not a word in most dictionaries," but contends that we "invent words and remix definitions every day" (p. 1). Thus, for Jarvis, "publicness" is the "act or condition of sharing information, thoughts, or actions...an ethic of openness" (p. 1).

8 See Jarvis (2011, p. 12-14) for a discussion of social media's role in the Egyptian revolution in 2011.

information discovery tools because they are freely available, subsidized by the attention users devote to them. Social media presents an important alternative to methods of information access that may not be economically sustainable. It has been my experience that information literacy instruction that incorporates social medial tools is often done in lieu of "traditional" electronic resources, especially proprietary databases. Accardi, Dabrinski, and Kumbier (2010) suggest that the turn toward nontraditional media in information literacy instruction is necessary because it destabilizes students' perceptions of "the library catalog and scholarly databases as texts for rote, instrumentalist lessons about authority" (p. xii). Of course, the distinction between social media and traditional databases is dissolving as many databases are starting to integrate social media sharing features into their content. Furthermore, we cannot ignore the changing landscape of publishing in higher education. The rising cost of proprietary database access is well documented, and as the economics of scholarly publishing change, our institutions may no longer be able to pay for the content we are used to accessing.[9] Thus, critical information literacy instruction should not solely focus on knowledge circulated through subscription databases, but also on a larger, metacritical awareness of how all information circulates across networks, inside and outside of the academy. Students will not have access to subscription databases after they leave college unless they attend graduate school, and they need to start trafficking with the tools that will be available to them after they graduate.

Finally, when we integrate social media into the information literacy classroom, we implicitly invite students to rethink the kinds of evidence they bring into their research. Social media is, by virtue of its openness, the marketplace for publically-important sources of information that become the basis for exploration of ideas in essays, speeches, and other forms of traditional academic discourse. Farkas (2011) identifies a problematic component of many college writing assignments, in which instructors demand that their students have only peer-reviewed sources of information. Clearly, scholarly evidence is an important part of academic and

---

9 Indeed, active resistance to exploitative models in academic publishing is already happening. In January 2012, mathematician Timothy Gowers (2012) released a pledge to stop publishing content in or refereeing content for any academic journals associated with Elsevier.

public discourse, but it is often not the appropriate kind of evidence that students should integrate into their essays. This directive only reinforces authoritative knowledge, and it does not encourage students to evaluate information according to its public importance. When students blindly look for peer-reviewed sources, they are merely trying to find a specific kind of source and plug it in, so as to discharge the requirements of an assignment. When they find information on a social media source, the act of discovery can parlay into the act of evaluation and eventually synthesis. As students connect ideas, they gain a strong sense of a source's role in public discourse.

Praxis: Curating Twitter Lists and Writing about Urban Decline in Detroit

Perhaps the most significant argument for social media's role in the information literacy classroom is that it encourages curation, an approach to culling, evaluating, and representing information that is fast becoming a fundamental literacy in the digital age. Networks that require curation assume that those who use social media are not passive consumers of knowledge, but instead are active organizers of the massive amounts of information available to them. By giving individual users control over the way ideas are presented, curation platforms liberate information-seeking from task-oriented projects, in which the learning transaction has a definite ending. Instead, curation requires that users approach learning as an ongoing process that can pay dividends in future situations. Any time we "like" something on Facebook, follow someone on Twitter, subscribe to an RSS feed, pin something on a Pinterest board, or give a "thumbs up" to a song we hear on Pandora, we are curating the flow of information we encounter, distilling it for ourselves and others in our networks. When we curate we make judgments about the quality of information we see, and we use the tools embedded within social media platforms to make that information useful to others.

In order to demonstrate how curation can drive engaged learning, I will conclude with an extended example from my own experience in the classroom. Recently, I taught an introductory literature course that took as a theme the dereliction of urban America in the wake of our declining industrial economy. During the semester, we read a variety of pastoral poems and novels in the British and American literary traditions that envision cultural decay as the inevitable result of a capital economy dependent on the exploitation of land and labor. I supplemented our primary readings with literary and cultural criticism, essays that modeled ways for students to interpret the literature we read in the context of the contemporary social and ecological problems we face. As a librarian, I was responsible for the information literacy instruction in this course, and I used that opportunity to teach information-seeking vis-à-vis social media platforms. For example, I required students to curate lists of Twitter feeds and update them throughout the semester. Since I asked the students to approach our readings and discussions from the vantage point of our current ecological problems, I encouraged them to find information from leading environmentalist outlets and gather what they found on topically-focused lists. Students learned how to locate the Twitter feeds of key publications (e.g., *The Climate Desk, Orion Magazine,* and *Nature*), prominent public intellectuals who have written about climate change (e.g., Michael Pollan, Al Gore, and Bill McKibben), and university initiatives that study nature and culture (e.g., Yale Environment 360 and the Stockholm Resilience Centre). Having been given a starting place, the students expanded their lists, supplementing them with sources that they could eventually incorporate into formal essays. We talked about the concept of information abundance on Twitter, and we discussed why the limits of human attention demand that we organize our Twitter networks into subcategories.[10] Students used several deductive tactics to add new feeds: they found accounts recommended through Twitter's algorithms, searched for keywords, or simply mined the public lists of other prominent intellectuals who are on Twitter.

One of the lasting benefits of Twitter that it helped our class eclipse was the "one shot" method of information literacy instruction that has been scrutinized in recent scholarship (Kvenild & Calkins, 2011). Periodically throughout the semester, I would call students up to the front of the

---

10 Many of the discussions we had about managing information abundance and focusing attention are summarized in Johnson (2012). See also Rheingold (2012), who ranks the "practical literacy of controlling attention" as one of the five central literacies of the digital age (p. 9).

classroom to showcase their lists and talk about the logic they had used to construct them. Students added or left off feeds for various reasons. For example, a local newspaper's Twitter account was a valuable source of information about environmental matters in our community, but it contained links to many other topics and was deemed to dilute the list. The metacritical commentary each student shared proved to be instructive to the rest of the class. More importantly, the curation process suggested to students that research is an always-ongoing, never complete process of discovery and organization. Twitter lists are like other social media platforms in that they can always be refined. There is not as much of a sense of finality when a list is "published"; rather, it is to be expected that students will discover more sources and will continually organize, grow, and refine their lists.

The Twitter assignment also served our class discussions and informal writing assignments. It was not uncommon for students to begin a blog entry or a formal essay with a discussion of a public problem that they first encountered on Twitter. The best example of this process of discovery came at the end of the semester. We had concluded the course by reading Rebecca Solnit's (2007) article, "Detroit Arcadia: Exploring the Post-American Landscape." In her work, Solnit describes the decline of Detroit, a city that lost over half of its population during the last half of the twentieth century. The automobile industry paradoxically facilitated the flight from Detroit's urban center and doomed the city as rising fuel prices and competition from foreign companies destroyed the workforce. Today, large swaths of abandoned lots and dilapidated houses cover the neighborhoods surrounding downtown Detroit, yet Solnit imagines the city as one with the potential to be transformed into a post-American landscape. The vacant plots of land are, Solnit (2007) argues, "the most extreme and long-term hope Detroit offers us: the hope that we can reclaim what we paved over and poisoned, that nature will not punish us, that it will welcome us home" (p. 73). At one point in her article Solnit describes a visit to the Catherine Ferguson Academy for Young Women, a school for teenage mothers that infuses urban farming into its curriculum.[11] The

---

11 For more information about the Catherine Ferguson Academy for Young Women, see the

school offers single mothers a chance to complete their high school education, all the while coupling that education with a chance for them to grow their own vegetables as a supplemental source of income.

Our class had just finished discussing "Detroit Arcadia" when a student named Lauren posted on the course blog. Lauren had been alerted by a tweet from *Grist Magazine* that the Catherine Ferguson Academy would be shut down because of a lack of funding from the Michigan state government, and she decided to write a brief blog article about the news (Zimmerman, 2011). Lauren begins by writing, "I know that class is basically over, but after doing some final research for my paper I happened to stumble upon this article on *Grist*" (Tinchey, 2011, para. 1). Because she had previously decided to connect to *Grist* on Twitter, she encountered current information that connected with our class reading. Lauren aptly points out that "a school with a 90% graduation rate and a 50% college acceptance rate for its *pregnant* students sounds like a good thing to me" (para. 2). As Lauren's admission that "class is basically over" suggests, her argument is occasioned not by the requirement of the course, but instead by the need to weigh in on an issue of social justice that had been brought to her attention. Her ongoing curation work fostered this connection and compelled her to write.

I see the connection that Lauren made between her Twitter list and her ability to write as an engaged public intellectual as the best possible result of library instruction and pedagogy that begins with curation and ends with active resistance to unjust social practices. Lauren cultivated a network of information that allowed her to encounter relevant, timely sources, related to the themes of our course but independent from any specific assignment. The information-seeking and organizational skills we learned in class transferred into a moment of public presentation that was not tied to a class grade, but instead seemed motivated by a genuine concern over social negligence. Admitting that the class is over, Lauren synthesized her experience with the literature to make public a case for a socially just cause. I am not so naïve as to think that a single blog post by a student significantly influenced public policy in Detroit. Nevertheless,

---

documentary *Grown in Detroit: Teen Moms Become Urban Farmers* (Poppenk & Poppenk, 2009).

I can say that because of the network of information Lauren created, she was able to join the critical mass of public dissatisfaction with Michigan's unjust funding principles. Over the 2011 summer months, the Detroit Public School System responded to angered citizens and rolled the Catherine Ferguson Academy into a privately-operated charter school system (Dawsey, 2011). Although a privately-operated charter is a less than an ideal solution, the protests allowed for the Catherine Ferguson Academy to remain open and serve a vital need in Detroit's community. The kind of learning and writing that emerges from information discovery on social networks is the foundation of participatory democracies. It invites learners to draw boundaries around spheres of knowledge and present content to other people in ways that can catalyze real social progress.

References

Accardi, M. T., Dabrinski, E., & Kumbier, A. (Eds.). (2010). *Critical library instruction: Theories and methods*. Duluth, MN: Library Juice Press.

Arum, R., & Roksa, J. (2011). *Academically adrift: Limited learning on college campuses*. Chicago, IL: University of Chicago Press.

Association of College & Research Libraries (ACRL). (2000). Information literacy competency standards for higher education. Retrieved from http://www.ala.org/acrl/standards/informationliteracycompetency

Barber, B. R. (1998). *A passion for democracy: American essays*. Princeton, NJ: Princeton University Press.

Bivens-Tatum, W. (2012). *Libraries and the Enlightenment*. Duluth, MN: Library Juice Press.

Bobish, G. (2011). Participation and pedagogy: Connecting the social web to ACRL learning outcomes. *The Journal of Academic Librarianship, 37*(1), 54-63.

Click, A., & Petit, J. (2010). Social networking and web 2.0 information literacy. *International Information Library Review, 42*(2), 137-42.

Davidson, C. N. (2011). *Now you see it: How the brain science of attention will transform the way we live, work, and learn*. New York, NY: Viking.

Dawsey, C. P. (2011, June 16). Detroit school for pregnant, parenting teens to stay open as a charter. *Detroit Free Press*. Retrieved from http://www.freep.com/article/20110616/NEWS01/110616032/Detroit-school-pregnant-parenting-teens-stay-open-charter

Delbanco, A. (2012). *College: What it was, is, and should be*. Princeton, NJ: Princeton University Press.

Durrani, S. (2008). *Information and liberation: Writings on the politics of information and librarianship*. Duluth, MN: Library Juice Press.

Farkas, M. (2011, October 27). "I need three peer reviewed articles" or the freshman research paper. [Web log post]. Retrieved from http://meredith.wolfwater.com/wordpress/2011/10/27/i-need-three-peer-reviewed-articles-or-the-freshman-research-paper/

Farkas, M. (2007). *Social software in libraries: Building collaboration, communication, and community online*. Medford, NJ: Information Today, Inc.

Grassian, E. S., & Kaplowitz, J. R. (2009). *Information literacy instruction: Theory and practice*. New York: Neil-Schuman.

Giroux, H. (2007). *The university in chains: Confronting the military-academic-industrial complex*. Boulder, CO: Paradigm Publishers.

Gowers, T. (2012, February 8). A more formal statement about mathematical publishing. [Web log post]. Retrieved from http://gowers.wordpress.com/2012/02/08/a-more-formal-statement-about-mathematical-publishing/

Habermas, J. (2006). Political communication in media society: Does democracy still enjoy an epistemic dimension? The impact of normative theory on empirical research. *Communication Theory, 16*(4), 411-26.

International Federation of Library Associations (IFLA). (2005). *Beacons of the information society: The Alexandria proclamation on information literacy and lifelong learning*. Retrieved from http://archive.ifla.org/III/wsis/BeaconInfSoc.html

Jacobs, H. L. M. (2008). Perspectives on information literacy and reflective pedagogical practice. *The Journal of Academic Librarianship, 34*(3), 256-62.

Jacobs, H. L. M. (2010). Posing the Wikipedia "problem": Information literacy and the praxis of problem-posing in library instruction. In M. T. Accardi, E. Dabrinski, & A. Kumbier (Eds.), *Critical library instruction: Theories and methods* (pp. 197-199). Duluth, MN: Library Juice Press.

Jarvis, J. (2011). *Public parts: How sharing in the digital age improves the way we work and live*. New York: Simon & Schuster.

Jefferson, T. (1966). "To George Wythe, August 13, 1786." In G. C. Lee (Ed.), *Crusade against ignorance: Thomas Jefferson on education* (pp. 97-100). New York: Teachers College Press.

Johnson, C. A. (2012). *The information diet: A case for conscious consumption*. Sebastopol, CA: O'Reilly Media.

Kvenild, C., & Calkins, K. (Eds.). (2011). *Embedded librarians: Moving beyond one-shot instruction*. Chicago, IL: Association of College and Research Libraries.

Kopp, B. M., & Olson-Kopp, K. (2010). Depositories of knowledge: Library instruction and the development of critical consciousness. In M. T. Accardi, E. Dabrinski, & A. Kumbier (Eds.), *Critical library instruction: Theories and methods* (pp. 55-67). Duluth, MN: Library Juice Press.

Lynch, R. (2012, February 3). Komen learns the power of social media: Facebook, Twitter fueled fury. *Los Angeles Times*. Retrieved from http://latimesblogs.latimes.com/nationnow/2012/02/facebook-twitter-fueled-fury-against-in-susang-komen-for-the-cure-.html

Mackey, T. P., & Jacobson, T. E. (2011). Reframing information literacy as a metaliteracy. *College & Research Libraries, 72*(1), 62-78.

Obama, B. (2009). National Information Literacy Awareness Month, 2009: A Proclamation. Retrieved from http://www.whitehouse.gov/assets/documents/2009literacy_prc_rel.pdf

Pawley, C. (2003). Information literacy: A contradictory coupling. *Library Quarterly, 73*(4), 422-452.

Poppenk, M., & Poppenk, M. (Directors). (2009). *Grown in Detroit: Teen moms become urban farmers* [Motion picture]. Netherlands: filmmij.

Reece, E. (2011). The schools we need. *Orion Magazine, 30*(5). Retrieved from http://www.orionmagazine.org/index.php/articles/article/6401/

Rioux, K. (2010). Metatheory in library and information science: A nascent social justice approach. *Journal of Education for Library and Information Science, 51*(1), 9-17.

Rheingold, H. (2012). *Netsmart: How to thrive online.* Cambridge, MA: MIT Press.

Sehr, D. T. (1997). *Education for public democracy.* Albany, NY: SUNY Press.

Shapiro, J. J., & Hughes, S. K. (1996). Information literacy as a liberal art: Enlightenment proposals for a new curriculum. *Educom Review, 31*(2). Retrieved from http://net.educause.edu/apps/er/review/reviewArticles/31231.html

Solnit, R. (2007). Detroit arcadia: Exploring the post-American landscape. *Harper's Magazine, 315*(1886), 65-73.

Strauss, J. (2011, October). An interview with Henry Giroux: Youth movement in a culture of hopelessness. *Truthout.* Retrieved from http://www.truth-out.org/interview-henry-giroux-youth-movement-culture-hopelessness/1318092302

Taylor, M. C. (2010). *Crisis on campus: A bold plan for reforming our colleges and universities.* New York: Alfred A. Knopf.

Tinchy, L. (2011, June 8). Michigan farming high school shutting down. [Web log post]. Retrieved from http://thepastoral.wordpress.com/2011/06/08/michigan-farming-high-school-shutting-down

Zimmerman, J. (2011, June 8). Amazing urban farm school for teen moms will be shut down. *Grist.* Retrieved from http://www.grist.org/list/2011-06-08-amazing-urban-farm-school-for-teen-moms-will-be-shut-down

Critical Information Literacy in the College Classroom: Exploring Scholarly Knowledge Production through the Digital Humanities

Andrea Baer
King's College

In recent years librarians such as James Elmborg and Heidi L. M. Jacobs, looking to the connections between information literacy and studies in rhetoric and composition, have drawn attention to the inherently political and social nature of information literacy (IL) and information literacy instruction (ILI). Calling for a more critical pedagogical *praxis* for ILI, Elmborg and Jacobs assert that a holistic and critical understanding of IL, one which recognizes and embraces IL's political and social significance, must extend beyond rubrics and must involve more complex ways of exploring the relationships between information, society, and politics.

Given that formal ILI most often takes place in the college or university classroom, the implications of a critical praxis for IL seem particularly relevant to academic libraries, where students are often advised regarding scholarly practices and the use of scholarly sources. Although the aim of ILI in these contexts is most often to foster critical thinking and inquiry (and although this aim is frequently met in many respects), a great deal of academic library instruction neglects to draw attention to the subjective nature of academic publications, and to the fact that academic scholarship, like all information, is born out of social and political structures that are not immune to bias and power relations.

As a growing number of librarians and educators argue for a more critical praxis for ILI, one which encourages students to critically evaluate all information and to consider it in relation to social, political, and rhetorical contexts, ILI must go beyond making general distinctions between scholarly and non-scholarly sources which often elide the complexities of knowledge production.[1] Instead, a strong critical and socially-conscious

---

1 Among others, the work of James Elmborg (2004, 2006), Heidi L. M. Jacobs (2008), Cushla Kapitzke (2003a, 2003b), Christine Pawley (2003), Maria T. Accardi, Emily Drabinski, and Alana

ILI praxis emphasizes the inherently biased nature of *all* information, and invites students to explore information as reflective of the specific rhetorical and sociopolitical situations in which it is created, shared, and responded to.

While many librarians and educators agree in principle with the idea of a critical praxis for ILI, knowing how to implement such an approach remains a difficult question. Drawing on Elmborg's conception of academic information literacy, I argue in this chapter that the digital humanities (DH) – understood perhaps most simply as the intersection between humanities scholarship and digital technologies – offers rich possibilities for fostering critical information literacy more broadly and academic information literacy more specifically through a critical pedagogical praxis. Because much of DH engages in alternative scholarly practices (such as the use of digital media, recognition of alternative forms of scholarship such as digital tools and experiments, and new models of publishing and peer review), DH presents numerous openings for exploring with students traditional and emerging scholarly practices, as well as ways that academic discourse and scholarship are influenced and shaped by social, political, institutional, and structural contexts. After considering ILI in relation to academic information literacy, I will discuss what DH in particular can contribute to ILI. Finally, I close with ideas for the classroom which address the sociopolitical dimensions of scholarly discourse and practices through the lens of DH.

Academic Information Literacy in the College Classroom

In higher education, a particularly important aspect of critical information literacy is what James Elmborg has called "academic information literacy." As Elmborg (2006) explains, "If literacy is the ability to read, interpret, and produce texts valued in a community, then academic information literacy is the ability to read, interpret, and produce information valued in academia" (p. 196).

Academic information literacy involves not merely recognizing and

Kumbier (2010), Troy Swanson (2004, 2005, 2010), and Dane Ward (2006) has placed particular emphasis on the importance of a critical pedagogy for information literacy instruction.

reproducing scholarly discourse, but also thinking critically about the creation and use of scholarship. As Elmborg (2006) states, academic information literacy "involves the comprehension of an entire system of thought and the ways that information flows in that system. Ultimately, it also involves the capacity to critically evaluate the system itself" (p. 196). From this perspective, the university and scholarly communities are not the embodiment of truth, but rather one part of the complex social and political world in which we live.

Many college and library classes, however, often imply that academic sources require little scrutiny, based on the presumption that academic work is always well-researched and well-argued. Elmborg's conception of academic information literacy suggests that effective information literacy instruction goes beyond simple distinctions between scholarly and popular sources, as educators encourage deeper understandings of scholarly work, practices, and communities.

Deeper understandings of academic discourse require reflection on the institutional, structural, and sociopolitical contexts which largely shape academic work. Academic information literacy should not be a thought-less acceptance of all aspects of academic structures and discourse. To the contrary, a critical approach to academic information literacy offers openings for examining and perhaps even challenging that very system. Similarly, academic information literacy need not deny the experience that many individuals have of feeling "uninitiated" or excluded from the academic world. Rather, academic information literacy can help individuals to recognize the circumstances in which experiences of exclusion arise, and potentially to challenge those conditions from which some individuals feel alienated. To foster such approaches to information literacy educators need pedagogical approaches that invite students at once to become part of academic discussions and to analyze scholarly discourse from a critical perspective.

Elmborg (2006) convincingly argues that academic librarians can and should play a central role in promoting academic information literacy. He poses the question

Should librarians "serve" the academy by teaching its literacy skills unquestioningly, or should librarians participate in the critical reflection undertaken by "educators," a reflection that leads us to challenge, if necessary, the politics of academic exclusion, and to participate in the creation of new and better academic models? (p. 197)

If we agree that our role as librarians is to encourage both higher-level thinking and social consciousness, then the answers to these questions are clear. How we go about serving students, however, is a much more open question.

Critical Pedagogy for Academic Information Literacy

Critical pedagogy, a philosophical and pedagogical approach informed by the work of theorists like Paulo Freire and Henry Giroux, offers a valuable framework for information literacy instruction which emphasizes critical thought and social awareness, including within the academic context. Advocates of critical pedagogy posit that education should foster critical thought and inquiry, in particular in regards to the social, political, and institutional forces that shape our worlds and our experiences. For Freire (2002), this occurs not through content-focused teaching (what he calls the "banking concept" of education), but rather through students' active dialogue, reflection, and engagement in real-world problems. Through such education students take charge of their own learning and may develop "critical consciousness" (p. 73). This critical consciousness, according to Freire, involves awareness of how political, social, and structural conditions affect oneself and others, on both local and global scales.[2]

Such awareness is crucial to academic information literacy, for to understand and to engage critically in academic studies, one must examine and sometimes question the institutional, social, and power structures that largely shape academic discourse and scholarly practices. But if one finds academic discourse difficult or even alienating (as many students appear to do), it may be especially hard to trust one's own experiences and ideas about scholarly work.

Critical pedagogy may prove a particularly powerful approach in the

---

2 It is worth noting that for Freire critical consciousness ultimately moves beyond social awareness to social action. This chapter, however, focuses primarily on fostering social awareness.

face of the intimidation that many students experience when they first encounter scholarly discourse. Because critical pedagogy emphasizes the value of students, their experiences, and their voices, many students may find assurance when encouraged to speak openly about both their intellectual and their emotional experiences in response to academic scholarship, especially if they have previously been frustrated with or felt alienated from academic discourse. Along with students' reflections on their personal experiences with academic work, they may begin to view their personal understandings of and relationships to academic work in new ways, and perhaps to find meaningful connections between scholarly work and their own lives.[3]

Imagine, for example, a classroom of students who have been told repeatedly that academic writing is proper and that informal ways of speaking are incorrect, without being encouraged to consider how notions of propriety and correctness are culturally and politically situated. What if those students were exposed to critiques of academia as elitist, or to arguments that academic discourse is not the single "correct" way of speaking but simply one linguistic style that has emerged from a specific context? When students are encouraged to consider the academic world in its sociopolitical context, they are better positioned to understand, to engage in, and to effect change in scholarly practices that have grown out of a complexity of sociopolitical and institutional structures, some of which do not align always with ideals of equality and social justice.

How might library instruction facilitate critical awareness of academic practices, and where might students begin to examine academic discourses and practices in a way that is accessible to individuals with limited exposure to academic scholarship? There is, of course, no single answer to these questions, and any given approach will have its own particular strengths and limitations. That said, I propose that the digital humanities, approached through the framework of critical pedagogy, presents especially

---

3 Conversations about students' relationships to academic work are, of course, not always easy. This may be particularly true in diverse classrooms in which individuals have varying degrees of familiarity and comfort with scholarly discourse (particularly since this level of familiarity sometimes corresponds with other factors such as social class). As Mary Louise Pratt has argued in "Arts of the Contact Zone" (1991), such moments of unease can be some of the richest opportunities for meaningful learning; they are also among the most challenging.

rich possibilities for introducing students to academic practices, while also encouraging critical thought and self-reflection on those practices. Because DH at once highlights and challenges traditional scholarly practices, particularly in response to ongoing technological and social changes, it presents unique openings for exploring academic discourse in relation to the social, political, and structural contexts that largely shape it.

In discussing what DH might offer to critical information literacy instruction, I will first consider how DH often both exposes and reflects sociopolitical structures and power relations that are central to the production and sharing of knowledge within academia. This will feed into a discussion of how DH can challenge and/or affirm traditional scholarly practices in the humanities, such as blind peer review and the privileging of the print monograph. Finally, I will present class activities and discussion topics intended to foster critical and academic information literacy.

The Digital Humanities

Digital humanities (DH), an emerging and complex concept, can be understood perhaps most simply as the intersection between humanities scholarship and digital technologies. This definition, however, does not capture the complexity of DH, a term which also implies new approaches to and attitudes about academic scholarship and the role of the university. These emerging practices include (but are by no means limited to) digital publishing, digital media, collective editing, hybrid models of peer review, new standards and procedures for tenure and promotion, and digital pedagogy and digital literacies.

These issues, of course, are inextricable from the social, political, institutional, and technological contexts and structures that largely shape academic practices. The complex relationships between these contexts and structures are reflected in many of DH's central concerns, including the use of digital tools and media, recognition of digital and collaborative scholarship, and alternative publishing models like open access and collaborative editing. An understanding of the practices and debates surrounding such issues is, I contend, essential to academic and critical information literacy, particularly in the digital age.

The relevance of DH to academic and critical information literacy is evident in the many questions and debates within DH. What within the digital environment counts as scholarly activity? Should peer review be an open process to which anyone can contribute, or does such openness compromise the authority of academic writing? Should venues like Wikipedia and Twitter have a part in academic discussions, or do such tools trivialize or "dumb down" scholarly discourse? In what ways might digital technologies serve as openings and/or barriers to democratic systems that support open information and free expression? Are there dangers in viewing technology and digital tools as neutral, and if so how can we make more transparent the ways that digital tools and structures are shaped by cultural bias or philosophical perspective? Does hacking as a means of political engagement have a place in academia? These are all questions raised within the expansive areas of DH.

Projects associated with DH span a wide range of interests. One example is MediaCommons, described as a "community network for scholars, students, and practitioners in media studies" which explores new forms of digital publishing (MediaCommons, n.d.). MediaCommons' digital publishing projects, which take a variety of shapes, are intended not simply to increase digital content, but also to shift the structures of traditional publishing.

As MediaCommons makes evident, the structures and practices of publishing can be understood in political terms. For example, in the humanities the single-authored print monograph historically has been considered superior to other modes of writing, such as digital and open access publications and less formal academic writing such as blogs, collaboratively written wikis, and self-published digital books. MediaCommons, however, argues that humanities scholars need to respond to a rapidly changing and largely digital culture with new modes of publishing and communication. As is explained in the MediaCommons' "About" page,

> Our hope is that the interpenetration of these different forms of discourse will not simply shift the locus of publishing from print to screen, but will actually transform what it means to "publish," allowing the author, the

publisher, and the reader all to make the process of such discourse just
as visible as its product. (MediaCommons, n.d.)

This emphasis on transparency in the publishing process draws attention to the dynamic and social nature of publications, which involve not
just the author and publisher but also readers and interested communities. MediaCommons' consideration of the reader appears to be realized
in its projects, which use open peer review and invite reader comments
and active engagement in discussions. Through these new approaches to
academic work, the editors and contributors at MediaCommons hope that
"new communities will be able to get involved in academic discourse, and
new processes and products will emerge, leading to new forms of digital
scholarship and pedagogy" (MediaCommons, n.d.). Many of these approaches may help to open discussions to a wider community and may
challenge scholarly practices that reinforce more hierarchical structures
and that tend to limit opportunities for reader input.

The potential for DH to raise awareness of power relations and structures
Endeavors like MediaCommons illustrate not only how academic practices like publishing and information sharing are changing, but also how
such activities must be understood in relation to the structural, institutional, and sociocultural contexts that surround them. As MediaCommons
points to the values of collaboration, openness, and even democracy, it
demonstrates the often overlooked connections between how a community
creates and shares knowledge and how individuals view themselves in
relation to larger political, social, and institutional structures.

The potential for DH to raise awareness of power relations and structures
in academia is also evident in the work of THATCamp (The Humanities
and Technology Camp), an "unconference" at which "humanists and
technologists at all skill levels learn and build together in sessions proposed
on the spot" (THATCamp, n.d.). The impromptu nature of this event is
intended to foster creativity and spontaneity, and to contrast the more formal style of most academic humanities conferences. The egalitarian model
which participants aspire to is evident in THATCamp's About webpage,
which explains that the event is "non-hierarchical[,] non-disciplinary[,]
and inter-professional" (THATCamp, n.d.). The less formal culture of
THATCamp reflects a growing interest held by many within DH in

breaking down boundaries between disciplines, institutional structures, and the university and the general public.

As in evident in the work of THATCamp and MediaCommons, many DH projects illustrate how tensions between traditional and emerging scholarly practices are closely tied to the social and power structures of academia. In so doing, such projects provide openings for discussing the politics and power relations of information and knowledge production in academia.

This is not, however, to say that DH erases social hierarchies and therefore offers a utopian model of scholarly engagement. While many in DH strive for a more egalitarian, open, and collaborative community, hierarchical power and social structures are clearly present in many (and on some level probably all) DH debates and scholarship. The fact that DH communities often aspire to a new social order, however, presents opportunities for thinking deliberately about the roles of power and social structure in communication and information practices.

The Appeal of Digital Humanities in Critical Information Literacy Instruction

Since DH has grown largely out of some scholars' frustrations with traditional approaches to scholarship and academic promotion that are sometimes associated with hierarchical structures and more narrow conceptions of scholarship, it offers a unique opening for exploring the academic arena as a complex and often contentious space in which varying perspectives and agendas are at play. As digital and emerging scholarly practices have been met with some resistance and skepticism by academics within and outside of the humanities, DH also calls attention to political and social issues and agendas that affect many disciplines today.

Issues in DH lend themselves particularly well to a critical pedagogy that explores students' personal experiences both at the university and in various digital environments. Students who are more versed in the digital world may tap into their knowledge, skills, and interests, while also being challenged to consider their relationships to technology, digital environments, and various digital communities in new ways. At the same time, DH's focus on the intersections between technology and culture and between the university and the broader public encourages individuals to consider how their connections to information are profoundly influenced and often shaped by the contexts and communities in which they encounter and interact with that information.

Because DH often challenges traditional scholarly practices, as well as the exclusivity of academic language, it may also be refreshing to students who might otherwise feel frustrated or alienated by scholarly discourse. As DH tends to involve critical examinations of established and alternative approaches to academic work, it may encourage individuals to consider the reasons for established scholarly practices, as well as potential opportunities and limitations of these conventions. Similarly, the very fact that much of DH work is intended to reach the general public provides natural openings for considering information in relation to power and social structures, communities and students themselves.

Addressing Multivocality within DH

My description of DH as generally embracing alternative models of scholarship, along with greater inclusivity of communities outside of academia, could be interpreted as part of an "us against them" mentality, in which DH is presented as the positive and progressive force standing against regressive traditionalists. This is *not* my intent. To represent academia and DH in such a dualistic way would be a disservice to students which encourages all-or-none thinking rather than critical thought.

While I do believe in many of the ideals and principles commonly associated with DH (e.g., making scholarship accessible to a wider audience, challenging elitist tendencies that are often part of university structures), and while I am excited about many possibilities that DH offers to scholarship and to education, I do not view DH as a perfect model of what all scholarship should or must be. Rather, I would argue that concepts, practices, and communities related to DH can be explored in ways that foster critical inquiry about *all* information sources and the rhetorical circumstances in which those sources are produced.

DH is incredibly multi-faceted and complex, just as is academia more broadly. Indeed, much of DH literature centers on disagreements about what the digital humanities is and what it should or should not do. (Among those debates is the question of whether DH scholars engage sufficiently in social and political issues, or if technological tools actually become obstructions to doing so). The breadth and range of DH, as well as the debates both within and beyond it, demonstrate in large part the opportunities it presents for critical inquiry into academia and scholarly practices. An exploration of DH helps to communicate the actual diversity of philosophies and scholarly practices within academia, and challenges the notion of a monolithic university representative of a coherent group or a universal truth. With this in mind, I find it important when comparing DH to more traditional scholarly practices to acknowledge the diversity and breadth within both DH and the university more generally. Such acknowledgement affirms the varying voices, approaches, and interests evident not only in DH, but also in so many communities. Too often such multivocality is overlooked, and the sense of a consensus may discourage students from questioning ideas or expressing dissenting views.

Acknowledgement of multivocality is similarly essential to an open class environment that allows for critical dialogue and opposing views. As John Trimbur argues, allowing for a "rhetoric of dissensus" is particularly important in the classroom, as it helps students to "demystify the normal workings of discourse communities," operations which often involve silencing difference (as cited in Leverenz, 1994, p. 168). Such an approach, as Carrie Shively Leverenz (1994) explains, can "enable teachers and students to go beyond a mere replication of established knowledge-making communities to a critique of those communities' practices" (p. 168). As Leverenz's idea of a "dissensus pedagogy" suggests, when dissonances and heterogeneity are recognized and perhaps even celebrated, students may not only get a fuller picture of academic institutions; they may also feel more comfortable to voice their own ideas, regardless of whether those views seem to align with a given group.[4]

---

4 It is notable that Leverenz (1994) focuses on the challenges of dissensus pedagogy in the multicultural classroom. She considers how dissensus pedagogy in practice (rather than in theory) is complicated by the rootedness of established institutional and sociocultural structures in the

Class Activities & Resources

The activities and resources described in this section point to concrete ways of exploring DH in order to foster critical understandings of scholarly practices, academic institutions, and scholarly information sources. The activities, informed by critical pedagogy, ask students to reflect on not only the social and political contexts of scholarly practices and discourse, but also on connections between academic work and students' personal experiences.

Each activity can be built upon, expanded, or otherwise modified, depending on the needs and circumstances of a given class. For many of the activities, I have suggested related resources and readings. These sources are by no means comprehensive, and other materials may prove more appropriate, depending on an instructor's focus and goals.

1: Defining Digital Humanities: Exploring the Impossible Question "What Is Digital Humanities?"

Adequately defining a concept like the digital humanities is incredibly difficult, and in some respects impossible, since DH encompasses so many viewpoints and areas of study. Given this reality, how does one effectively introduce a term that resists definition, and present it in a way that opens discussion of scholarly practices as reflections of the social, political, and structural dimensions of the university? In order to open deeper discussions of how DH relates to such issues, a class may begin by establishing a broader understanding of DH as a concept. The difficulty of defining DH, while possibly frustrating, reflects its rich potential for the IL classroom. The complexity of the concept of "digital humanities" highlights the reality that academia is not a monolithic entity, but rather includes communities and individuals with both overlapping and diverging interests and concerns.

The fact that the term "digital humanities" has no clear definition and

---

academy (many of which students have already come to accept without question). Unfortunately, the scope of this chapter does not allow for a detailed discussion of dissensus pedagogy in practice, though sensitivity to the challenges of encouraging dissensus is vital to the pedagogy and activities herein described.

is to a great extent open to interpretation also underscores the idea that scholarship and scholarly practices, like all forms of information, are situated within particular sociopolitical and structural contexts and within communities of individuals with both common and diverging interests and concerns. At the same time, work in DH reflects how communities and their practices evolve in response to numerous factors, including technological and social changes.

To open a discussion on defining DH, an instructor might first explain to students that DH is a diverse field, and that individuals often disagree on what it is and is not. The instructor might then indicate that an awareness of various definitions of DH will enable the class to explore many of the issues and concerns raised in DH in greater depth.

Students might then compare different definitions.[5] A class might examine where these definitions converge and diverge, and what these overlaps and differences suggest about academic culture and practices, including their relationships to digital environments. Part of this discussion would address how social and technological changes can be related to institutional and social structures.

Salient discussion points might include: the use of digital environments and digital tools for communication; the growing role of online communities for academic discussion (and in particular how these may affect social and power structures); evolving publishing models and the value placed on print vs. electronic sources; and the concept of scholarly work as a "social undertaking" (see Kirschenbaum's (2010) definition of DH).

To connect the discussion more directly to students' experiences, a class might also consider whether any of the issues expressed in the reviewed definitions of DH have clear relevance to their own lives (possible topics might include digital communication; online personas; digital privacy; the digital divide; methods of consensus building – particularly in relation to peer review or wiki creation; and inclusion/exclusion from a given group due to differences in ideology, politics, social practices or use of language).

---

5 Varying definitions of the term "digital humanities" are abundant. Potentially useful sources include *Wikipedia* (n.d.a), Smith (2009, February 1), Bobley (2011, February 1), Kirschenbaum (2010), and Presner, Schnapp, Lunenfeld, et al. (2009, June 22).

2: Defining the DH Community

As the varying definitions of DH make clear (see Activity 1), those "doing" DH do not always agree on what it is. To deepen class discussions about scholarly debate and scholarly communities, instructors may ask students to read and to discuss debates about how DH is conceptualized.

There is a plethora of materials that might be used. I offer below three sources which are all part of a somewhat contentious discussion, begun in 2011, about who should and should not be considered a DH scholar (or a "DHer"). These sources can help to initiate a conversation about the politics, power dynamics, and interpersonal relations that are central to communication both within and outside of the academy.

In Ramsay's (2011b) "Who's In and Who's Out," he argues that in order to be a digital humanist one must build in some capacity. For him, simply using digital tools or theorizing about them does not make one a DH scholar. He also contends that despite common efforts within DH to be all-inclusive, the reality is that the humanities "is not some airy Lyceum. It is a series of concrete instantiations involving money, students, funding agencies, big schools, little schools, programs, curricula, old guards, new guards, gatekeepers, and prestige" (Ramsay, 2011b).

Ramsay's argument provides an opening for considering the value and the limitations of defining a given community or discipline, and how such definitions reflect both concrete realities and power relations of social and institutional structures. Ramsay, writing in response to critiques of this talk, also published a follow-up essay, "On Building," which may provide content for further discussion (Ramsay, 2011a).

In Mullen's (2010, April 29) "Digital humanities is a spectrum; Or, we're all digital humanists now," Mullen responds to Ramsay's talk "Who's In an Who's Out" by arguing that all scholars use digital tools and materials in some capacity, and that DH should therefore not be viewed as something from which an individual is either included or excluded.

THATCamp's (n.d.) description of its "unconferences," available on their "About" page, presents an additional perspective on what it means to participate in DH and to create highly inclusive, collaborative, and non-hierarchical communities.

Among the questions students might explore when discussing these readings are:

• How do these arguments work to include and/or exclude certain individuals or groups?
• How do the arguments reflect established and/or changing power and social structures within the humanities?
• What is the value of establishing definitions of a discipline, sub-discipline, or other academic pursuit? What are the limitations of developing such definitions?

3: DH Manifestos

A number of manifestos for DH have been written, some of which use playful and often purposely hyperbolic language to express legitimate concerns about the future of scholarly practices and higher education. These documents offer a humorous way of identifying central (and often political and institutional) concerns among DH scholars. It is notable that many of these documents have been created collaboratively, as is the case for much of the work in DH.

Listed below are two such manifestos. The first was created at THAT-Camp Paris 2010, and is relatively serious in tone. The second, written by Todd Presner, Jeffrey Schnapp, Peter Lunenfeld, and numerous others (2009, June 22), takes a clearly hyperbolic tone.

• Dacos, M. (2011, March 26). "Manifesto for the digital humanities." *THATCamp Paris 2010*. Retrieved from http://tcp.hypotheses.org/411
• Presner, T., Schnapp, J., Lunenfeld, P., et al. (2009, June 22). "The digital humanities manifesto 2.0." Retrieved from http://www.humanitiesblast.com/manifesto/Manifesto_V2.pdf

Possible discussion questions include:

• What central issues, concerns, and/or debates of DH are evident in these manifestos?
• How are power structures, political forces, and institutional structures represented in the DH manifestos? What attitude(s) do the authors suggest they have towards politics and institutional structures

in academia?

• What is your emotional response to the DH manifestos? How might other audiences relate or respond to the manifestos (e.g., a fellow DH scholar, a humanities academic unfamiliar with DH, a university administrator, a publisher of a peer-reviewed subscription journal, a Wikipedia editor, etc.)?

• Can you relate any specific issues raised in the DH manifestos to your own experiences with or beliefs about using information or technology? If so, what parallels can you draw? How do the concerns articulated in the manifestos compare to your own?

• What is a manifesto, and what is/are its purpose(s)? What are some examples of manifestos that have been used throughout history? What tone and rhetoric are used in these documents, and to what ends?

Students might explore these questions individually or in groups, and then report back to the class. The Wikipedia (n.d.b) entry for "Manifesto" includes a list of notable manifestos that might be useful for this activity. It may be particularly interesting to contrast the uses of tone and rhetoric in various manifestos, such as Marx and Engels' Communist Manifesto and "The Vow of Chastity," a manifesto written by Dogme 95, a movement of avant-garde filmmakers started by Danish film directors Lars von Trier and Thomas Vinterberg (1995).[6]

Follow-up activity: Manifesto writing. Discussions might be coupled with groups' writing their own manifestos, whether for DH or for another community or concept. Afterwards the class might discuss how their experiences creating the manifesto collaboratively might have differed from writing such a document individually. Did participants experience disagreements, consensus, and/or acceptance of dissensus? Did they take on various roles in the group? Did this process affect how students think about the challenges, debates, or concerns within both DH and academia more broadly?

---

6 "The Vow of Chastity" is a tongue-in-cheek manifesto which offers an effective exercise in analyzing tone, and rhetorical purpose and strategy. Before discussing this document with a class it is advisable to have some background information on the film movement Dogme 95.

4: Exploring Models of Peer Review and Digital Scholarship

While much of academic library instruction suggests that peer reviewed sources are of higher quality than other types of publication, there are growing questions about the value and sustainability of traditional models of blind peer review, particularly in the DH community. Discussions of peer review address concerns about whose voices get heard or silenced, whether the opinion of a single identified "expert" is superior to the collective views of a wider audience, and what dangers or possibilities alternative approaches to traditional blind peer review might present. Issues to consider include the purposes, advantages, and disadvantages of various forms of review. MediaCommons, discussed earlier in the section "Digital Humanities," is a prime example of how various forms of peer review are intertwined with social and institutional structures and power relations. The project uses a complex peer-to-peer reviewing system that allows all users to review others' work, but which does not weigh all reviewers' comments equally. Another significant aspect of the review system is the requirement that in order to publish through MediaCommons one must first become an active reviewer of its publications (Fitzpatrick, 2009). Such processes and guidelines for review point to the review process as a powerful force within the MediaCommons community, its structure, and its work. For a more detailed explanation of MediaCommons' review process, see Kathleen Fitzpatrick's (2009) *Planned Obsolescence: Publishing, Technology, and the Future of the Academy.*

To explore how the peer review and publishing processes relate to power and social structures, a class might begin by reading the "About MediaCommons" webpage, which explains the community's purpose and approaches (MediaCommons, n.d.). Students could discuss what makes this approach to publishing distinct from other forms of academic publication, and how the project's practices reflect the communities and social structures involved in the endeavor. To take discussion farther, students might explore some of MediaCommons' most prominent features: "In Media Res," "MediaCommons Press," and "The New Everyday." Each is accessible from MediaCommons homepage at http://mediacommons. futureofthebook.org.

Another valuable resource for discussions of peer review is the science journal *Nature*'s (n.d.) series of twenty-three articles about the peer review debate. Though this journal is not directly related to digital humanities, its experiments with and debates about peer review clearly address concerns vital in the humanities and across academic communities.[7]

Conclusion

The above ideas suggest the great potential for exploring DH in order to support academic information literacy and critical evaluation of all information sources, regardless of whether those sources are considered academic or humanities-specific, and regardless of the format or context in which the information appears. By no means do these activities address all aspects of DH that are central to academic information literacy. Indeed, there are numerous concerns of digital scholarship that I have not touched upon here. I hope that these activities and sources provide practical strategies, while also serving as catalysts for other teaching ideas.

Because DH exists in a unique space, somewhere in between the "traditional" world of academia and that of the "mainstream" blogosphere, it offers great potential for exploring scholarly discourse not as a unified way of thinking, but as a diversity of approaches which nonetheless tend to share some common assumptions and practices. When students examine the conversations, practices, and communities found within DH, they are introduced to a variety of scholarly practices and debates that they can in many respects relate to and compare to their own experiences within and outside of academia, and in both the digital and the analog realms.

As DH scholars often directly address political and institutional issues surrounding scholarly practices, including the roles of technologies and digital communities, DH proves particularly fruitful for fostering academic

---

7 Additional resources relevant to a discussion of peer review include P. Cohen (2010, August 23), D. Cohen (2010, March 5), Updike (2006, June 25), Lehrer (2010, December 13), Engber (2005, April 5), Solomon (2007), Karush (2011, March 10), Clark (2006, December 20), and Salzman and Ruhl (2006). It is worth noting that the majority of the above listed sources (though not all) lean more favorably towards alternatives to traditional peer review. It may prove worthwhile to discuss with students reasons that publications made available through the "visible" Web might be more likely to express this perspective.

information literacy that will likely have resonance to students in the digital age. In connecting academic work to their own lives, students can develop understandings and abilities central to information literacy which extend beyond the more technical aspects of information use. Through such engagements students may develop deeper, more reflective, and more socially aware approaches to evaluating, using, and creating information, whether within or outside of the university.

References

Accardi, M. T., Drabinski, E., and Kumbier, A. (Eds.) (2010). *Critical library instruction: Theories and methods.* Duluth, Minnesota: Library Juice Press.

Bobley, B. (2011, Februrary 1). "What is digital humanities?" Retrieved from http://www.neh.gov/ODH/ODHHome/tabid/36/EntryId/156/What-is-Digital-Humanities.aspx

Clark, M. (2006, December 20). Peer-to-peer: Report on *Nature*'s peer review trial. [Web log post]. Retrieved from http://blogs.nature.com/peer-to-peer/2006/12/report_of_natures_peer_review_trial.html

Cohen, D. (2010, March 5). The social contract of scholarly publishing. [Web log post]. Retrieved from http://www.dancohen.org/category/promotion-and-tenure/

Cohen, P. (2010, August 23). "Scholars test web alternative to peer review." *New York Times.* Retrieved from http://www.nytimes.com/2010/08/24/arts/24peer.html?_r=3&partner=&pagewanted=all

Dacos, M. (2011, March 26). Manifesto for the digital humanities. Retrieved from http://tcp.hypotheses.org/411

Elmborg, J. (2004). Literacies large and small: The case of information literacy. *International Journal of Learning, 11,* 1235-1239.

Elmborg, J. (2006). Critical information literacy: Implications for instructional practice. *The Journal of Academic Librarianship, 32*(2), 192-199.

Engber, D. (2005, April 5). Quality control: The case against peer review. *Slate.* Retrieved from http://www.slate.com/articles/health_and_science/medical_examiner/2005/04/quality_control.html

Freire, P. (2002). *Pedagogy of the oppressed* (30th ed.). (D. Macedo, Trans.). New York: Continuum.

Jacobs, H. L. M. (2008). Information literacy and reflective pedagogical praxis. *The Journal of Academic Librarianship, 34*(3), 256-262.

Karush, M. (2011, March 10). Guest post: Defending current practice. [Web log post]. Retrieved from http://theaporetic.com/?p=1714

Kapitzke, C. (2003a). (In)formation literacy: A positivist epistemology and a politics of (out)formation. *Educational Theory 53*(1), 37-53.

Kapitzke, C. (2003b). Information literacy: A review and poststructural critique.

Australian Journal of Language and Literacy, 26(1), 53–66.

Kirschenbaum, M. G. (2010). What is digital humanities and what's it doing in English departments? *ADE Bulletin, 150,* 55-61.

Fitzpatrick, K. (2009). *Planned obsolescence: Publishing, technology, and the future of the academy.* New York: New York University Press.

Lehrer, J. (2010, December 13). The truth wears off: Is there something wrong with the scientific method? *The New Yorker.* Retrieved from http://www.newyorker.com/reporting/2010/12/13/101213fa_fact_lehrer

Leverenz, C. S. (1994). Peer response in the multicultural composition classroom: Dissensus—a dream (deferred). *Journal of Advanced Composition, 14*(1), 167-186.

MediaCommons. (n.d.). About MediaCommons. Retrieved from http://mediacommons.futureofthebook.org/about-mediacommons

Mullen, L. (2010, April 29). "Digital humanities is a spectrum; Or, we're all digital humanists now." Retrieved from http://lincolnmullen.com/blog/digital-humanities-is-a-spectrum/

Nature. (n.d.) Peer review: Debate. Retrieved from http://www.nature/com/nature/peerreview/debate

Pawley, C. (2003). Information literacy: A contradictory coupling. *The Library Quarterly, 73*(4), 422-452.

Pratt, M. L. (1991). Arts of the contact zone. *Profession, 1991,* 33-40.

Presner, T., Schnapp, J., Lunenfeld, P., et al. (2009, June 22). The digital humanities manifesto 2.0. Retrieved from http://www.humanitiesblast.com/manifesto/Manifesto_V2.pdf

Ramsay, S. (2011a). On building. Retrieved from http://lenz.unl.edu/papers/2011/01/11/on-building.html

Ramsay, S. (2011b). Who's in and who's out. Retrieved from http://lenz.unl.edu/papers/2011/01/08/whos-in-and-whos-out.html

Salzman, J., & Ruhl, J. B. (2006) In defense of regulatory peer review. *Washington University Law Review, 84*(1), 1-61.

Simmons, M. H. (2005). Librarians as disciplinary discourse mediators: Using genre theory to move toward critical information literacy. *portal: Libraries and the Academy, 5*(3), 297-311.

Smith, K. (2009, February 1). "Q&A with Brett Bobley, Director of the NEH's Office of Digital Humanities (ODH)." Retrieved from http://hastac.org/node/1934

Solomon, D. J. (2007). The role of peer review for scholarly journals in the information age. *The Journal of Electronic Publishing, 10*(1). http://dx.doi.org/10.3998/3336451.0010.107

Swanson, T. A. (2004). A radical step: Implementing a critical information literacy model. *portal: Libraries and the Academy, 4*(2), 259-273.

Swanson, T. A. (2005). Applying a critical pedagogical perspective to information literacy standards. *Community & Junior College Libraries, 12*(4), 65-77.

Swanson, T. A. (2010). Information is personal: Information literacy and personal epistemology. In M. T. Accardi, E. Drabinski, & A. Kumbier (Eds.),

Critical library instruction: Theories and methods (pp. 265-277). Duluth, Minnesota: Library Juice Press.

THATCamp. (n.d.). About. Retrieved from http://thatcamp.org/about/

Updike, J. (2006, June 25). The end of authorship. *The New York Times.* Retrieved from http://www.nytimes.com/2006/06/25/books/review/25updike.html

von Trier, L., & Vinterberg, T. (1995, March 13). The vow of chastity: Dogme manifesto. Retrieved from http://ifsstech.files.wordpress.com/2008/06/the_vow_of_chastity.pdf

Ward, D. (2006). Revisioning information literacy for lifelong meaning. *The Journal of Academic Librarianship, 32*(4), 396-402.

Wikipedia. (n.d.a). "Digital humanities." Retrieved from http://en.wikipedia.org/wiki/Digital_humanities

Wikipedia. (n.d.b). Manifesto. Retrieved from http://en.wikipedia.org/wiki/Manifesto

The Tyranny of Tradition:
How Information Paradigms Limit Librarians' Teaching and Student Scholarship

Carrie Donovan
Indiana University

Sara O'Donnell
University of Northern Colorado

The changing nature of scholarly information can primarily be attributed to a move away from the print-based paradigm that favors hierarchies established and maintained by academic publishers toward an environment in which authors share knowledge openly, even if it is undeveloped or unpopular, without the need for the approval or support of traditional publishing mechanisms. The ramifications of these changes, which call into question traditional processes for classifying and accessing scholarship, are often manifest in librarians' teaching through a renewed and revised focus on information evaluation. The impact of scholarly communication on discrete library instruction initiatives may not seem important, until one considers the greater information literacy movement and its potential for furthering education reform by subverting the dominant print paradigm that has heretofore shaped library instruction.

In the higher education context, information literacy adopts the roles and responsibilities of teaching ethical and effective information use within specific scholarly discourse communities, for which practices vary from discipline to discipline. Unfortunately, it can also serve to perpetuate the commodification of information and the negation of student empowerment by reinforcing age-old practices of information seeking and evaluation based on the privileging of certain information sources over others. In order to flatten information hierarchies and lend agency to scholars whose work goes unrecognized or unapproved by traditional mechanisms of peer review, librarians must embrace their roles as advocates and educators in order to upend the process of knowledge creation as an economic endeavor that allows product to trump purpose. This chapter identifies and justifies the ways in which librarians may apply the principles of scholarly communication to information literacy, with a focus on information democratization and student empowerment, to address the breakdown of traditional paradigms.

A Democratic Education

Library instruction programs must be examined in the context of which they are a part–universities and colleges. The goals of such institutions inform the objectives of information literacy instruction. So what exactly is the value of higher education? Naturally, the precise answer to this question varies by geography, by institution, and even by individual. That said, we believe that there are some steadfast principles that do, or at least ought to, guide all activities in institutions of higher education. A core principle of higher education is democracy. Democracy in this sense does not simply imply that everyone is entitled to an education. It also speaks to the nature of the content and delivery of instruction. Instruction should not be used to cement given patterns of knowledge; rather, it should allow for the questioning and subversion of those very patterns through the nurturing of a critical stance toward information (Claus, 1981; Dewey, 1929; Molander, 2002; Weinstein, 2004). This Socratic model of instruction enables students to succeed academically and, moreover, ensures their preparedness for successful participation in a democratic society. The cultivation of critical thinking is imperative to democracy as it allows the individual to step outside of their given paradigm to evaluate it from a perspective that is more authentically their own. Only in this way can the perpetuation of dominating claims to truth be undermined, allowing for the emergence of new ideas. Clearly there are social implications to the powers of critical thinking beyond the development of a new scientific method or a unique reading of Shakespeare. Higher education has the capacity–indeed, the responsibility–to cultivate individuals who will question unjust or oppressive social structures and practices. Weinstein (2004) writes, "Civic education must, first and foremost, create citizens who are educated into a system that allows for rejection. It should teach that the power of the state is neither primary nor absolute" (p. 239). Higher education is tasked with preparing students for responsible citizenship, not merely conveying decontextualized systems of knowledge or isolated skill sets (Freire, 1985).

One way for higher education to achieve the democratic ideal is to reposition the student at the center of the learning process. This move, already taking place in many college classrooms, entails shifting from a top-down instructional style–what Freire (2000) calls "narrative sickness," in which "[t]he teacher talks about reality as if it were motionless, static, compartmentalized, and predictable" (p. 71)–to a bottom-up style that privileges student experience and perspective. This latter approach bears more of a resemblance to an encounter with Socrates than a typical lecture-based course. It favors dialogue and questioning above the dissemination of facts. A bottom-up approach serves first to break down the student-instructor power relationship, supporting a more equitable learning partnership, one that Jaros (2009) defines as "co-construction of knowledge"(p. 192). Secondly, it legitimates a multiple-perspectival approach to information evaluation and interpretation, giving power to student experiences. Thirdly, it encourages good habits: questioning, exploration, and curiosity. According to Dewey (1929), "education is itself a process of discovering what values are worth while *[sic]* and are to be pursued as objectives" (p. 74). Dewey advocates education as a tool for discovery, not merely the dissemination of facts. The value of higher education then, is that it provides a safe-haven for exploration in a society that is often more focused on ends than means.

What this suggests for libraries, and particularly for those librarians who provide information literacy instruction, is that we cannot simply proceed with business as usual. Librarians must be proactive in breaking from the paradigms of scholarly communication as it is currently taught. The values inherent in the scholarly publishing community enforce the authority of the academy, while excluding learners and their use of information. Bourdieu (1967) writes that education creates mental patterns and categories that situate individuals in and toward culture. We must ensure that the frame we provide for the learner is one of freedom and authority, not oppression and coercion. It is necessary for instruction librarians to employ a use-centered approach to information literacy in order to establish authority in its proper home–with the student.

Use-Centered Instruction

Bizup (2008) writes,

> If we want students to adopt a rhetorical perspective toward research-based writing, then we should use language that focuses their attention not on what their sources and other materials are (either by virtue of genres or relative to some extratextual point of reference) but on what they as writers might *do* with them. (p. 75)

Bizup shifts the focus from the information *source* to the information *use*. The locus of control is reallocated to the student as an author, moving us away from traditional structures of scholarly authority that prioritize the nature of the information source itself. If we are to fully inculcate students into the world of scholarship, it would be wise to emphasize use more consistently in information literacy instruction.

Although as information professionals we have long known that information cannot effectively be evaluated out of context, actually implementing a use-centered approach is quite a different task. It entails a certain unbalancing of expectations, creating what Weinstein (2004) terms "cognitive conflict." Cognitive conflict is the agents' awareness of their ability to choose among competing options, and the parallel knowledge that such a choice will not lead to any resolution or cognitive relief as such (p. 242). Rather than simply equipping the student with a set of skills, information literacy instruction ought to embrace a model that supports the creation of cognitive conflict. It is in this space of choice and uncertainty that students can fulfill their potential as scholars and truly engage in dialogue with their peers. This process shares many of the characteristics of "tacking," a sailing maneuver that allows boats to sail into the wind. They sail first toward starboard, then toward port, and back again in a zigzag motion that can seem chaotic, but is in reality a purposeful strategy for moving forward through adverse conditions. Similarly, the state of cognitive conflict allows students to progress toward genuine reflective thinking–not in a straight line, but with detours along the way that serve to push them into roles of responsibility and empowerment.

The principle of cognitive conflict is by no means new. Vygotsky's (1978) "zone of proximal development" (p. 86) approach advocates the benefits of discomfort as a means to kick-start learning. Peers and experts (in this case, instruction librarians) serve as support for students as they navigate new experiences, but ultimately these mentors must provide only enough assistance to prevent students from entering into a state of anxiety. The zone of proximal development provides an opening for students to push beyond their current level of understanding and ultimately gain intellectual independence. It is in this space that students will realize they even have the option to engage with and alter structures they previously assumed to be permanent mainstays of academia (Weinstein, 2004). If we want to produce individuals that are contributors to, not just consumers of information, this is a necessary state to induce in them. It moves students from static observers to dynamic participants in learning. As the term implies, any process that involves cognitive conflict is bound to be an uncomfortable one – and one that is undoubtedly difficult for students and instructors alike. As educators, we want to ease frustrations, instill skills, and provide answers. But it is precisely the space of questioning that leads to more effective information evaluation. Ultimately, it allows students to become fully embedded in the world of scholarship and to embrace the ideal of self-authorship. This is the direction in which information literacy ought to move. Rather than providing students with an external point of reference, future scholars need to explore their own goals as primary focal points for information gathering and use.

The rhetorical process espoused by Bizup advocates the power of language to structure students' thinking and orientation toward themselves and scholarly materials. Green and Smith (1999) note a similar trend in their interviews with first-year composition students: "[W]e need to account for the ways in which writers use language to represent tasks, a language that is all too often based on a legacy of schooling that privileges recitation of received information, not the purposeful use of information"

(p. 151). It is the goal of information literacy to shake students out of the big-T "Truth" mindset and into the flexible and often frustrating world of genuine scholarly communication. Information literacy is not a toolbox you can flip open and select the "right" tool to find the "right" source. It is much more chaotic and uncomfortable. It is a process that students are continually building upon as they work to become more fully themselves.

Empowered Authorship

In order to properly empower students to take responsibility for their education and enter the world as fully prepared and responsible citizens, it is necessary to create a sense of authorial identity that extends beyond the classroom. Authorship is a state that has repercussions for more than just the writing process. It is a state that works to inculcate a sense of authority in students in which they see themselves as primary players in scholarly dialogue (Pittam et al., 2009; Christensen, 2011; Gerald et al., 2004; Green and Smith, 1999; Hodge et al., 2009; Kapitzke, 2003; Magolda, 1999) as well as the dialogue of liberal democratic citizenship itself (Weinstein, 2004). Magolda (1999) states that "[Self-authorship] is simultaneously an ability to construct knowledge in a contextual world, an ability to construct an internal identity separate from external influences, and an ability to engage in relationships without losing one's identity" (p. 12). Self-authorship, then, is not just about writing better five paragraph essays or choosing more appropriate sources, but instead about preparing students for membership in the world as conscientious and empowered citizens—citizens capable of making decisions reflective of internal beliefs, not swayed by dominating and potentially oppressive social patterns. In terms of information literacy, this means cultivating students' ability to evaluate sources from a perspective that is their own rather than one that is conferred on them from outside persons and institutions. This requires a dramatic mental shift on the part of both student and instructor. Often it requires students to throw almost two-decades' worth of imposed author-ity into question before they realize they can be contributing members to information structures. The goal is to create equitable relationships between students and educators, rather than relationships of power. The re-situation of students with respect to academic publishing patterns is a powerful way in which to reorient student authority inwards. The creative force of authorship, in which students put pieces of themselves out into the world and become part of the fabric of the world, provides the ultimate source of scholarly empowerment. Authorship is a locus of power that imbues students with a unique authority and perspective in and toward the world. It is in this way that we can legitimate student scholarship and give them entry into discourse in a meaningful way.

Crafting this sense of self-authorship requires giving students a voice in the classroom and enabling a genuine democratic discourse between students, instructors, and experts in the field. Students must see themselves as a creative force, not just a receptive one. In order to give students voice we must respect and acknowledge the ways in which they currently receive and filter information. Dialogue requires that all parties are acknowledged and that their "primordial right to speak their word" (Freire, 2000, p. 88) is honored. Kapitzke (2003) writes that "youth in consumer societies negotiate and construct their interests and identities" through multiple channels that are often not considered academically sound (such as music, text messages, YouTube videos, and the like) (p. 51). Before we can expect students to engage in new ways of communication and enter into academic citizenry we must first legitimate their existing modes of communication as reasonable entryways into the world of information. Librarians must recognize students' knowledge claims as a valued starting point for exploration, if we are not to alienate them from the scholarly process. The lines we draw between peer-reviewed and not, or between scholarly and popular send the message, "This is legitimate; you are other." We need not open up the world of information uncritically, but we must respect and be aware of the ways that students orient themselves toward information in order to empower them to use it more responsibly. Academia is only one culture among many with its own traditions, languages, and rites that are by no means monolithic. There are institutional and cultural issues at play that subvert other legitimate forms of literacy that arise outside the accepted realm of commodified academic publishing. That does not mean that academic literacy as currently practiced is *illegitimate*, only that it is not the *only* legitimate form of literacy (Henderson and Hirst, 2007; Kapitzke, 2003). By allowing students the freedom and space to question a given authority, we enable them to construct new forms knowledge.

New Information Paradigms

The proliferation of online information and the resulting implications for scholarly communication allows us to approach information literacy from a student-centered framework, unlike the earliest proponents of information literacy whose educational approaches were primarily driven by information access as stipulated by publishers and corporations. Paul Zurkowski (1979) was among the first to conceive of information as a commodity that should be treated as a national economic asset, stating that it was incumbent upon academic and governmental agencies to ensure access to information via information aggregators and publishers. Having accounted for the important role of the private sector in information literacy education, he equated an individual's and a nation's "wealth" as one that generates information, and therefore power and prosperity, for all its citizens (Badke, 2010). Such privileging of information systems as the constructs that control not only access to information, but the power it can bring, becomes increasingly less relevant in a non-print based model of information creation and dissemination in which readers, researchers, and authors now take a more direct role in the flow of information beyond the strict structures of publishing. New texts are fluid (Gounari, 2009) in their form, content, and audience, which undermines previous conceptions of information as a rules-driven, one-way mode of communication. In this emerging information paradigm, positions of power are shifting to accommodate for the ubiquity of information and the increasingly egalitarian process by which information is created, disseminated, and evaluated.

New information technologies also necessitate a contextual approach to information seeking, use, and evaluation that can be construed as a departure from the format-based approach that previously guided the means by which various types of knowledge were produced and reproduced (Gounari, 2009). In an environment that allows immediate and far-reaching access to knowledge, the act of evaluating or judging the quality of information cannot be based on any singular factor, but on a broad-based understanding of the process by which knowledge is created, shared, and revised in an open community. In this process, peer review maintains its governance as the premier process for the validation of new ideas. However, more egalitarian modes for producing and sharing information have brought about similarly open methods of review that question traditional notions of expertise. Even in the scholarly information environment, changes to the nature and structure of information blur the lines between formal and informal publication types and content creators in such a way that information quality is no longer simply a question of provenance or authorship.

In speaking of traditional methods of information evaluation, librarians often refer to those that were prevalent and relevant in an age of information in which format dictated quality, due to the strict structures of scholarship imposed by academic publishers. Fundamental to this system was the notion of *authority*, a common criterion for evaluation of information for both novice and experienced scholars. Widely acknowledged as the phenomenon by which the work of specialists is judged by other specialists (Wilson, 1991), authority perpetuates the elite nature of scholarly communities to the extent that new voices or opposing ideas are not always welcome. Often manifest in the form of peer review, this power of authority is so widely accepted as to become endemic to the culture of academe (Mark, 2011b). Unfortunately, information seeking that is guided by authority, rather than what the knowledge creator hopes to do with the information, does not always serve to propel scholarship into original and creative directions. In addition, acknowledging research from experts and the sources through which they communicate as "the best," alienates novice researchers, strips them of agency, and denies them access to participation in the conversations of specialists, thereby limiting their potential for genuine learning through the research practices unique to scholarly communities. Being acknowledged and being able to participate in social practice is necessary for identity development (Riedler & Eryaman,

2010); in this way meaning is negotiated such that the playing field levels between teachers and students, between expert and novice researchers.

The historical and cultural conventions of scholarly environments that celebrate and reward the successful review by experts in a particular field are prevalent in the nature and structure of scholarly information today; however, these conventions are being called into question by new generations of learners and new modes of information access. Based on a traditional paradigm in which librarians set up dichotomous frameworks for interpreting and evaluating knowledge, including scholarly vs. popular, dominant and non-dominant, and authoritative and non-authoritative, the print-based structure of identifying scholarship is weakened in a web-based world of information (Swanson, 2004), because it promotes source format as the criterion for selection and evaluation above all others. Such simplified mechanisms for understanding knowledge structures and practicing information evaluation are rendered irrelevant by the seemingly straightforward searching made popular by Google and adopted, more recently, by academic libraries through meta-search and discovery services. This method of information retrieval creates a new information gathering strategy, defined by Marcia Bates (1989) as "berrypicking." Throughout this process, a student would gather information in small increments, which would then lead the individual further until their personal store of information grows like berries picked and placed in a bucket (Williams, 2007). The berrypicking practice of information gathering is especially common with digital content but can render non-traditional information sources difficult to evaluate for meaning and quality. Researchers who rely on evaluative criteria from the print-based information paradigm in order to make sense of the complex digital world of information will come up short. Accordingly, learning the processes for information evaluation that are based on checklists are no longer a service to students whose world of information is not easily defined by elements such as authority, currency, relevance, and publisher. Such criteria limit students' creativity and curiosity in discovering new knowledge, as well as in their application of ideas that fall outside the approval process of established scholarly communities.

Instead of suffering disappointment when faced with students whose evaluative decisions do not reflect those of previous generations of research-ers, librarians should be among the most vocal advocates for students to make choices based on the contextualization of information for their own research and writing. As information mediators, librarians are well acquainted with assignments that only serve to alienate students from the research process by setting it up as a linear exercise of asking questions and finding answers. As described by Norgaard (2004), the traditional research paper is focused on product, rather than process. Helping countless frustrated students navigate research assignments that require a certain number of scholarly sources without reason or justification, librarians are uniquely positioned to understand and support new frameworks for information evaluation that could allow for students to be more engaged and responsible for decision-making in the access, selection, and use of information for their own research and writing. Ceasing to acknowledge traditional scholarly information structures as the definitive guidelines for information evaluation allow research-based assignments to become an opportunity for learning, rather than an exercise in finding specific types of information sources and struggling to weave them into a coher-ent narrative.

Faculty and instructors design research assignments with strict parameters regarding the type of sources students should consult; these requirements are often put in place to encourage students' use of the "best sources" for their research needs. Few, if any, li-brarians would disagree with the value in students' use of quality sources, but it is time for us to redefine our notions of quality to encompass knowledge that is created in social spaces and ideas that are formulated and proven beyond the traditional means of schol-arly peer review. If librarians stop simply equating quality sources with "library-vetted" sources (Mark, 2011a), students will learn to recognize, assess, and value the subjectivity inherent in most forms of scholarship. Understanding that sources communicate hard facts in addition to personal meaning will challenge students to evaluate information contextually, including the influences and circumstances of the author, publisher, and selector of that information. Students who employ this inclusive approach to assessing information will determine source quality based on the facts they read and the meaning they intuit, as well as how the source might be used according to their own individual research and writing needs. Personalizing the research process in this way will encourage students' active participation as scholars in a context in which information seeking and use may have a greater purpose in improving the world and their place in it, rather than as a means to an end (i.e. find a particular number of scholarly sources). In this new paradigm, source use, not source type, would ideally guide students' choices.

Information Literacy Revitalized

Looking at librarianship through a lens of activism and progressivism, evidence of revolutionary movements is apparent through the increasing acknowledgement of alternative modes of research, publication, and review. Librarians have a long history of advocating for the underrepresented, the underserved, and the disenfranchised when it comes to ensuring access to knowledge and information (Samek, 2001; Dalrymple, 2002; Preer, 2006; Raber, 2007; Morrone & Friedman, 2009). With near ubiquitous access to digital information, librarians have supported a growing movement toward making online content open to a broader readership. Open access is defined as peer reviewed academic work made freely available online and created without the intention of the author to profit financially (Park & Qin, 2007). The movement toward democratizing information, especially in support of initiatives related to scholarly communication and open access, situates librarians as agents of change in the evolving information landscape.

Open access appeals to librarians' service orientation and progressive sensibilities as a means to make information broadly available, while simultaneously minimizing the role of publishers in the process of bringing knowledge to the masses. Responding to economic influences that dictate the access and flow of information, academic librarians have led the charge on many campuses to challenge the traditions of scholarly publishing and reclaim the work of local communities of scholars. Through the creation of scholarly repositories for digital content, librarians have created a mechanism for authors to maintain a modicum of control over their own works and for libraries to make research available to a broader audience without the intervention of scholarly publishers and their exclusive processes.

With librarians heavily involved in issues related to open access and digital content management in higher education, it would make sense that the democratic values inherent in these projects would trickle down to the teaching of novice researchers, but this is not always the case. Librarians often perpetuate the very structure of publishing which they seek to upend in the development of digital repositories and open access initiatives through information literacy instruction by continuing to hold to the dichotomous paradigms of "scholarly vs. popular," "primary vs. secondary," "refereed vs. not." While not unhelpful in describing different kinds of information sources, these dichotomies superimpose an artificial hierarchy of knowledge, creating haves and have-nots of the information world. Some sources are established as legitimate whereas others are somehow lesser, to be browsed and absorbed, but never mentioned in scholarly work. The *peer-reviewed* limiter that appears in many academic databases represents the epitome of dichotomous thinking, as it does not take into account the various review processes that may fall outside this strictly defined category and it eliminates the student researcher's own thinking and decision-making as a potential participant in the review process.

As educators, we seek inspiration to invigorate our information literacy instruction with active learning and student-centered teaching. While continual renewal and reflection on the many ways in which we engage students in the process of research is good pedagogical practice, a firm grounding in the greater potential and purpose of librarians' teaching is just as important. As the instructional goals of academic librarians continue to engage educators on a broader scale, the need to create a theoretical underpinning, or an informed pedagogical praxis as Heidi Jacobs (2008) recommends, becomes even more important. Such a framework will ensure the centrality of information literacy to student learning in higher education and to the future of scholarship in the digital world going forward. The driving forces of open access, as a movement concerned with power and democracy, are essential to the emerging role of librarians as publishers and educators. In both capacities, open access principles offer guidelines for engaged and participatory praxis on the part of librarians.

At a minimum, instruction librarians would do well to follow the conversations surrounding the open access movement in order to develop an informed strategy toward educating the next generation of scholars and researchers about their role in securing rights and ensuring access to the knowledge they work so hard to create. Ideally, instruction librarians would also engage colleagues in considering how the fundamentals of open access could be applied to instructional scenarios. It is no surprise that librarians are leaders in the open access movement, but in order to further its success, we must incorporate the tenets of open, social, engaged research into the information literacy initiatives that will shape future generations of scholars. If we take the opportunity to create classrooms and learning environments that acknowledge information as political and learning as a social, collective process in which students and teachers engage in learning together, information literacy will remain a powerful education reform movement.

Empowering students to make informed decisions regarding information sources based on their potential use, rather than on antiquated and decontextualized evaluative criteria, will complete this newly defined cycle of information creation and dissemination. Like open access, teaching students to engage with knowledge and information in order to shape their unique ways of thinking and their own process of learning is a means of empowerment by placing the onus of the scholarly community squarely back in the hands of knowledge creators. Our ability to see the connections between and across disciplines positions librarians uniquely to teach about the consistencies, trends, and pitfalls in publishing in a variety of subject areas (Knievel, 2008). Having a background in collaborative teaching and consensus building will help librarians create integrative, supportive academic communities with information literacy education and open access principles as their guideposts.

Some of the best ways for instruction librarians to incorporate this new framework into their teaching is to start with what they know: the traditional paradigm. If a literature search formerly asked students to think about a particular topic in a very systematic way that first engaged reference sources and background information, an approach informed by new information environments would subvert the linearity of the process and encourage students to gather and identify information sources from a broad range of perspectives at the very beginning stages of research. This would allow students to engage with a variety of authors to inform their own thinking, without the necessity of having found the sources within a particular information container or from a particular type of source or in any certain order. While seemingly haphazard and rudderless, the approach is actually quite similar to how students will experience information seeking in real-world contexts in which they will be required to engage with a wide variety of ideas, perspectives, and sources.

Similarly, if an instructional scenario in the traditional paradigm were guided by the cycle of information (i.e. what types of sources are created at the various stages of publication after a particular event), then a revised approach would undermine the position of importance afforded the publication process as a determinant for source selection and would instead create an opportunity for sources to be identified and evaluated based on the decisions and desires of the researcher. In this scenario the context used to provide meaning for the information seeking and evaluation process is not dictated by the publication cycle, but by the purpose of the creative output as defined by the student researcher. This is not to say that students would not benefit from knowing about the formalized structures of scholarly publishing and its associated language. In fact, researchers who are ignorant of labels such as "primary" and "secondary" and how their meaning shifts from discipline to discipline will have difficulty participating in fully formed scholarly communities and information literacy education must account for this. The structures of publishing are a reality of scholarship that demands acknowledgment, as the vocabulary is still used actively in classrooms today. It would be irresponsible not to educate students about the extant structures in the academic community. That said, it is also is important to emphasize that this is only one facet of information seeking, not *the* facet. Student-centered information literacy education entails giving students the appropriate tools while simultaneously framing the process in a use-centered way.

Additionally, consider a student who was educated about determining the perceived sphere of influence of a particular author or work by using cited reference searching. If this student were also introduced to the availability and value of alternative value measurements, or alt-metrics, the student would have a well-rounded and progressive approach to information evaluation that would apply to traditional as well as new modes of scholarship. In challenging the checklist approach for information evaluation, Meola (2004) does not recommend that librarians ignore peer review as an irrelevant means of evaluating scholarship; instead, he describes the power of revealing the inherently social nature of peer review and, by doing so, making its weaknesses and drawbacks transparent to student researchers. The same approach can be taken with cited reference searching.

With the instructional approach to information literacy grounded solidly in the open access movement, librarians would have a practical and a theoretical reasoning for demanding that information publishers and aggregators begin to accept these ways of thinking as widely-used and therefore important to include in the search functionality of databases and search engines. Experiencing the philosophical frameworks of open access and information literacy in familiar online search environments would reinforce their value to researchers and serve as a reminder of these approaches until they become common scholarly practice. Linking the philosophies of scholarly communication and information literacy will also serve the profession of librarianship in its quest toward developing a cohesive community of practice with shared guiding principles.

Conclusion

If information literacy is to be the means by which students come to understand the world of information, they must engage as equal and active participants in a conversation that encompasses the creation and dissemination of knowledge in a scholarly context. Students who feel their research output makes a contribution to scholarship in a particular discipline will fully understand and embrace the knowledge and skills that are foundational to information literacy, such as framing a research question, identifying authorship, and acknowledging the work of others, because they are more invested in the research process rather than simply fulfilling the requirements for a particular assignment. While librarians have a significant role in introducing and enculturating students to the process of finding, evaluating, and using information, we may be doing students a disservice if we do not acknowledge and validate students' research and writing as part this scholarly conversation. Situating students on the same ground as published authors and established scholars empowers them to truly embody scholarship in their own work. By embracing and applying the fundamental principles of open access to information literacy, librarians will find themselves one step closer to developing a pedagogical praxis that is both relevant and radical.

References

Badke, W. (2010). Foundations of information literacy: Learning from Paul Zurkowski. *Online, 34*(1), 48-50.

Bates, M. J. (1989). The design of browsing and berrypicking techniques for the online search interface. *Online Review, 13*(5), 407-424.

Bizup, J. (2009). BEAM: A rhetorical vocabulary for teaching research-based writing. *Rhetoric Review, 27*(1), 72-86.

Bourdieu, P. (1967). Systems of education and systems of thought. *International Social Science Journal, 19*(3), 338-358.

Christen, L. (2011). Finding voice: Learning about language and power. *Voices from the Middle, 18*(3), 9-17.

Claus, J. F. (1981). Radical reform within a liberal and democratic framework? Rawls and the radical critique of schooling. *Educational Theory, 31*(2), 153-165.

Dalrymple, C. (2002). Help for the advocacy-impaired librarian: A bibliography of resources on library advocacy. *Public Libraries, 41*(3), 158-165.

Dewey, J. (1929). *The sources of a science of education*. New York: Liveright Publishing Corp.

Freire, P. (2000). *Pedagogy of the oppressed*. (M.B. Ramos, Trans.). New York: Continuum International Publishing Group.

Freire, P. (1985). *The politics of education*. (D. Macedo, Trans.). South Hadley, MA: Bergin & Garvey Publishers, Inc.

Gounari, P. (2009). Rethinking critical literacy in the new information age. *Critical*

Inquiry in Language Studies, 6(3), 148-175.

Greene, S., & Smith, E. (1999). Teaching talk about writing: Student conflict in acquiring a new discourse of authorship through collaborative planning. In K.L. Weese, S.L. Fox, & S. Greene (Eds.), *Teaching academic literacy: The uses of teacher-research in developing a writing program* (pp. 149-174). Mahway, NJ: Lawrence Erlbaum Associates, Inc.

Henderson, R., & Hirst, E. (2007). Reframing academic literacy: Re-examining a short-course for "disadvantaged" tertiary students. *English Teaching: Practice and Critique, 6*(2), 25-38.

Hodge, D. C., Magolda, M. B. B., & Haynes, C. A. (2009). Engaged learning: Enabling self-authorship and effective practice. *Liberal Education, 95*(4), 16-23.

Jacobs, H. L. M. (2008). Information literacy and reflective pedagogical praxis. *The Journal of Academic Librarianship, 34*(3), 256-262.

Jaros, M. (2009). Pedagogy for knowledge recognition and acquisition: Knowing and being at the close of the mechanical age. *The Curriculum Journal, 20*(3), 191-205.

Kapitzke, C. (2003). Information literacy: A positivist epistemology and politics of outformation. *Educational Theory, 53*(1), 37-53.

Knievel, J. E. (2008). Instruction to faculty and graduate students: A tutorial to teach publication strategies. *portal: Libraries and the Academy, 8*(2), 175-186.

Magolda, M. B. B. (1999). *Creating contexts for learning and self-authorship: Constructive-developmental psychology.* Nashville, TN: Vanderbilt University Press.

Mark A. E. (2011a). Format as a false judge of credibility. *Communications in Information Literacy, 5*(1), 21-37.

Mark A. E. (2011b). Privileging peer review: Implications for undergraduates. *Communications in Information Literacy, 5*(1), 4-8.

Meola, M. (2004). Chucking the checklist: A contextual approach to teaching undergraduates web-site evaluation. *portal: Libraries and the Academy, 4*(3), 331-344.

Molander, B. (2002). Politics for learning or learning for politics? *Studies in Philosophy and Education. 21,* 361-376.

Morrone, M., & Friedman, L. (2009). *Radical reference: Socially responsible librarianship collaborating with community.* The Reference Librarian, *50*(4), 371-396.

Norgaard, R. (2004). Writing information literacy in the classroom: Pedagogical enactments and implications. *Reference & User Services Quarterly, 43*(3), 220-226.

Park, J., & Qin, J. (2007). Exploring the willingness of scholars to accept open access: A grounded theory approach. *Journal of Scholarly Publishing, 38*(2), 55-84.

Pittam, G., Elander, J., Lusher, J., Fox, P., & Payne, N. (2009). Student beliefs and attitudes about authorial identity in academic writing. *Studies in Higher Education, 34*(2), 153-170.

Preer, J. L. (2006). "Louder please": Using historical research to foster professional identity in LIS students. *Libraries & The Cultural Record, 41*(4), 487-496.

Raber, D. (2007). ACONDA and ANACONDA: Social change, social responsibility, and librarianship. *Library* Trends, *55*(3), 675–97.

Riedler, M., & Eryaman, M. Y. (2010). Transformative library pedagogy and community-based libraries: A Freirean perspective. In G. J. Leckie, L. M. Given, & J. E. Bushman (Eds.), *Critical theory for library and information science: Exploring the social from across the disciplines* (pp. 89-100). Santa Barbara, CA: Libraries Unlimited.

Samek, T. (2001). *Intellectual freedom and social responsibility in American librarianship, 1967–1974.* Jefferson, NC: McFarland.

Swanson, T. (2004). A radical step: Implementing a critical information literacy model. *portal: Libraries and the Academy,* 4(2), 259-274.

Vygotsky, L. S. (1978). *Mind in society: The development of higher psychological processes.* M. Cole, V. John-Steiner, S. Scribner, & E. Souberman (Eds.). Cambridge, MA: Harvard University Press.

Weinstein, J. R. (2004). Neutrality, pluralism, and education: Civic education as learning about the other. *Studies in Philosophy and Education, 23,* 235-263.

Williams, G. (2007). Unclear on the context: Refocusing on information literacy's evaluative component in the age of Google. *Library Philosophy and Practice, 9*(3), 1-10.

Wilson, P. (1991). Bibliographic instruction and cognitive authority. *Library Trends, 39*(3), 259-70.

Zurkowski, P. G. (1979). Information and the economy. *Library Journal, 104*(16), 1800-1807.

Liberatory Praxis:
Students and Teachers as Co-Learners

The Three-Credit Solution:
Social Justice in an Information Literacy Course

Anne Leonard
New York City College of Technology, CUNY

Maura A. Smale
New York City College of Technology, CUNY

Information literacy is more than simply searching library databases. Incorporating critical pedagogy and social justice into library and information literacy instruction has the potential to improve student learning by linking research skills to important and contested issues in the information landscape that will affect today's college students throughout their lives. Unfortunately, much library instruction by necessity occurs in individual, isolated sessions. While many librarians would like to address social justice in their information literacy instruction, the assignment-driven nature, course faculty preferences, and serious time constraints of many single instruction sessions (also known as one-shots) may be prohibitive (Kopp & Olson-Kopp, 2009, p. 61).

In this chapter we discuss a semester-length, three-credit information literacy course at New York City College of Technology (City Tech), the technical college of the City University of New York (CUNY). This course–LIB1201 Research & Documentation for the Information Age–is the first credit-bearing course to be offered in the Library Department at City Tech. This is not a library skills course: we do not spend the semester teaching undergraduates how to act like librarians. While we do teach using the online library catalog and databases, the acquisition of mechanical search skills is not our primary goal. Drawing on inspiration from similar courses at other colleges, we work with students to explore and interrogate the lifecycle of information in depth. In this course we have the time to encourage thoughtful engagement by students with a wide variety of information sources and media, as both content consumers and producers. Teaching this course enables us in our role, as academic librarians and college faculty, to engage in "a critical practice of librarianship—a theoretically informed praxis" (Elmborg, 2006, p. 198).

Critical Information Literacy and Social Justice

Over the last decade several seminal publications have defined, discussed, and explored critical information literacy as well as the important role of elements of social justice to a critically-informed instructional practice (Accardi, Drabinski, & Kumbier, 2009; Elmborg, 2006; Simmons, 2005; Jacobs, 2008; Patterson, 2009; Swanson, 2004a, 2004b, 2011). Critical information literacy is inspired by the critical pedagogy espoused by Paulo Freire (1970), among others; discussion of its theory and practice has become increasingly prevalent in the library and information science literature. Elmborg (2006) suggests a succinct goal for a critical pedagogy of information literacy instruction in his summary of Freire's work:

Rather than focus on knowledge acquisition, students identify and engage significant problems in the world. By developing critical consciousness, students learn to take control of their lives and their own learning to become active agents, asking and answering questions that matter to them and to the world around them. (p. 193) Adopting a critical pedagogy perspective in research and library instruction allows librarians to emphasize that information literacy is more than just a set of research skills and approved standards (Simmons, 2005; Jacobs, 2008, p. 258; Reed & Stavreva, 2006; Seale, 2010; Swanson 2004a). While the Association of College and Research Libraries' (ACRL) Information Literacy Competency Standards for Higher Education (ACRL, 2000) can be useful guidelines for creating information literacy lessons and assignments, Swanson (2004a) suggests that "these standards shortchange the impact information literacy can have on students by oversimplifying a complex process" (p. 66). Seale (2010) notes that the Standards are stripped of any politicized context, and that unsituated information study misses an opportunity to relate to untraditional, perhaps even user-generated, content that students encounter outside of the classroom (p. 229). Critical information literacy can take us beyond the focus on finding and gathering information that is so prominent in many sets of standards to encourage critical thinking and knowledge production among our students. As Simmons (2005) writes, "facilitating students' understanding that they can be participants in scholarly conversations encourages them to think of research not as a task of collecting information but instead as a task of constructing meaning" (p. 299).

Critical pedagogy encourages us to recognize students' prior knowledge, and reminds us that our students bring real and relevant life experiences into the classroom (Swanson, 2004a, p. 67). While students may come to college with highly varied experience in information-based research, facility with navigating, understanding, and using information is surely important for all students, and may be especially important for under-prepared students (Swanson, 2004b, p. 263-264). Our students do have experience in using information of many types—from websites to videos to newspapers, for example—but they may not have critically examined the information that is readily available to them on the internet or through the mainstream media. It is important for a critical information literacy to acknowledge the relevance of the wide variety of information that is available to everyone, as students need the ability to navigate all of the different types of information sources, not simply scholarly sources (Doherty & Ketchner, 2005, p. 7; Shanbhag, 2006, p. 1). Further, many students will not continue past their undergraduate degrees, and, since most scholarly publishing remains locked inside subscription-based article databases, it is imperative that students gain experience with information from many different sources and perspectives.

A critically-informed information literacy instruction can bring social justice issues to the forefront of the classroom by encouraging students to "explore the social construction of information" (Swanson, 2004a, p. 73). Students can interrogate information sources to determine how and why they were made, how they are intended to be used, whether there are benefits to their use, and whether anyone is excluded as authors or audience, among other questions (Doherty, 2007, p. 3; Franks, 2009, p. 46; Simmons, 2005, p. 308; Swanson, 2004a, p. 73). Librarians can encourage thoughtful engagement by students with a wide variety of information and media, as both content producers and consumers. Social justice is an important component of these discussions of the cultural, economic and political factors that affect information and media, and is a natural ally in the information literacy classroom.

Credit-Bearing Information Literacy Courses

Literature on the place of critical information literacy in credit-bearing library courses is emerging. Many of the courses described in the literature are one-shot research orientations or one-credit library skills courses in which instructors may lack the time to fully explore topics beyond classroom instructors' assignments or the functionality of library discovery tools. Even the Library of Congress subject headings used to describe these articles in the library literature do not fully address the topic; *information literacy--study and teaching* comes close, but does not evoke a critical approach to the study of information.

William Badke (2008), author of the textbook used in our course and a veteran teacher of and advocate for credit-bearing information literacy, asserts that information literacy is "foundational to what we mean by education" (p. 47) and is also essential to meet the research demands of many specialized careers (p. 49). While he recognizes the importance of research training and skills to a student's skill set, he clearly distinguishes library research skills learned in a decontextualized vacuum from information literacy that is learned through doing "real research" (p. 49). Badke asserts that information literacy is a "credible academic subject" that invites engagement with the "sociological and ethical implications" of information and its production, dissemination, and consumption (p. 49).

Our course concludes with a documentation project, in which small groups of students design an information tool, resource, educational game, gather competitive intelligence on comparable resources as well as substantial research on the topics their chosen form will cover, and document both the sources they use (including multimedia), as well as the process of creating, researching, and producing it. This problem-based approach, described by Peterson (2010), allows students to leverage their experience (as commuting college students, gamers, veterans, etc.) into building a relevant and useful information resource (p. 71). To Peterson the superficial engagement of one-shots is not ideal as students rarely get the opportunity to engage with a complex problem in a meaningful way or apply previous experience to begin to respond to it or solve it. Problem-based learning encourages students to begin to question relevant problems, yet may only be a truly realistic approach with the luxury of a three-credit information literacy course.

The Origins of LIB1201

Librarians are faculty in tenure-bearing lines at CUNY and the library is an academic department, so there is no procedural or policy impediment to offering a credit-bearing course. Indeed, several other library departments at CUNY colleges offer courses of between one and three credits on a range of research and information literacy topics, and one–Baruch College–offers an Information Studies minor for undergraduates (Newman Library, Baruch College, n.d.).

In Fall 2008, faculty members in the Entertainment Technology Department at City Tech who were developing a new degree track in Emerging Media Technologies contacted the Information Literacy Librarian (Smale). As described in the college catalog, this interdisciplinary program:

> integrates media design theory and practice, computational media models and principles, and engineering methodology and implementation. In collaborative learning workshops, students gain hands-on experience using media production tools, develop skills in rapid prototyping, system integration, teamwork, software knowledge, and the knowledge to evaluate the viability of new media technologies. (New York City College of Technology, n.d., p. 230)

The faculty who created this new program are keen to ensure that their students are both media and information literate, and that they have the opportunity to research, incorporate sources, write, and document their work both traditionally and using online technologies. An initial meeting included a faculty member in the English Department as well as faculty from the Library and Entertainment Technology Departments. While at first it seemed that perhaps the course would be team-taught by one faculty member each from English and the Library, we quickly realized that the focus of the course would primarily be research and documentation rather than composition, and thus the Library Department would be well-suited to offer the course.

Our course—titled LIB1201 Research & Documentation for the Information Age—was developed from October 2008 through January 2009. During the Spring 2009 semester the course proposal progressed through the College Council Curriculum Committee and other review channels. City Tech's college governance approved the course in April 2009, and it received approval at the university level soon thereafter. We offered the first section of the course in Spring 2010 and it has grown in popularity each semester since; during the Spring 2012 semester there were 2 sections which filled to capacity at 20 students each. At the time of this writing the course is now required for students in three degree-granting programs at the college in very diverse fields: Entertainment Technology, Chemical Technology, and Radiologic Technology & Medical Imaging. Additionally, students in other programs at the college may take LIB1201 to fulfill 3 credits of their Communications Core requirement or as an elective.

The past several years have also seen an increased emphasis on information literacy throughout the college, which is partially in response to the college's most recent Middle States accreditation visit in 2008. The City Tech Assessment Committee, composed of one faculty member from each academic department, selected information literacy as one of the General Education competencies to assess collegewide, and a pilot is currently underway in the 2011-2012 academic year. The availability of a research and documentation course taught in the Library Department has certainly contributed to keeping the importance of information literacy at the forefront of the college's attention.

Developing the Syllabus

Research & Documentation for the Information Age seeks to engage with this question posed by Elmborg (2006): "Is the library a passive information bank where students and faculty make knowledge deposits and withdrawals, or is it a place where students actively engage existing knowledge and shape it to their own current and future uses" (p. 193)?

In developing our course, we reviewed several information literacy courses at other colleges to familiarize ourselves with the content included and pedagogy used in a typical credit-bearing information literacy course. Two courses in particular were extremely valuable when creating our course: Information Literacy & Research Skills (INFS 1000), developed by Tom Eland (2011) at Minneapolis Community and Technical College, and Information Fluency (NDL 301), developed by Barbara Fister (2012) at Gustavus Adolphus College. These courses incorporate both research skills and critical information literacy and social justice components, including topics such as the political aspects of scholarly research and publishing, and the role of alternative presses and knowledge producers as compared to the mainstream media.

Our course goals for Research & Documentation for the Information Age, which appear on the syllabus, are:

> To introduce you to the theory and practice of research and documentation for all information and media, including:
>
> Cultural, economic and political factors that affect information and media;
>
> The organization of information in multiple formats;
>
> Developing methods for finding information that is relevant to you;
>
> Critically evaluating information and its sources;
>
> Copyright, fair use, and ethical use of information and media; and
>
> The role of documentation and citation in scholarly, professional, and public work.

In committing to these goals for our course, we acknowledge students' prior experiences with information and media, both in their academic careers and their lives outside of their college work. While many of our students have considered these topics before (for example, the ethical issues around downloading music), in our course we invite students to engage in critical conversation about these issues in the classroom and in their writing.

Though as open access advocates we realize that textbook publishing is highly problematic,[1] as mentioned above we have chosen to use a textbook for LIB1201: William Badke's *Research Strategies: Finding Your Way through the Information Fog* (as does Tom Eland's INFS 1000 course at Minneapolis Community and Technical College). The text is clearly written and a good introduction to the practical research and library skills components of the course, and includes sections on note taking and other writing competencies that we feel are a valuable reference for our students.[2] We supplement the textbook with a wide variety of scholarly, journalistic, and popular readings (articles, book chapters, and websites), videos, and other sources, many of which we learned about from the syllabi of other courses. Since our course is concerned with current information issues, there is ample opportunity for all of us, students and professor alike, to bring in additional sources to discuss as the semester progresses.

In the syllabus for LIB1201 we place a special focus on the use of on-line technologies such as collaborative publishing and social media tools. This focus stems in part from our initial discussions with faculty in the Emerging Media Technology program, though as librarians we also feel that it is important for all students to gain experience with these tools. As Mackey and Jacobson (2011) suggest, "(t)he emergence of social media and collaborative online communities requires a reframing of information literacy as a metaliteracy that supports multiple literacy types" (p. 62), including information literacy, media literacy, and visual literacies. Current online technologies enable students to participate in the creation and discussion of content in addition to consumption, and we take the

---

1 Among our many concerns with textbook publishing is the high price charged by textbook publishers (in the hundreds of dollars, in many cases), especially in light of the frequent release of new editions of textbooks every few years, often with very little new or changed content. While open access textbooks are beginning to be created, they are not yet available for all disciplines. We feel that the textbook we selected is a reasonable compromise: it is available new for approximately $20 and as a PDF for $10, and covers the basics of library and internet research well.

2 ENG1101 English Composition I is the prerequisite for our course; while our course is writing-intensive and provides students with many opportunities for both informal and formal writing, we do not spend significant time on composition in our course.

opportunity afforded by our course to encourage students to explore this participatory culture (McLeod & Vasinda, 2008). While our students may be familiar with these online technologies before taking our course, they may not have used them critically in their academic work.

Our selection of instructional technologies is congruent with our desire to move beyond library and research skills in LIB1201. City Tech and the CUNY system use Blackboard as the primary learning management system, but Blackboard is a closed platform in which students may only view the courses in which they are enrolled, and has no relevance to students outside of their college coursework. Using open online media tools in an instructional setting encourages students to engage with the course topics beyond their work for the class, and hopefully even beyond the course, and allows students to learn to work with technologies that they can continue to use outside of college.

We also want our students to gain experience in writing for different audiences and in different formats, and to have the opportunity for their work to be seen by a wider audience than merely the instructor and classmates. For these reasons we use a course blog. Students are required to publish short blog posts throughout the semester, often as a reading response or research journal, as well as to comment on their classmates' blog posts. While not all students embrace blogging to the same extent, one of our former students is now an established food blogger, which is highly relevant to both her course of study at the college (Hospitality Management) and her future plans. Collaborative online technologies have helped turn our library classroom into a place like the one Elmborg (2006) imagines, "where students actively engage existing knowledge and shape it to their own current and future uses" (p. 193).

Course Content and Pedagogy

As they consider registering for our course, students and their advisors read the description published in the college catalog:

> This course explores research and documentation for all media formats including text, images, sound, and multimedia. Students will examine

the full lifecycle of information, including: how information is produced and organized in both traditional and emerging media, locating information sources in a variety of media and formats, critical evaluation of sources, the ethics of information use, and documentation and citation of traditional and emerging media and technologies. Students will create and present research and documentation projects. (New York City College of Technology, n.d., p. 78)

As librarians turned classroom faculty, we bring years of experience with one-shot delivery to first-semester students in English Composition I, but significantly less experience teaching semester-long, credit-bearing classes; our most recent classroom experiences were as graduate students in LIS and other professional degrees at the master's level. We begin the semester with an introduction to the lifecycle of information and investigate issues around both medium (digital or print) and format (text, audio, or visual). This section of the course includes discussion on ownership and distribution of mainstream media and the range of alternatives; a half day devoted to the very small press–zines–opens some students' eyes to a wide range of authorship identities and introduces the radical idea that there is indeed an audience for any and every voice. By expanding the examination of the information lifecycle to include nontraditional forms, we encourage students to critique it and to "question the grand narratives that still exist within our educational structures" (Franks, 2010, p. 52).

The sequence of class meetings that cover issues in information and media could easily be expanded to an entire semester's worth of reading, discussion, and writing. Discussions in this sequence explore access, plagiarism, copyright and fair use, preservation, and privacy from interdisciplinary and multidisciplinary perspectives, addressing legal, ethical, and political aspects of each issue. We begin the exploration of issues with an overview of personal and institutional access to analog and digital information with emphasis on the digital divide. While the digital divide is a concept that students may have some familiarity with, their understanding of it is limited; many have not considered the urban/rural divide (West & Engstrom, 2010). Yet many students are personally familiar with an emerging method of bridging the digital divide: skipping the purchase of the home computer and the subscription to home internet service entirely and instead using a smartphone or mobile device and its data plan to substitute for many of a computer's functions (Smith, 2011).

Discussion of plagiarism includes a survey of students' beliefs and attitudes about plagiarism and includes a simple survey with yes/no questions. In discussion, students first supply the answer they think their instructor wants to hear, but through further discussion we reject a yes/no response construct and explore the "it depends" responses: *once I graduate, what does it matter if I sell my A papers to a term paper bank? Since I'm no longer a student, why is this an academic integrity infraction? And the paper belongs to me – as its author, why shouldn't I sell it?* The day's discussion also investigates recent examples of plagiarism of published authors.[3] Any conversation about copyright and fair use inevitably turns to recorded music, perennially a rich area where the students teach the instructor. Students are also introduced to the Right to Research Coalition (http://www.righttoresearch. org/), an international coalition of student organizations advocating for open access to scholarly research.

As the semester progresses, we study the organization of information, classification systems and taxonomies, and information retrieval in theory and practice. We compare taxonomies and folksonomies, Google Scholar and EBSCO. This section of the course most closely resembles a library skills course, and these discussions coincide with the students' initial research efforts towards the scaffolded research assignment. Students' growing familiarity with research resources is reflected by the annotated bibliography assignment. As we grade the annotated bibliographies, we can usually determine which research resources are the most fruitful; this valuable feedback loop halfway through the semester provides another point of access into a discussion about information discovery.

The course continues with readings and discussion about the role and importance of citation and documentation. Students investigate why citation styles have evolved, a question that rarely gets asked in any educational setting, and determine the most important criteria for a style they invent. The semester concludes with an assignment that puts students in the roles

---

3 We hesitate to use the term "real-world" plagiarists, because the world of academia is very real to students immersed in it.

of information evaluators, creators, and recorders as they work in small groups to develop a prototype for a research game, a research tool, or an information resource. By documenting the process of producing a group effort, the arc of locating and evaluating resources similar to the one they propose, and by properly documenting and acknowledging every type of information source they use—from images to multimedia to websites, articles, and books—students take on the roles that they have read about and discussed: author, researcher, recorder, beta-tester, and presenter.

Assigned readings and viewings may come from the information literacy "canon" of fundamental, elementary, and essential readings on core information literacy topics, and are also very much driven by current cultural phenomena. The fact that scholarly sources on a specific, recent event may not yet exist well illustrates the earliest arc of the information lifecycle. Scholarly articles are assigned in a targeted way, both to introduce a more abstract or theoretical concept and also to illustrate the concept of scholarly communication itself. Students are encouraged to share news articles they find, though in practice this is very informal and rarely drives class discussion, since sharing of articles is not formally required for the class participation grade.

Students show a remarkable ability to relate course content to their experiences. On the class day designated for discussion of print and digital alternative press, each semester we discuss the structure of media ownership; specifically, the "Big Six" media giants and their diverse holdings in print, digital and broadcast media (Free Press, 2009). Students frequently ask about the media of other nations: *"Who owns Al-Jazeera?"* Their curiosity about corporate ownership of media and information distribution companies informs what they identify as critically important for others to know about the research process; one group of students included correct identification of library database vendors as a point-scoring feature in a research game they prototyped for their final project. These students now consider learning about library database corporate ownership a prerequisite to using these research tools, and have moved from passive consumption of information to a critical analysis of research tools.

The idea that media ownership could influence the promotion or suppression of a news story resonates with students and encourages reflection upon censorship they have encountered. Inspired by the suggestion that censorship exists, we engaged in an animated discussion about language; specifically, bitch, fag, and the N-word, and how these terms are used in mainstream media, which in this case they identify as a voice that alters the meanings of these terms from their vernacular. The concept of gatekeeping (Badke, 2011, pp. 5-8) regularly stirs a collective sense of justice in the students; they perceive it as an institutionalized form of potential censorship rather than as a means to disseminate high quality, trustworthy information. At the start of the semester, the students' "critical consciousness" (Freire, 1970) is generally inconsistently expressed; by the conclusion of the semester, students demonstrate a more developed critical consciousness. We would like to develop an assignment or instrument to determine whether it was there all along and unexpressed until late in the term, or more confidently expressed as a result of development of confidence in their own interpretation of course material.

The size of the class is dictated by the library's available space; a well-designed but small classroom and flexible/modular space. Since we have room for just 20 students, we can foster a seminar environment where questions and discussion are encouraged. We make an effort to conclude each topic or section with an opportunity for students to reflect critically on the topic and offer their perspectives. Seasoned teachers at any level know that "Any questions?" all too often invites stony silence; we stimulate discussion with invitations to comment and share knowledge–even knowledge gained outside of an academic context–on relevant issues.

Assignments that Incorporate Social Justice

Assignments and classroom activities engage students' critical perspectives on the study of information and also recognize that their own experiences creating content, synthesizing new knowledge, and even responding to classroom activities are legitimate. Throughout the course, students contribute to the course blog in the form of reading response blog posts, comments on classmates' posts, and research journal blog posts. The research journal posts are responses to a prompt that asks them to delve into their experiences as scholars and researchers and describe them, comparing it to their past experiences (and thus validating those experiences). One research journal prompt asks students to compare their search process and results among various library databases and commercial search engines; encountering the paywall for access to scholarly content often incites complaints and frustrated comments. While encountering the paywall in class discussion is often easily breached, the same experience outside of higher education illustrates that access to some scholarly content is often restricted.

On the day that alternative media and publishing are discussed, we bring several zines to class for students to examine. Working in small groups, students select a zine. They are asked to identify its theme, main idea, or reason for existence, to recall when and where they have encountered a similar point of view, and record their thoughts on the author's motives and address the question "why a zine?" By sharing their thoughts and judgments on these examples of the very small press and seeing the concept of authorship reframed, students begin to see themselves as potential authors with a voice and an audience.

As the course investigates the importance of evaluating information, one class day is devoted to a research game. In the research game, students self-organize into teams and compete against each other to locate and evaluate high quality online information sources that they would use to answer a question posed by the instructor, based on criteria the students crowdsource in the previous class. The question is chosen carefully and used as an opportunity to both raise students' awareness of political and economic forces that influence their status as students and also to introduce a complex question requiring highly developed internet search skills and keen critical abilities to evaluate. The question is often controversial, local, and overtly political; economic conditions of recent semesters made it essential to ask "How will cuts in New York State's budget affect CUNY?" and "How would forgiving student loans help stimulate the economy and correct the current economic recession?" Such questions encourage students to reflect upon their situation as students at a large urban public institution, and also as citizens, taxpayers, and participants in a democracy.

Grappling with Neutrality

As instruction and reference librarians we strive to be neutral as we guide students to resources while teaching them to evaluate those resources for quality and relevance. As we take on another role, that of classroom instructor, we rediscover neutrality in the act of evaluating students' work: we seek evidence that they have synthesized their sources to create new knowledge and have properly documented all sources they have used.

Yet we cannot be neutral when we bring our progressive values to the information literacy classroom. Core values of the profession, codified by the American Library Association (2004), align with many of the topics discussed in the course: access, privacy, and preservation. Taking a position on issues critical to libraries may also mean taking the same position on issues critical to the free and ethical exchange of information. We are not teaching library skills, and we are not teaching librarianship to undergraduates, yet the values of the profession permeate our teaching, and, because of this, we cannot be neutral about ethical issues around information.

While we are introducing students to topics in the course that are shaped by our own progressive values and adherence to critical pedagogy, we believe that it is important to give students experience with these views, as they run counter to the mainstream media and consumer values with which students are saturated throughout their lives.

Looking to the Future

We recognize that an entire semester to fully interrogate issues of information and media is a luxury that many librarians may only dream of, and many libraries may not believe they have the staff capacity to institutionalize. Exploring this belief with the intent to uncover the means to develop and sustain a credit-bearing information literacy course is a worthwhile effort. By not having to privilege skills over issues, librarians who also teach one-shots or research workshops may see ways to engage critically with the content in shorter instruction opportunities. By sharing the experience of facilitating a semester of reading, discussion, writing, and projects on information literacy and social justice, academic librarians gain vital experience that our other principal constituency–classroom faculty–prizes: sustained teaching and evaluation.

It is our intent to continuously evolve and improve our course by including current and relevant issues, constantly maintaining awareness of scholarly trends as well as news. We will continue to bring current and relevant information practices into the undergraduate classroom; in the near future we plan to use the course as the framework to publish an open access undergraduate research journal where students will use open peer review to evaluate their classmates' contributions. We may explore developing additional information literacy courses, or collaboration with other departments at the college to co-teach capstone research courses. We look forward to both continuing and new opportunities to work with our undergraduate students on information literacy and social justice issues in this course and beyond.

Our course offers a setting for library instruction, in addition to our work at the reference desk and in one-shots, in which we can encourage student exploration of the social justice issues implicit in information literacy. As such, teaching the course has been a valuable addition to our own practice as academic librarians. Building on our experiences teaching a course that does not privilege skills over issues, we now look for ways to engage critically with information literacy as we teach during one-shots, research workshops, and other shorter instruction opportunities. We enthusiastically work towards a future in which our work in library instruction takes on a more socially activist stance, the better to work with our students on current and future challenging information issues and develop a library–and a locus for learning at the college–that is a complex and interactive information space.

References

Academic publishers have become the enemies of science. (2012, January 16). *The Guardian*. Retrieved from http://www.guardian.co.uk/science/2012/jan/16/

academic-publishers-enemies-science

Accardi, M. T., Drabinski, E., & Kumbier, A. (Eds.). (2010). *Critical library instruction: Theories and methods.* Duluth, MN: Library Juice Press.

American Library Association. (2004). Core values of librarianship. Retrieved from http://www.ala.org/offices/oif/statementspols/corevaluesstatement/corevalues

Association of College and Research Libraries. (n.d.). Information literacy competency standards for higher education. Retrieved from http://www.ala.org/acrl/standards/informationliteracycompetency

Badke, W. (2008). Ten reasons to teach information literacy for credit. *Online, 32*(6), 47–49. Retrieved from http://www.infotoday.com/online/default.shtml

Badke, W. (2011). *Research strategies: Finding your way through the information fog.* Bloomington, IN: iUniverse.

Doherty, J. J. (2007). No shhing: Giving voice to the silenced: an essay in support of critical information literacy. *Library Philosophy and Practice.* Retrieved from http://cors0812.unl.edu/LPP/doherty2.pdf

Doherty, J. J., & Ketchner, K. (2005). Empowering the intentional learner: A critical theory for information literacy instruction. *Library Philosophy and Practice.* Retrieved from http://unllib.unl.edu/LPP/doherty-ketchner.pdf

Eland, T. (2011). INFS 1000: Information literacy & research skills. Retrieved from http://library.minneapolis.edu/courses/infs1000/syllabus/INFS_1000_syllabus.doc

Elmborg, J. (2006). Critical information literacy: Implications for instructional practice. *The Journal of Academic Librarianship, 32*(2), 192–199.

Fister, B. (2012). NDL 301: Information fluency. Retrieved from http://infofluency.wordpress.com/assignments-and-grading/

Franks, S. (2010). Grand narratives and the information cycle in the library instruction classroom. In M. T. Accardi, E. Drabinski, & A. Kumbier (Eds.), *Critical library instruction: Theories and methods* (pp. 43-54). Duluth, MN: Library Juice Press.

Free Press. (2009). Ownership chart: The big six. Retrieved from http://www.freepress.net/ownership/chart/main

Freire, P. (1970). *Pedagogy of the oppressed.* New York: Continuum.

Jacobs, H. L. M. (2008). Information literacy and reflective pedagogical praxis. *The Journal of Academic Librarianship, 34*(3), 256–262.

Julien, H., & Williamson, K. (2011). Discourse and practice in information literacy and information seeking: gaps and opportunities. *Information Research, 16*(1). Retrieved from http://informationr.net/ir/16-1/paper458.html

Kopp, B. M., & Olson-Kopp, K. (2010). Depositories of knowledge: Library instruction and the development of critical consciousness. In M. T. Accardi, E. Drabinski, & A. Kumbier (Eds.), *Critical library instruction: Theories and methods* (pp. 55-67). Duluth, MN: Library Juice Press.

Mackey, T. P., & Jacobson, T. E. (2011). Reframing information literacy as a metaliteracy. *College & Research Libraries, 72*(1), 62–78.

McLeod, J., & Vasinda, S. (2008). Critical literacy and web 2.0: Exercising and negotiating power. *Computers in the Schools, 25*(3/4), 259–274.

New York City College of Technology. (n.d.). 2011-2013 college catalog. Retrieved from http://www.citytech.cuny.edu/catalog/index2.html

Newman Library, Baruch College. (n.d.). Credit courses: Information studies minor. Retrieved from http://newman.baruch.cuny.edu/services/creditcourses.html

Patterson, D. (2009). Information literacy and community college students: Using new approaches to literacy theory to produce equity. *The Library Quarterly, 79*(3), 343–361.

Petersen, E. (2010). Problem-based learning as teaching strategy. In M. T. Accardi, E. Drabinski, & A. Kumbier (Eds.), *Critical library instruction: Theories and methods* (pp. 71-80). Duluth, MN: Library Juice Press.

Reed, S. L., & Stavreva, K. (2006). Layering knowledge: Information literacy as critical thinking in the literature classroom. *Pedagogy, 6*(3), 435–452.

Rollins, D. C., Hutchings, J., Goldsmith, M. U. D., & Fonseca, A. J. (2009). Are we there yet? The difficult road to re-create information literacy. *portal: Libraries and the Academy, 9*(4), 453–473.

Seale, M. (2010). Information literacy standards and the politics of knowledge production: Using user-generated content to incorporate critical pedagogy. In M. T. Accardi, E. Drabinski, & A. Kumbier (Eds.), *Critical library instruction: Theories and methods* (pp. 221-235). Duluth, MN: Library Juice Press.

Shanbhag, S. (2006). Alternative models of knowledge production: A step forward in information literacy as a liberal art. *Library Philosophy and Practice, 8*(2). Retrieved from http://unllib.unl.edu/LPP/shanbhag.htm

Shapiro, J. J., & Hughes, S. K. (1996). Information literacy as a liberal art: Enlightenment proposals for a new curriculum. *Educom Review, 31*(2). Retrieved from http://teaching.uncc.edu/sites/teaching.uncc.edu/files/media/files/file/InstructionalTechnologies/InformationLiteracy.pdf

Simmons, M. H. (2005). Librarians as disciplinary discourse mediators: Using genre theory to move toward critical information literacy. *portal: Libraries and the Academy, 5*(3), 297–311.

Smith, A. (2011). 35% of American adults own a smartphone: One quarter of smartphone owners use their phone for most of their online browsing. Washington, D.C.: Pew Research Center. Retrieved from http://pewinternet.org/~/media/Files/Reports/2011/PIP_Smartphones.pdf

Swanson, T. (2004a). Applying a critical pedagogical perspective to information literacy standards. *Community & Junior College Libraries, 12*(4), 65–77.

Swanson, T. (2004b). A radical step: Implementing a critical information literacy model. *portal: Libraries and the Academy, 4*(2), 259–273.

Swanson, T. (2005). Teaching students about information: Information literacy and cognitive authority. *Research Strategies, 20*(4), 322–333.

Swanson, T. (2011). A critical information literacy model: Library leadership within the curriculum. *Community College Journal of Research and Practice, 35*(11), 877–894.

West, J., & Engstrom, J. (2010). *How the other half lives: Touring the Digital Divide* [PDF document]. Retrieved from http://www.librarian.net/talks/sxsw10/

Hip-Hop and Information Literacy:
Critically Incorporating Hip-Hop in Information Literacy Instruction

Dave Ellenwood
University of Washington Bothell

As an information literacy (IL) educator and instruction librarian in a higher education setting, it is easy to recognize the significant role that IL plays in the academic success and lives of college students. Many instruction librarians seek innovative methods to teach these important skills to students, and a new body of critical literature on IL is asking questions about the theory and practice of IL instruction. Are instruction librarians delivering lessons in a culturally responsible, socially responsible, and pedagogically engaged manner? As librarians grapple with these questions, hip-hop music and culture has maintained increased popularity in U.S. society across racial and cultural boundaries, but particularly among youth of color (Sullivan, 2003; Kitwana, 2005, p. 99-100). Additionally, hip-hop has inspired my personal growth as well as challenged my teaching style to critically engage with the curriculum and issues of social justice. As popular hip-hop artist and business mogul Jay-Z once said, "hip hop has done more than any politician to improve race relations" (DeCurtis, 2009), and if we include it in IL curriculum, it can work as a bridge to many students' previously established IL skills to help introduce tough, but important topics. This chapter will demonstrate that hip-hop can be used in IL instruction to teach students critical IL skills and foster constructive conversations about oppressive forces in the world and a range of social justice issues. Building from existing IL learning structures as practical guides that can be expanded and supplemented to incorporate critical pedagogy, social justice-oriented discourse, and alternative visions of IL, this chapter will outline several practical strategies, tools, and activities for introducing hip-hop into IL workshops.

Hip-hop and library instruction may seem like a curious combination to many readers, but there are several conceptual connections between this odd couple. Separate paths brought me to hip-hop and librarianship, but I find both compelling for similar reasons: cultural knowledge, social justice, and critical perspectives. I started listening to hip-hop in kindergarten while living in a suburb of Hartford, Connecticut, but the music and culture grabbed me permanently in middle school when my brother, home from college, introduced me to several "conscious" rappers whose well-crafted rhymes and infectious beats spoke to me in a way that no other music previously had. Through these rappers' enlightening verses, I was introduced to some of the themes that are prevalent in the consciousness of those marginalized by society, including young African Americans and Latinos, among others. Although oppression was not evident in my experience as a middle-class white male from the suburbs, it was largely evident in the experiences of youth of color that grew up around me and throughout the world. Through progressive verses ranging from simple stories to complex critiques of capitalism, militarism, police brutality, etc., I was able to gain knowledge about other peoples' lives and of their sophisticated ideas and critiques on society. For example, the following rhymes from Brother Ali, written and produced during the Iraq War, connected the U.S. tax structure with racism, militarism, and the complacency of middle class citizens:

> You don't give a **** about the bum
> standin' on the corner with a sign bleedin' from his gums
> Talkin' 'bout you don't support a crackhead
> What you think happens to the money from your taxes?
> **** the government's an addict
> With a billion dollar a week kill brown people habit...
> And even if you ain't on the front line
> When master yells crunch time, you're right back at it
> Man look at how you're hustling backwards
> At the end of the year add up what they subtracted
> 3 out of 12 months of your salary paid for that madness, man that's sadness
> What's left? Get a big *** plasma
> To see where they made Dan Rather point the damn camera
> Only approved questions get answered
> Now stand your *** up for that national anthem
> (Ali, 2007)

Verses like Ali's urge listeners to ask questions about his lyrical themes and provide a critical perspective that may be applied to information acquired during the research process. A listener inspired by Ali might inquire further about what he refers to as the government's "billion dollar a week kill brown people habit" by asking, for instance, about the racialized rhetoric used by the government leading up to the Iraq war. The education that I received from hip-hop lyrics like these influenced the subject matter that I pursued in my own studies as well as my current approach to instruction librarianship. Similarly, teaching students how to recognize and build upon their IL skills in a higher education context matches my interest in social justice because people need to be able to critically navigate information sources in order to make informed personal and political decisions. This chapter demonstrates how using hip-hop in the IL classroom promotes social justice by engaging with cultural knowledge and introducing critical perspectives.

Literature Review

Although the Association of College and Research Libraries' (ACRL) Information Literacy Competency Standards for Higher Education (2000) are a useful structure for the everyday practices of instruction librarians, they possess several shortcomings. An emerging influential segment of the LIS literature challenges the ACRL Competency Standards by theorizing a critical perspective on IL as both an alternative to the ACRL Standards as well an expansion of their original offerings. For example, Elmborg (2006) critiques the format and cultural boundaries of the written text-based ACRL Competency Standards' concept of literacy. Instead, he advocates multiple literacies by defining IL as "the ability to read, interpret, and produce 'texts' appropriate and valued within a given community" (p. 195). Situated in a cultural context, one can imagine a vast amount of IL criteria limited only by the number of existing communities and valuable texts. These texts are not simply confined to print materials, but can take on other formats beyond the written word. Elmborg continues to describe texts as including "any objects that are intentionally inscribed with meaning and subsequently 'read' and 'interpreted' by members of communities" and can exist in any format: visual, aural, or tactile (p. 195), an argument that opens up space for hip-hop styles, lyrics, and sounds to be considered texts. Furthermore, Norgaard (2003) maintains that the term literacy implies a deficit model in which students are not already skilled with information, but he argues, that "college students have developed fairly complex (if not always effective, appropriate or productive) ways of accessing and using information" (p. 126) well before they enter computer labs for IL instruction. Given this notion, students have learned to grapple with information through experiences prior to entering higher education, and in a context in which hip-hop is an influential phenomenon, they may have internalized information practices that are specific to or influenced by hip-hop culture. For example, authority or credibility in hip-hop culture largely emanates from experiencing social struggle (Hess, 2005) as opposed to the process of peer-review and institutional validation that generally characterize authority in academia. This notion of authority might impact a student's perception of academic writing on a host of issues (e.g. poverty and race) if the student does not view the author as having empirical experience with the material.

IL benefits from being situated in cultural context, but it also must be viewed through the lens of critical pedagogy and social justice. Jacobs (2008) supports Elmborg's and Norgaard's claims about IL and culture, but goes further to argue that when we limit IL's "potential to outcomes and standards, we run the risk of minimizing the complex situatedness of IL and diminishing–if not negating–its inherent political nature" (p. 258). This is not to say that standards, outcomes, and assessments are disposable, but theory, action and reflection about issues that directly impact students' lives and communities are valuable as well. Making the concept of IL more flexible, allowing for a more contextualized Freirean practice of problem posing (Freire, 2000) in IL instruction, can build bridges to students' own IL skills and expand upon them. Ward (2006) purports that IL education must involve fostering a deep personal connection with information in various forms and he even uses a rap music-based classroom example to show how IL can inspire college students towards the greater good. Ward and his faculty collaborator play the Black Eyed Peas song "Where is the Love" to spark conversation about "the paradox of valuing human compassion and yet contributing, albeit indirectly, to the creation of a culture that hurts our fellow humans" (p. 400). Additionally, media literacy scholars Malott and Porfilio (2007) connect this critical and social justice perspective utilizing hip-hop and other transgressive social movements' potential as sites of liberatory education for both students and educators (p. 583).

It is difficult to validate and engage non-dominant cultures, world-views, and identities when institutions of higher education tend to privilege certain cultural norms, practices and forms of intelligence over others. Elmborg (2006) invokes Gee to argue that schools privilege a certain class of students, through honoring and validating the specific cultural practices of those students, while simultaneously parents in the middle and upper economic echelon socialize their children to embody the values that translate into success in a school environment. This process generates an environment in which minority students are marginalized when schools disregard their values (p. 194). If students are not steeped in the dominant set of values then it can disadvantage their ability to succeed in an academic environment that privileges other students. These students are often deemed deficient or unprepared, but instead of further marginalizing these students with this deficiency model, it might be more productive to interrogate schools and curriculums themselves to see whether they "are a large part of the problem, especially when they become conservative protectors of traditional, authoritative knowledge and cease to respect students as people capable of agency and meaning making in their own right" (Elmborg, 2006, p. 194). More specifically, Elmborg (2006) notes Gardener's work with the concept of multiple intelligences stating that "'traditional schools' have privileged verbal and analytical thinking while discounting other kinds of intelligence" and they do not allow for the inclusion of "diverse abilities that people bring to learning" at many levels (p. 195).

Higher education professionals, including librarians, are not oblivious to this type of discrimination in colleges and universities, but we have difficulty creating multicultural environments. For example, Whitmire has published several articles examining the state of library usage by students of color at academic libraries here in the United States. In her study, Whitmire (2003) demonstrates that as minority enrollment has increased in higher education, minority student use of library resources has also increased. On first glance, this figure is positive, but coupled with increased use is an increased sense of discomfort for students of color visiting the library. Another study conducted by Whitmire (2004) explains that minority students experience a variety of micro-aggressions, "defined as subtle insults directed toward people of color," (p. 363) when they visit the library. One African American library user who participated in the study said that:

> Last time we went to the library . . . to study . . . obviously, it's finals time . . . people are going to study. But when we walked in there looking for somewhere to sit down, it's like . . . they've never seen African American people before in their lives, or they've never seen African American people study before! (p. 363)

An environment that promotes reactions to minority students like this is unacceptable in a multicultural society, and is a disservice to both the students of color who may feel this way and to the white students who will inevitably be a part of a global community that requires cooperative experience and interaction with diverse groups. Whitmire's study is one of many indications that concerned librarians have important work to do in order to continue fostering a successful multicultural environment in today's academic library. This can be done thoughtfully in the instruction classroom and hip-hop is one avenue for strategically engaging with issues of race and privilege.

Hip-hop culture is relevant to many of the students who attend IL sessions and students are likely familiar with it because of its popularity with youth and young adults, its controversial qualities, and the meaningful social impact that it has had on many communities. After its formation in the early 1970's, hip-hop quickly grew into a national and international phenomenon, increasing in prominence throughout the United States as well as in hundreds of countries around the globe. It began as an art form developed and performed primarily by African Americans and Afro-Caribbean youth combining graffiti artists, rappers, break-dancers (Rose, 1994, p. 2) and DJ's in New York City. Hip-hop founding father DJ Kool Herc stated that hip-hop "has bridged the culture gap. It brings white kids together with black kids, brown kids with yellow kids" (Chang, 2006, p. xi). Despite powerful signs of hip-hop's potential to create social progress, it simultaneously exhibits oppressive sub-currents of sexist, homophobic, and violent activity. But, some argue that the commodification of hip-hop produces the majority of these problematic manifestations (Asante, 2008; Rose, 2008, p. 2-5). And often, as Rose (1994) contends, the media has chosen to focus on these incendiary aspects of hip-hop without providing the social context in which "everyday struggles over resources, pleasure, and meanings take place" (p. 2). The media conversation about some questionable aspects of hip-hop, absent of context, has promoted widespread negative attitudes towards hip-hop (Chang, 2006; Rose, 1994; 2008). However, several scholars (Chang, 2006; Flores-Gonzalez, 2006; Kitwana, 2002) have discussed the connection between hip-hop, activism, and positive social change. For example, a group of activists based in Atlanta, Georgia, responded to heavy criticism of rap music and the "War on Youth" marked by large-scale media attacks on hip-hop, which culminated in a Senate Judiciary hearing on the subject, by organizing hip-hop devotees in Atlanta "to defend hip hop and constructively critique it" (Chang, 2006, p. 453) in several public forums. Possibly due to the negative media portrayal of hip-hop, higher education has been slow to embrace it, but given hip-hop's cultural significance, social justice orientation, and critical perspectives, it has the potential to benefit college students in and out of the classroom.

As mentioned earlier, hip-hop music does contain a significant amount of sexist content and objectifying imagery, and when broaching the subject in a classroom that is diverse in terms of race and gender there will be strong reactions in response to these themes. A negative or any other reaction to sexism in hip-hop music, especially from women who are largely targeted, is completely understandable. Although Sharpley-Whiting (2007) reverently recognizes the importance of hip-hop for young women of color and others, she notes the problematic gender dimensions of hip-hop videos in which "overexposed young black female flesh…is indispensable to the mass-media-engineered appeal of hip hop culture" (p. 11). The "very public celebration and commercial trafficking in such images and behaviors has made them appear normal, acceptable and entertaining" and these public displays of sexism "hammer away at self-esteem" for all women, especially women of color (p. 12). Additionally, bell hooks (1998) repudiates the objectification of women throughout popular art and argues that "the sexist, misogynist, patriarchal ways of thinking and behaving that are glorified in gangsta rap are a reflection of the prevailing values in our society, values created and sustained by white supremacist capitalist patriarchy" (hooks, 1994, p. 116). She calls for "a rigorous feminist critique and interrogation of the sexis[m] and misogyny expressed" in rap music and that African American men too should be held "accountable for their sexism" (p. 116). However, she also warns that "this critique must always be contextualized or we risk making it appear that the problems of misogyny, sexism, and all the behaviors this thinking supports and condones, including rape, male violence against women, is a black male thing" (p. 116). These controversial and potentially offensive elements of hip-hop do not disqualify hip-hop from being a liberatory tool for the classroom, and furthermore, directly confronting these issues can be beneficial to students' intellectual and personal growth. Pough (2004) argues that the pedagogical "possibilities for using rap in the fight against sexism" (p. 194) are numerous and the music can be used in the higher education classroom as a "medium for putting these issues on the table" (p. 195). In Pough's experience including hip-hop in the curriculum, she found it "allowed students to explore sexism in popular culture as well as the race and class issues that sexism is connected to" (p. 199). The lively and passionate debates held in her classroom "provoked a discussion that went beyond the dismissive 'this is sexist, therefore this is bad' response" and "complicated the discussion and disrupted dismissive attitudes" (p. 199). Although these themes may promote lively discussion and liberatory intellectual experiences, it is important to be cognizant of and sensitive to potential objections to sexist material in hip-hop.

Educators at a variety of levels have employed hip-hop as a pedagogical tool to critically engage students in discussions about several issues relevant to their lives in addition to sexism. Akom (2009) discusses his use of hip-hop culture in the higher education classroom by employing a Critical Hip Hop Pedagogy or CHHP. CHHP, in an attempt to bypass the deficit model of education, seeks to teach students through youth-driven participation and to engage students through a group research process in which students contribute equally to the project. Additionally, it "foregrounds race, racism, gender, and other axis of social difference" in its research projects as well as "seeks a balance among critical thinking, reflection, analysis, and action" among other key principles (p. 56). One implementation of CHHP involves a program called "Inside the Hip Hop Studio" which is a public forum in which "scholars, students, artists, activists, community members, and…the media gather to engage in intellectual and personal explorations of the intersections of hip hop and racial attitudes, sex, sexuality, substance abuse, violence, political activism, civic engagement, and social change" (p. 59). This program acts as a bridge between academia and students' lives. Students get the opportunity, in an academic setting, to intellectually and respectfully engage with members of the community that they revere and to discuss issues that matter to them and that impact their lives. Akom argues that this addresses and transforms previous social science research surrounding communities of color that focuses on deficits and problems instead of assets, and strives to highlight and build upon the positive components of communities (p. 60). Akom argues that by applying his CHHP, educators can create a curriculum in which students "unlearn their stereotypical knowledge of race, class, gender, sexual orientation, and other axes of social difference while analyzing, problem solving, and theorizing what it means to be part of a diverse" (p. 63) community of learners. In other words, hip-hop can be used as a tool in the academy for students to intellectually address social problems through a student-centered approach that increases social awareness around issues such as race, gender, and poverty.

Furthermore, Kim (2011) has shown how implementing hip-hop in the classroom should be from a critical perspective, not divorcing hip-hop from its cultural and social justice context. Kim chronicles the hip-hop influenced pedagogy of an instructor named Florence in Illinois and demonstrates Florence's critical approach in which she views hip-hop as the language and culture of the African American youth. She uses hip-hop themes in her class that are relevant to youth struggles. Florence argues that "she uses hip-hop as a tool for validation of 'where they're at, and then bring them'" into a more analytical and academic conversation (p. 164). Kim is skeptical of non-critical, cookie-cutter uses of hip-hop in the classroom environment. She notes that pre-written curricula using hip-hop themes alone are generally weak, stating that "whether it offers pre-created hand-outs pairing rap lyrics with canonical texts, increased SAT vocabulary, or improved student engagement, most of these programs package hip-hop in overly simplified ways" (p. 173). Kim accurately argues that these amount to "shaking on a little hip-hop or pop culture" to help traditional curriculum relate better to students who are frustrated with the current educational materials. Instead, the structure of curriculum that includes hip-hop culture must be oriented towards liberation and social justice.

Teaching IL using a form of critical hip-hop pedagogy requires an important caveat, namely that the teacher consider the identities of the students in the class, as well as their own positionality, or position in relation to the class. Specifically as a white man, what are some of the issues that I must maintain awareness of while I engage students with hip-hop and issues of race, gender, and poverty? Greenfield (2007), who is also a white man engaging hip-hop in higher education, argues that this is a crucial component of teaching about a culture in which one is considered an "outsider," and the experience of thinking through one's privilege and outsider status can result in transforming the teacher and the curriculum while simultaneously engaging students in material that can be educationally liberating. One of the significant consequences of not being reflexive in this context is to enable a classroom environment that both privileges the teacher's values, teaching and learning styles, and perpetuates practices that disadvantage other groups of learners that don't match the teacher's primary style (p. 231). By foregrounding issues of race, age, and gender, Greenfield "wanted to indicate [his] willingness to actively examine [his]

positionality in the classroom and to encourage critical analysis of the dimensions of identity and authority" (p. 234). By being forthcoming with his
biases and perspectives about hip-hop, he created space for students to be
aware of these and at the same time contribute knowledge to the discussion.
As a teaching librarian with limited face-time with students I cannot
establish the same rapport as a professor who has the entire term to develop relationships, but there are a couple of simple ways that I attempt
to positively navigate my positionality. First, and very importantly, I
take hip-hop seriously. As Lankes (2011) argues, when librarians engage
other cultures "we must honor the norms of the conversations in terms
of intellectual property and indeed propriety" (p. 124). Making light of
hip-hop style, language, and music is common and often customary in
white spaces, but in diverse classes this dynamic is likely to alienate students who really identify and care about the subject. Additionally, it is
important to recognize that as a white man I don't own hip-hop culture
and it is likely that I will be considered an outsider. For example, when I
first started teaching IL I would tell students that my second goal in life,
aside from being a librarian, was to be a rapper, which would always be
met with laughter and disbelief. But, when this young white man who
does not have an entirely hip-hop influenced clothing or speech style
consistently asserted his love for the genre, students could understand
that I respected the art form. Lastly, it is important to create space for
students to have their own views on hip-hop music and culture whether
they are positive or negative. One way that I attempt to accomplish this is
through transparency, demonstrating how my own views are impacted by
my identity as a white man. This self-disclosure process renders my views
open to challenges from students and encourages collective knowledge
creation. Given the potential for charged language to arise around gender
and race, it is important to be especially sensitive to student reactions, and
to ensure that a wide variety of perspectives and experiences are heard
in class discussions.

Hip-Hop Activities in IL Instruction

To develop a set of practical hip-hop-oriented activities that can be critically used to teach IL skills and highlight issues of social justice, I used the ACRL IL Competency Standards (2000) as a general structure from which to expand and to supplement. The remainder of the chapter will use the structure of the ACRL Competency Standards, performance indicators, and sample learning outcomes. This section is additionally influenced by the structure and style of Kimball and O'Connor's (2010) column on employing music to teach IL. This section seeks to demonstrate how hip-hop can be used to teach general analytical IL skills by using a problem-posing and social justice orientation in an IL session. It will discuss potential portions of class plans and activities that incorporate hip-hop music and culture, help students think critically about oppression and power relations, and finally push beyond the analytical to what Ward (2006) calls "lov[ing] the question" (p. 398).

Standard one states that a student should be able to determine the "nature and extent of the information needed" (ACRL, 2000). This is an essential aspect of the information process because it comprises the "getting started" phase of a research project and this standard has a lot of potential for incorporating hip-hop. According to Project Information Literacy, one of the phases of research that students struggle with most is getting started (Head & Eisenberg, 2009, p. 7). The difficulty may lie in librarians' and faculty's inability to help students connect to the topics that have impact on their own lives. Freire (2000) argued that educators need to have a problem posing agenda in which students study and research the real-life issues that are important to them. As an instruction librarian, I would not require students to solely use hip-hop as a research topic, but I can use it as a tool in the classroom to raise issues that they might find interesting and then branch out to other topics. In this sense, hip-hop is a bridge between academic research and students' existing knowledge (Hallman, 2009), and this bridge is built with materials that will encourage discourse about oppression and other social issues. Furthermore, I can use it to model my own enthusiasm for critical inquiry into issues of social justice and cultural knowledge.

Under the first standard, one outcome states that an information literate student "develops a thesis statement and formulates questions based on the information need" (ACRL, 2000). This outcome can fit directly into a problem-posing pedagogy if instructors urge students to ask questions that are relevant to students' lives. It works especially well when there is strong coordination between the instruction librarian and the faculty member because both parties can guide students towards a question that is interesting to them during the topic selection phase. One way that I urge students to pose a question that is personally relevant is to discuss my own experience with hip-hop and how it led to my own interest and inquiry with several topics like racial profiling, segregation, or progressive educational methods. This modeling can help students begin thinking about what they want to learn more about, which can be difficult, especially when they may have felt as though their personal issues, values and/or knowledge has not been validated in the academic environment. This process can break through students' difficulty getting started and may ignite their intrinsic motivation to learn more about an issue that they care about. In a class in which I suggested researching hip-hop and racial identity, a student chose the topic because he could personally relate to it. Students are likely to think that hip-hop is not an academically appropriate topic, but when the professor or the librarian validates it, this sends a message that researching hip-hop or any topic that is important to students is worthwhile.

An information literate student, according to the first ACRL Competency Standard, is able to differentiate between primary and secondary sources. This often-necessary learning outcome is an opportunity to use socially relevant hip-hop documents to demonstrate how primary and secondary literature are conceptualized in academia. Arguably, in an academic context rap songs are mostly comprised of primary sources. When describing the difference between primary vs. secondary sources librarians might try using the song "Changes" by Tupac Shakur (1998) as an example of a primary source and then use Brown's (2005) scholarly article which posits that African American traditional values are reaffirmed through Tupac's music. Librarians should play a section of the song for the class, ask students to identify certain themes within the music and extract those themes from specific lyrics, and ask students if they had any thoughts about or reactions to the themes in the song. The song is peppered with racial themes, for example, the war on drugs and the black power movement. Early in the track Tupac rhymes:

> First ship 'em dope and let 'em deal to brothers.
> Give 'em guns, step back, and watch 'em kill each other.
> "It's time to fight back", that's what Huey said.
> Two shots in the dark, now Huey's dead.
> (Shakur, 1998)

In these lines Tupac is expressing frustration and hopelessness in connection to the drug epidemic and the cruel manner in which the police murdered African American leaders like Huey P. Newton. To initiate conversation about the song, librarians might ask questions such as: Are Tupac's claims true? Has the government supported the drug and arms trade in communities of color? Or, how have prominent black leaders been targeted by violence in U.S. history? Students may want to further investigate the veracity of Tupac's claims and these discussion questions could transform into student research papers, but these lyrics can also be used to clarify the meaning of primary and secondary sources. Brown's article compares the works of Tupac with many themes and values in African American culture and history. Librarians might have students read sections of the article that discuss the lyrics and similar themes generated from "Changes." After the discussion students should understand that in an academic context the article is a secondary source in which Brown relies on rap lyrics from "Changes" as primary source material to craft arguments. Engage students in a discussion about how we privilege primary sources and secondary sources with different types of authority. For example, primary sources are often important voices presenting real accounts of events or raw data and secondary sources are often perceived as the well crafted, intellectually produced collection and analysis of primary sources. Rap songs can defy both of these categories because rappers can narrate events using hyperbole and can craft assessments of a body of rap-based or other relevant texts. For example, in the context of the hip-hop community "Changes" might be considered a secondary source. Primary sources are generally firsthand accounts of events, but Tupac is not claiming to have been present at Newton's death. Instead, he is crafting an argument using historical events as evidence for the government's racist activities, albeit, he is not visibly employing common academic methodologies, presenting documented evidence, or using a standardized system of peer-review. Additionally, librarians could introduce newspaper sources and blog posts about "Changes" or Tupac in general. These would show the range of types of information written and produced about the song and the artist, further providing context for any research questions that might be asked about the song.

Lastly, the first standard asks that students consider the "costs and benefits of acquiring the needed information" and the "feasibility of acquiring a new language or skill (e.g., foreign or discipline-based) in order to gather needed information and to understand its context" (ACRL, 2000). The objective leaves space for students to focus on the often-disparaged language of rappers. This language, generally produced by poor and working class youth of color, has traditionally been stigmatized in educational environments because it does not match the dominant style of communication, but is a valid and rich linguistic form (Sanchez, 2010). In diverse classroom settings, there will likely be a spectrum of experience with such language, some students will be intimately familiar with the language and others will not. Additionally, rappers can code lyrics in a manner that listeners might only understand in a local, cultural, regional, or even individual context. In these instances rap lyrics can be interpreted by consulting a local, regional or cultural insider, or in the case of the latter we can use rappers' own analysis and annotations of their music as a tool to dissect it. In Decoded (2010), the rapper Jay-Z provides context for many of his influential songs through annotations which can act as a starting point for an IL activity. One idea developed in conjunction with University of Washington Bothell faculty member, Georgia Roberts, is to play a clip of a Jay-Z track and then project the decoded verse for the class to view. Librarians could then discuss the political undertones of many of the annotations and break students into groups to annotate a separate rap

verse, perhaps using Jay-Z's same annotation style, using various information sources. Librarians should have students pay particular attention to
social and political themes within the lyrics and have them present their
annotations to class to allow for discussion of relevant themes that arise.

Going beyond the structure of the ACRL Competency Standards, it
is important that instruction librarians look outside the analytical elements of research and engage with some of the intangible or affect-based
aspects of information. This means validating students' need to take a
break from the analytical to simply enjoy or experience a piece of hip-hop
culture. Ward (2006) calls for librarians to create a space in the classroom
in which we simply listen and "do not analyze it" (p. 400). However,
Michael Eric Dyson, scholar, religious leader, and professor of sociology
warns his students in his course focused on the sociological implications
of Jay-Z's oeuvre that it "is not a class meant to sit around and go, 'Oh
man, those lyrics were dope,'" (Richards, 2011, p. 1). Dyson's warning is
a self-conscious attempt to guard the course from potential criticism that it
lacks intellectual merit, which is a fair strategy given the manner in which
hip-hop has traditionally been treated, but it ultimately divorces music
from one of its more important functions, which is enjoyment and affect.
Both of these elements should have a place in a classroom environment,
allowing for intellectual and deep non-analytical connections to music.

The second ACRL Competency Standard requires students be able to
"access information effectively and efficiently" (ACRL, 2000). Suggested
outcomes for this standard are that students can weigh the positives and
negatives of various research methods that they utilize to answer or solve
their research need and to create a well-rounded research strategy that
will help them accomplish their aim. The term "access" is a key term and
can conceptually guide our students to understanding inequalities in a
society in which access to information translates to power.

One avenue for incorporating hip-hop culture into IL instruction for the
second standard is to address students' ability to design effective search
strategies by modeling the construction of a question related to hip-hop.
Generally, I strive to include a controversial topic to address this standard,
a strategy that I have used in IL workshops because students have an im-

mediate reaction. I tell students that I tend to choose research topics that I find interesting and relevant to my life and because I love hip-hop many of my female friends ask me the question: "Does hip-hop music promote sexist attitudes among youth?" Before dissecting this question together, I give students time to discuss their own thoughts on the subject with the class and then demonstrate to them how to dissect the question into main concepts, which generate keywords for searching. In the process of having students develop a list of synonyms, inevitably, one student suggests a colloquial term that would likely not be searchable in a library database. This is an opportunity to transition to a conversation about controlled vocabulary and how library databases tend to include technical or academic terminology as opposed to slang terms. Contextualizing this within the history of libraries and classification in the U.S. as a largely white, wealthy, middle and upper class undertaking would be helpful for students to understand the social dimensions of controlled vocabulary in library databases and searching.

The third Standard requires students to think critically about the authority of texts that they encounter in addition to incorporating new information into their knowledge base (ACRL, 2000). In terms of learning outcomes, this means that students can summarize and extract information from texts, can apply criteria to texts to determine if they are adequately authoritative to include in an academic paper, and can interpret what they read and discuss it with their peers. Many instruction librarians address this standard by describing the criteria for determining peer-review as well as the criteria for assessing the authority of web-based resources. Both of these skills are valuable when approaching academic research, although some are beginning to question the need of emphasizing peer-review to undergraduates because these texts are difficult to read and most students are not likely to become academics or author academic texts (Mark, 2011). However, hip-hop offers several examples from which to address the issue of authority and incorporating information into our knowledge base.

It is important to teach students how to identify and verify if a text is peer-reviewed and give them skills to evaluate those readings, but this should be placed in the context of social power and privilege. Although the authority of peer-reviewed journal articles can potentially be viewed as a hierarchical imposition in which the intellectual elite creates knowledge for the less-educated masses, this is the ultimate standard of academic publishing. To produce successful work in the academic context, no matter their cultural identity, scholars largely rely on peer-reviewed journal articles. As noted by Delpit (1987), the skills heralded by dominant societal groups are important to teach, not because they are more valuable, but because some skills provide access to institutions in which one can prosper. When introducing the issue of authority of peer-reviewed sources to students, discuss it within the context of power and privilege, but also mention that this is the standard that is used in higher education. Ask students how individuals and communities create knowledge in alternative ways. Show students a news article that is critical of rap's influence on youth. The following is a list of several hip-hop-based questions that might inspire students to consider the impact of authority on race, representation and inequality:

• Does the author display a bias?
• Do you think there might be any prejudice, deception, or manipulation in the article? In what broader cultural context was this article published?
• Do you think that articles like this might lead to discriminatory views about hip-hop and its cultural adherents?

Using group discussion to engage with this outcome also addresses a separate outcome focused on demonstrating an "understanding and interpretation of the information through discourse with other individuals" and subject-area experts. In fact, when using hip-hop as a tool for IL we can accomplish both by having students discuss this amongst their peers in a group discussion and by consulting experts on the issue since several students are likely to have significant hip-hop knowledge. This outcome connects with several activities outlined in this chapter including the activity pairing "Changes" with the Brown article in which students discuss issues of social relevance while teaching other students and the instructor. This process gives some students the opportunity to be "experts" and allows others to consult their expertise.

The fifth and last ACRL Competency Standard requires students to understand "many of the economic, legal, and social issues surrounding the use of information and access and uses information ethically and legally" (ACRL, 2000). This standard is increasingly important as we access more information digitally and in more complex ways, but it does seem to have a punitive, potentially oppressive tone. It asks students to know the rules around plagiarism and copyright, but it largely ignores the possible inequalities perpetuated by copyright law. This is a topic that easily accommodates a hip-hop discussion, but it is imperative that instructors include a critical perspective about power and property.

Kimball and O'Connor (2010) describe a hip-hop inspired activity that can be used to teach students about copyright issues. They state that:

> The issues of plagiarism, copyright, and intellectual property could be discussed using any rap or hip-hop song that includes samples of other songs. This example could be contrasted with a "mash-up," in which two or more songs are combined without any new input. For example, Kanye West's "Gold Digger" uses a sample from Jamie Foxx's interpretation of the Ray Charles song "I've Got a Woman." The sample sets the tone for the song and provides some of the lyric underpinnings, but West is clearly the author of the song. This could be contrasted with a mash-up in which "Gold Digger" and Walter Murphy's "Fifth of Beethoven" are combined. Though clever, this mash-up is not a new creative work.
>
> The difference between using excerpts to reinforce your arguments (sampling) and co-opting others' work (blending two songs into a mash-up) should be clear to students. While the musical examples are being played, students could record their observations and then discuss them in small groups. Starting with a musical form that most students are familiar with to teach a complex issue like copyright helps students extend their knowledge (p. 318).

It is useful to contextualize this activity in hip-hop culture's discourse surrounding copyright. On one hand, rappers and music DJ's are keenly aware of intellectual property evidenced by the phrase "don't bite," meaning "write your own lyrics without stealing someone else's." However, there is awareness within hip-hop of being targeted with unreasonable copyright laws that limit creativity. Michael Franti's (2001) line, "stealin' DNA samples from the unborn and you comin' after us because we sampled a James Brown horn," demonstrates the sensitivity to a perceived hypocrisy and overreach of copyright law.

Conclusion

These activities and discussion prompts can be altered and manipulated, expanded and pared down to match many IL instruction contexts. They have the ability to engage college students in critical dialogs, problem posing research endeavors, raise issues of social justice in ways that may not have been possible in the classroom previously, and engage in non-analytical encounters with information. Hip-hop is a bridge to all of these concepts because it appeals to youth, contains valuable cultural knowledge, and is controversial. But, ultimately, it is not about hip-hop, and as Kim (2011) concludes her chapter, "this *is* bigger than hip hop" (p. 174). Issues of race, gender, poverty, capitalism and social justice are crucial to our students' education and any way that we can develop to include them in IL training is worthwhile. Employing hip-hop in the classroom will help instructors think about their positionality and how they are perceived by students. This process will likely develop librarians' relationships with students in new directions, directions in which librarians can participate in their own liberatory praxis while simultaneously promoting the liberation of their students.

References

Association of College and Research Libraries (ACRL). (2000). Information literacy competency standards for higher education. Retrieved from http://www.ala.org/acrl/standards/informationliteracycompetency

Akom, A. A. (2009). Critical hip hop pedagogy as a form of liberatory praxis. *Equity & Excellence In Education, 42*(1), 52-66.

Asante, M. K. (2008). *It's bigger than hip-hop: The rise of the post-hip-hop generation.* New York: St. Martin's Press.

Brother Ali. (2007). Uncle Sam Goddam. On *The undisputed truth* [CD]. Minneapolis, MN: Rhymesayers Entertainment.

Brown, T. J. (2005). Reaffirming African American cultural values: Tupac Shakur's greatest hits as a musical autobiography. *Western Journal Of Black Studies, 29*(1), 558-573.

Chang, J. (2006). *Can't stop, won't stop: A history of the hip-hop generation.* New York: Picador.

DeCurtis, A. (2009). Jay-Z's secrets for personal success. *Best Life, 6*(3), 74.

Delpit, L. D. (1987). Skills and other dilemmas of a progressive black educator. *Equity and Choice, 3*(2), 9-14.

Elmborg, J. (2006). Critical information literacy: Implications for instructional practice. *The Journal of Academic Librarianship, 32*(2), 192-199.

Franti, M., & Spearhead. (2001). Oh my god. On *Stay human* [CD]. San Francisco: Six Degrees Records.

Flores-González, N. (2006). Latino youth culture and community action. *Latino Studies, 4*(3), 321-325.

Freire, P. (2000). *Pedagogy of the oppressed.* New York: Continuum.

Greenfield, D. (2007). What's the deal with the white middle-aged guy teaching hip-hop? Lessons in popular culture, positionality and pedagogy. *Pedagogy, Culture & Society, 15*(2), 229-243.

Hallman, H. L. (2009). "Dear Tupac, you speak to me": Recruiting hip hop as curriculum at a school for pregnant and parenting teens. *Equity & Excellence In Education, 42*(1), 36-51.

Head, A. J., & Eisenberg, M. B. (2009). *Finding context: What today's college students say about conducting research in the digital age.* Project Information Literacy Progress Report, The Information School, University of Washington. Retrieved from http://projectinfolit.org/

Hess, M. (2005). Hip-hop realness and the white performer. *Critical Studies in Media Communication, 22*(5), 372-389.

Hooks, B. (1994). *Outlaw culture: Resisting representations.* New York: Routledge.

Hooks, B. (1998). Selling hot pussy: Representations of black female sexuality in the cultural marketplace. In R. Weitz (Ed.), *The politics of women's bodies: Sexuality, appearance, and behavior* (122-132). New York: Oxford University Press.

Jacobs, H. L. M. (2008). Information literacy and reflective pedagogical praxis. *The Journal of Academic Librarianship, 34*(3), 256-262.

Jay-Z. (2010). *Decoded.* New York, NY: Spiegel & Grau.

Kim, J. (2011). Is it bigger than hip-hop? Examining the problems and potential of hip-hop in the curriculum. In V. Kinloch (Ed.), *Urban literacies: Critical perspectives on language, learning, and community* (pp. 160-176). New York, NY: Teachers College Press.

Kimball, K., & O'Connor, L. (2010). Engaging auditory modalities through the use of music in information literacy instruction. *Reference & User Services Quarterly, 49*(4), 316-319.

Kitwana, B. (2002). *The hip hop generation: Young blacks and the crisis in African American culture.* New York: Basic Civitas Books.

Kitwana, B. (2005). *Why white kids love hip-hop: Wanksters, wiggers, wannabes, and the new reality of race in America.* New York: Basic Civitas Books.

Lankes, R. D. (2011) *The atlas of new librarianship.* Cambridge, Massachusetts: MIT Press.

Malott, C., & Porfilio, B. (2007). Punk rock, hip-hop and the politics of human resistance: Reconstituting the social studies through critical media literacy. In D. P. Macedo & S. R. Steinberg (Eds.), *Media literacy: A reader* (pp. 582-592). New York, NY: Peter Lang.

Mark, A. E. (2011). Privileging peer review: Implications for undergraduates. *Communications in Information Literacy, 5*(1), 4-8.

Norgaard, R. (2003). Writing information literacy: Contributions to a concept. *Reference and User Services Quarterly, 43*(2), 124-130.

Pough, G. D. (2004). *Check it while I wreck it: Black womanhood, hip-hop culture, and the public sphere.* Boston: Northeastern University Press.

Richards, C. (2011, November 3). Jay-Z 101: Georgetown sociology course focuses on rap star. *The Washington Post*, pp. C01.

Rose, T. (1994). *Black noise: Rap music and black culture in contemporary America.* Hanover, NH: University Press of New England.

Rose, T. (2008). *The hip hop wars: What we talk about when we talk about hip hop—and why it matters.* New York: Basic Civitas Books.

Sánchez, D. M. (2010). Hip-hop and a hybrid text in a postsecondary English class. *Journal of Adolescent & Adult Literacy, 53*(6), 478-487.

Sharpley-Whiting, T. D. (2007). *Pimps up, ho's down: Hip hop's hold on young Black women.* New York: New York University Press.

Shakur, T. (1998). Changes. On *Greatest hits* [CD]. New York, N.Y.: Death Row Records/Interscope Records.

Sullivan, R. E. (2003). Rap and race. *Journal Of Black Studies, 33*(5), 605-622.

Ward, D. (2006). Revisioning information literacy for lifelong meaning. *The Journal of Academic Librarianship, 32*(4), 396-402.

Whitmire, E. (2003). Cultural diversity and undergraduates' academic library use. *The Journal of Academic Librarianship, 29*(3), 148-161.

Whitmire, E. (2004). The campus racial climate and undergraduates' perceptions of the academic library. *portal: Libraries and the Academy, 4*(3), 363-378.

Forces of Oppression in the Information Landscape:
Free Speech and Censorship in the United States

Lua Gregory
University of Redlands

Shana Higgins
University of Redlands

"Only by posing real problems in the world can we encourage students to see themselves as actors in the world" (Elmborg, 2012, p. 92).

In a chapter titled, "Critical Information Literacy: Definitions and Challenges" from the compilation *Transforming Information Literacy Programs: Intersecting Frontiers of Self, Library Culture, and Campus Community* (2012), James Elmborg challenges librarians to resist an uncritical use of Freirean pedagogical theory in their teaching practices:

> I have never been able to see twenty-first century students as 'oppressed' in the Freirian sense. They generally do not accept their powerlessness in the world...we need to find new ways to name this new kind of student's dilemma and to pose the problem of their condition to the students themselves. (pp. 92-93)

Elmborg's primary concern is that we have adopted wholesale a pedagogical theory and praxis that was deeply rooted in a particular time and place. If we are to develop a critical information literacy praxis grounded in Freire's philosophy of education (Jacobs, 2008; Olson-Kopp & Kopp, 2010; Elmborg, 2004; Elmborg, 2012) then we need to "account for the translation of his work" (Elmborg, 2012, p. 90) into our specific contexts. Indeed Freire's work should be "re-invented in the contexts in which his readers find themselves, thereby enjoining a contextually specific translation across geographic, geopolitical, and cultural borders. [...] In fact, Freire urged his readers to reinvent him in the context of their local struggles" (McLaren, 2000, p. 164). For many of us the specific context within which we teach and learn is the U.S. higher education system, working with traditional and non-traditional aged undergraduate students, ranging from working class to upper-middle class socio-economic backgrounds. Our situatedness varies from rural to urban, from public to private institutions, from west to east and north to south, from community college to Ivy League, and so forth. However, there are several threads common to discourses critical of education in the United States, many of which immerse the student in a neoliberal construction of education (Giroux & Giroux, 2004; Giroux, 2012; McLaren, 2011).[1] Most of our students now enter higher education with a common language of use value and return on investment in relation to schooling, a valorization of individual freedom, and a 'banking' conception of education resulting from No Child Left Behind. Disciplinary faculty, writing faculty, and librarians (with faculty status or not) may in significant numbers embrace Freirean pedagogical strategies but critical reading/writing/information literacy/viewing/ consciousness-raising is not the 'bill of goods' our students have been sold. Certification and employability are the keywords connected with the purpose of higher education; the language of business prevails for legislators and parents alike in their calls for returns on the investment of a college education.[2]

The focus on economic value, in relation to education, is the 21st century students' dilemma. What is particularly worrisome is that neoliberal discourse, which favors market value and corporate needs, begins to eclipse other goals of education. This is a topic that Henry Giroux (2004) explores in *The Terror of Neoliberalism: Authoritarianism and the Eclipse of Democracy*. He reminds us that:

> Education is not only about issues of work and economics but also about questions of justice, social freedom, and the capacity for democratic agency, action, and change as well as the related issues of power, exclusion, and citizenship. Education at its best is about enabling students to

---

1 You only have to watch the news, read major newspapers, and stay abreast of articles, webinars, and workshops offered through various higher education resources (Chronicle of Higher Education, Inside Higher Ed, EDUCAUSE, etc.) to recognize neoliberal critiques of higher education and the calls for efficiency, accountability, flexibility, entrepreneurship, and returns on investment.

2 As one example of the imbrication of corporate discourse with education, the language of the Association of College & Research Libraries publication *Value of Academic Libraries: A Comprehensive Research Review and Report* (2010) reflects an immersion in and a response to the language of business pervading higher education.

take seriously questions about how they ought to live their lives, uphold the ideals of a just society, and act upon the promises of a strong democracy. These are educational and political issues and should be addressed as part of a broader concern for renewing the struggle for social justice and democracy. (p. 159)

In this chapter, we will consider neoliberal discourses as a primary mechanism of oppression in our students' lives and affecting their abilities to fully engage in the educative process. In the fall semester of 2010, we, Lua Gregory and Shana Higgins, taught a first-year seminar titled, "Bleep! Censorship and Free Speech in the U.S." In this seminar we and our students examined the limitations of our own culture, government, and institutions in relation to the First Amendment, free speech, and censorship. Our students were more accustomed to looking outward for examples of social injustice and rights limitations. It is much easier to become invested in injustices happening at a remove, than to examine our own complicity in states of oppression in the workings of late capitalism in the U.S. Taking Elmborg's challenge as a starting place, this chapter explores the following questions: What real problems do students of today face, especially in relation to information production, dissemination, and consumption within a neoliberal and corporate society? In what ways are U.S. students oppressed? How do these problems "encourage students to see themselves as actors in the world"? We suggest that not only are students "caught in a problematic educational system" (Elmborg, 2012, p. 92) but they are also oppressed by a neoliberal ideology and capitalist economic system that together narrow the diversity of ideas and information.

Forces of Power and Oppression

The root of the word "oppression" is the element "press." *The press of the crowd; pressed into military service; to press a pair of pants; printing press; press the button...* Something pressed is something caught between or among forces and barriers which are so related to each other that jointly they restrain, restrict or prevent the thing's motion or mobility. Mold. Immobilize. Reduce. (Frye, 1983, p. 2)

Power and oppression are inextricably linked in a grotesque dance of control over others' actions, thoughts, and ways of being. In general, those with power are able to press, force, coerce, immobilize, and constrain. There are many lenses through which we could examine power and oppression: via political thought, from a sociological perspective, as a feminist, as a matter of ethics, etc. Oppression is not a discrete experience but rather "occurs at the group or macro level, and goes well beyond individuals. Sexism, racism, classism, ableism, and heterosexism are forms of oppression" (Sensoy & DiAngelo, 2012, p. 40). Oppression is constituted historically, ideologically, culturally, and institutionally. Power can take shape in various forms, but when we position it in relation to social justice, it "refers to the ideological, technical, and discursive elements by which those in authority impose their ideas and interests on everyone" (Sensoy & DiAngelo, 2012, p. 52). In her book *Analyzing Oppression*, Ann E. Cudd (2006) argues:

> that material forces, by which I mean physical violence and economic domination, initiate a vicious cycle of harm that subjugates the oppressed to one or more privileged groups. These forces work in part by coercing the oppressed to act in ways that further their own oppression. Direct forces externally affect the choices of individuals, while indirect forces shape the background social beliefs and desires with which we perceive and behave toward others. The most important and insidious of these indirect forces is an economic force that acts by means of the oppressed persons' own preferences and rational choices. (p. 26)

It is this indirect economic force that shapes "the oppressed persons' own preferences and rational choices" that concerns us most. In relation to our 21st century undergraduate students, economic oppression is a strong force in their lives, especially as it intersects with information and media flows, and knowledge production and dissemination.

Capitalism as Economic Oppression

One of the most striking effects of capitalist economic oppression is the division of society into economic classes, which is brought about by institutional coercion and constrains the choices available to individuals and social groups. Durrani (2008) explains, "working class people as a whole are historically excluded from enjoying the social wealth created by their labour. Hence the [capitalist] system creates a class that is automatically excluded from wealth, power, education and information" (p. 145). Social class hierarchies are reflected in discussions of the "information divide" or "knowledge divide." Access to information and knowledge production is largely dependent on affluence: the affluence of your family determines your access to high quality educational institutions, the affluence of your community determines the resources available through your library, and the affluence of your nation in part determines its access to data and information sources for research and development. Likewise affluence is linked to the means of production of data, information, and knowledge. Thus in a capitalist economic system, free market capitalism, in which some have more capital (means) to be used in the production and dissemination of goods, affluence begets affluence even in relation to information and knowledge. Therefore if we do not provide our students with "a critical lens and critical language for looking at capitalism, they make assumptions about it, such as assuming that capitalism and democracy are the same thing, which they are not. It is a big part of the overall structure of oppression" (Sleeter, 2011, p. 71).

The oppressive aspects of a capitalist economic system are often far more complex than conscious maneuvers by those in authority to impose their will on those with less power. For example, the complexity of systemic coercion that takes place within various systems and institutions leads many of us to participate (sometimes) unwittingly in oppression, whether implicitly consenting to others' or our own oppression. Cudd (2006) explains that an "institution (economic system, legal system, norm) is coercive if the institution unfairly limits the choices of some group of persons relative to other groups in society" (p. 131). Thus, when we consider a capitalist economic system we can see how it limits the choices of people who do not have the material power to make exchanges within that system. And we can recognize the perceived limitation of choices with which neoliberal discourses constrain us. Neoliberal policy has been so effectively linked to ideas of individual freedom, and through this conception of freedom to democracy that many of us have failed to notice that "[t]hirty years of neoliberal freedoms have…produced immense concentrations of corporate power in energy, the media, pharmaceuticals, transportation, and even retailing (for example Wal-Mart)" (Harvey, 2005, p. 238). In effect, our choices and freedoms when it comes to information are often linked back to the market, which constrains that which is available through consolidation and the privilege of affluence.

Neoliberalism: 'To Believe in an Objectionable Ideology'

Ideology is the set of beliefs, values, and attitudes that legitimate the interests of dominant groups to exercise their privilege over others ("Ideology," 2000). For Cudd (2006) ideology refers to "political, social, and scientific theories" that enforce tradition and is enacted by those "who have an interest in maintaining the tradition or convention that the ideology upholds" (p. 170). At times, an ideology becomes objectionable when a theory is "false" or "exaggerated," meaning it has been "carried beyond its intended domain of application" (p. 170), is commonly believed, and creates barriers to change. To believe in an objectionable ideology is to be in a state of false consciousness (Cudd, 2006, p. 178).

False consciousness as defined by Jost (1995) is "the holding of false or inaccurate beliefs that are contrary to one's own social interest and which thereby contribute to the maintenance of the disadvantaged position of the self or the group" (p. 400). Jost recognizes that false consciousness can take many forms, including a failure to perceive injustice and disadvantage, justification of social roles, false attribution to blame, identification with the oppressor, resistance to change, and fatalism. All these manifestations of false consciousness are disturbing, but fatalism is particularly unsettling when we think of the ramifications of its hold on an individual. When one is fatalistic, one believes that the current political system is impossible to change and that "protest is futile" (Jost, 1995, p. 405).

In *Ideology Matters*, Freire connects fatalism with the market and neoliberal discourse in the following way:

> We need to say no to the neoliberal fatalism that we are witnessing at the end of this century, informed by the ethics of the market, an ethics

in which a minority makes most profits against the lives of the majority. In other words, those who cannot compete, die. This is a perverse ethics that, in fact, lacks ethics... I do not accept...history as determinism. I embrace history as possibility [where] we can demystify the evil in this perverse fatalism that characterizes the neoliberal discourse in the end of this century. (as cited in Freire, 2000, pp. 25-26)

In the above quote, Freire updates the notion of oppression in relation to the 21ˢᵗ century student. Whether or not our current students consciously "accept their powerlessness in the world" (Elmborg, 2012, pp. 92-93), they have likely accepted neoliberal discourses in which the ideals of dignity and individual freedom have been co-opted for the purposes of driving free-market capitalism (Harvey, 2005). In the name of freedom, neoliberalism "seeks to create an individual that is an enterprising and competitive entrepreneur. It is in this format that neoliberalism today forms the basis of social reality, the episteme" (Kaščák & Pupala, 2011, p. 148). And within this episteme oppression becomes a choice of sorts; Cudd (2006) calls

this phenomenon 'oppression by choice,' in order to highlight the twin facts that it is a force of oppression, and yet comes about through oppressed persons' choices. This force of oppression is particularly invidious because the oppressed choose the conditions under which they suffer. Everyone may seem content, and suggesting that there is oppression or victimization is likely to be met with hostility by privileged and oppressed groups alike. So it is deeply entrenched in the functioning social institutions of the society. (p. 146)

21ˢᵗ century students suffer from a false consciousness and fatalism insofar as they do indeed "accept their powerlessness in the world" in multiple ways. 1) They assume they are free to choose, that their individual freedoms are boundless, without questioning the choices from which they choose. 2) They have a limited understanding of activism. 3) They assume our government and corporate America tell the truth, and are the watchdogs of the best interests of the people. They are trapped within a neoliberal episteme.

Why Should Librarians Care?

Or better yet, how can librarians *not* care? As individuals who connect people with information in the spirit of our professional core values such as intellectual freedom, free access to information, democracy as it hinges on an informed citizenry, the public good, social responsibility, and the First Amendment's protection of free expression, we must care. It is inescapable that we consider the many different ways our current economic system shapes not only how information is produced and disseminated, and who or what is behind these processes, but also how mainstream neoliberal ideology influences the quality of information and the scope of perspectives available in order to support or enforce oppression. Indeed, Giroux (2010) emphasizes that:

> In a society that remains troublingly resistant to or incapable of questioning itself, one that celebrates the consumer over the citizen (or simply reduces one to the other), and willingly endorses the narrow values and interests of corporate power, the importance of the university as a place of critical learning, dialogue, and social justice advocacy becomes all the more imperative. (p. 186)

Information literacy, the processes by which an individual determines additional information is needed for a given task and the skills needed to access, critically evaluate, and synthesize information, is also affected by neoliberalism and its related societal and economic forces. Barriers to effective use of information may be cultural, socioeconomic, policy related, and due to the increasing corporatization of information, may be distorted or simply not accessible. Challenging this, a small but significant number of librarians have called for the need to develop collections with alternative resources (Berman & Danky, 1982-2001; Dilevko & Grewal, 1997; Gisonny & Freedman, 2006). A growing number of librarians, scholars from various disciplines, and disciplinary associations are making a case for the revision of what we mean by authority (Jensen, 2007; Seale, 2010; Swanson, 2004). Still other librarians have argued for the need to consider the socioeconomic and political powers that constrain the production and distribution of information and knowledge (Kapitzke, 2003).

How then, can we address Elmborg's recent call to pose real problems to our students so they may see themselves as actors willing to struggle for and imagine "a more just world" (Giroux, 2010, p. 182) while also incorporating a critical stance toward capitalism and neoliberal ideology into critical information literacy instruction? In the following sections we will outline discussions and activities that highlight our attempt to engage students with issues of free speech and censorship in a first-year seminar. By posing the problems of free speech and censorship issues in the United States, from colonial period to 2010, we, in part, met Elmborg's challenge. Throughout the semester we encouraged students to think about "why do we do what we do, in whose favor and in favor of what, or against whom or what" (Freire, 2004, p. 112)?

Consciousness-raising in a First Year Seminar

"How can I change my present in order to live in the future with courage, commitment, and a critical disposition that can make the world a better place for all those who suffer and are oppressed?" (McLaren, 2011, p. 103).

First Year Seminars at the University of Redlands are meant to be small, interdisciplinary, seminar-style courses that introduce incoming freshman to "what it means to be in a liberal arts college, allowing [them] to see and understand life from various perspectives" (University of Redlands, 2012, p. 1). This classroom space provides an opportunity to acknowledge our past and the experiences that make us who we are. Sometimes this process is difficult when, for example, people "from privileged groups tend to have little awareness of their own dominant identity, of the privileges it affords them, of the oppression suffered by the corresponding disadvantaged group, and of how they perpetuate it" (Goodman, 2000, p. 24). The seminar is also an opportune moment to begin to introduce students to social justice issues. Their beliefs and worldviews will be challenged in this new educational environment. What better moment to begin to orient them toward a critical consciousness with the goal of inspiring them to be active in the world.

In Freirean pedagogy, critical consciousness is the state of both being aware of the conditions in which one lives and of active engagement toward changing those conditions. Shor (1993) describes Freirean critical consciousness as having four qualities: awareness of how power is organized and exercised in society, critical literacy, recognizing and challenging normalized behaviors and values, and taking action to initiate change toward more just relations (pp. 31-32). Free speech and censorship issues are lenses through which one can initiate critical consciousness by considering neoliberal discourses and ascertaining why certain types of information are available for access and not others; what kinds of free speech struggles are fought daily and what these struggles mean for our First Amendment rights; how corporate power structures control media information; and how free speech is suppressed in various environments (work, school, or public spaces).

Beginning with the First Amendment

We grounded the class in the ideas and rights for all individuals as outlined in the foundational document for democracy in the United States, the First Amendment. We began by asking students to reflect on an aspect of the First Amendment and wrote it out in its entirety on the whiteboard as a reminder of what is included and of the simplicity of the language.

> Congress shall make no law respecting an establishment of religion, or prohibiting the free exercise thereof; or abridging the freedom of speech, or of the press; or the right of the people peaceably to assemble, and to petition the government for a redress of grievances.

A recent study by the First Amendment Center (2012) found that 27% of respondents could not list any of the rights guaranteed by the First Amendment; the percentage of respondents who could name freedom of the press and the right to assemble has declined over the past decade. Our students clearly reflected this decline in their demonstrated understanding of what could and should be published freely and in their misunderstanding of the illegality of demonstration and protest in public spaces. Although we entered into discussions on all five freedoms throughout the semester, we explored freedom of the press deeply, especially as it related to forms of censorship.

Media Journal Assignment and Media Oligopolies

[T]he common discussion of censorship as portrayed in the mainstream media does not really explore the underlying factors that contribute to censorship. It is too often simplistically framed and fails utterly to probe into the abiding consolidation and hegemony in media production facing our democracy.
(McDonald, 2008, p. 9)

Currently, a small percentage of corporations own the means of news media production, otherwise known as a media oligopoly. Since media oligopolies support a lack of diversity in perspectives and thus reinforce a dominant cultural perspective, individuals are subject to a form of ensorship. Media news outlets have been on the path to consolidation into the hands of a few corporations for quite some time. Edward S. Herman and Noam Chomsky (1988) elaborate on the symptoms of a corporate controlled media in their Propaganda Model, which highlights the influence that inequalities in wealth and power have on "mass-media interests and choices" (p. 2). The main issue of concern to us here is of the "size, ownership, and profit orientation of the mass media" (p. 3) outlets as the first "filter" that news goes through before dissemination. Herman and Chomsky state that because news media outlets are very large businesses, owned by a few corporations that are linked together through the market, that the news these goliaths produce is naturally biased to reflect the shared interests of major corporations as well as banks and the government (p. 14). To get a sense of what this looks like over time, in 1983 90% of U.S. media was owned by 50 companies while now it is owned by only six: General Electric, News Corp., Disney, Viacom, Time Warner and CBS. This concentration of media ownership is a serious problem that our government officials are failing to address. However, one recent exception is a speech by Vermont senator Bernie Sanders (2012), who explained that when you have a few "large media conglomerates owning and controlling what the American people see, hear and read, you have a very real threat to the kind of the democracy that many of us want."

The lack of diversity in news media affects both individuals and institutions such as libraries that serve the public good and aim to promote democratic ideals by enabling an informed citizenry through free access to information. The American Library Association, Intellectual Freedom Committee Subcommittee on the Impact of Media Concentration on Libraries published a report in 2007 titled Fostering Media Diversity in Libraries: Strategies and Actions, that "encourages librarians to oppose media concentration" because "consolidation negatively affects libraries" (Nappo, 2009, p. 419). According to this report, "A central purpose of the First Amendment is to protect marginal views" (p. 10). As information professionals we need to be active agents to oppose consolidation in order to advocate for a wide range of viewpoints. Advocating for change extends to educating the public, our users and our students. Lilburn (2007) poses a key question,

> should the focus of information literacy teaching be on giving students the tools and skills needed to work around conditions that impose barriers to access to information, or should the focus be shifted and expanded to address and directly confront those conditions? (p. 4)

Much of our work as instruction librarians involves teaching students to navigate barriers to finding the information they need for a particular project or assignment. In the first year seminar, "Bleep! Censorship and Free Speech in the U.S.," we were able to directly confront the conditions that suppress students' access to a wide and varied range of perspectives in the news media.

Our media news journal assignment was one such effort in both posing and confronting the real world problem of media ownership. Students were broken up into groups and assigned a media news outlet to follow for a couple weeks. In their journal, students would list the top stories on the front page of the news website, then summarize those stories, and finally analyze whether or not these stories were important to them. In each class during the two-week period of the assignment, students shared their media news outlets and top stories with the class in order to compare and contrast as a group. In essence, we hoped one outcome from these activities would be that students could identify the conditions created by oligopolistic media control.

In the two weeks that students discussed the top news stories from the BBC, CNN, Fox News, the New York Times, and Al Jazeera they identified a lack of diversity in news stories, particularly from CNN, Fox News, and the New York Times. Students in the class felt that the stories from these news outlets seemed to be mostly "fluff" or of a "scare-mongering" flavor rather than presenting the details of an event in a measured manner. The students decided that news media outside of the United States, the BBC and Al Jazeera seemed "more educational." The students were all surprised by the reportage from Al Jazeera, insofar as it provided stories not covered, or not prominently covered, in other news outlets and different perspectives that they found useful to understanding reportage in other news outlets. But most surprising for students was that Al Jazeera wasn't as "radical" as they initially presumed.

In addition to the media journal assignment, we examined and discussed the "limits" of free speech as it relates to public information gathering and dissemination. Debuting in 2006, WikiLeaks anonymously published classified and other secret information provided by various whistleblowers. In 2010 the WikiLeaks website released video footage titled Collateral Murder in which a U.S. Apache helicopter gunman shot and killed eleven people including two Reuters employees (Bradley Manning Support Network, n. d.). The release of this video resulted in shocked awareness around the world. Thereafter, WikiLeaks began to release documents on the wars in Iraq and Afghanistan, as well as later working with known media outlets to release classified diplomatic cables. We drew from the ideas of Swanson (2004) and Cope (2010) to shape classroom discussion on WikiLeaks. Cope urges a "collective questioning of how information is constructed, disseminated, and understood" and that "certain sources are 'authoritative' because authorities have decided that they are" (p. 25). Swanson states that information "should be viewed as a social construct used to transfer ideas. It is created with a purpose that we can evaluate and judge" (p. 265). Questions we explored with students in class, putting ourselves, as Elmborg (2012) encourages, "on the level of students as co-questioners, co-doubters, even co-dreamers" (p. 94) included: What is the purpose of an information dissemination organization such as WikiLeaks? What purposes do whistleblowers serve? Should whistleblowers be protected? If all the information in WikiLeaks had been available to the American public, and to the world, via mass media outlets, would recent history have played out in the same way?

Information released by WikiLeaks is valuable in understanding many current events, including the unveiling of how the modern news media functions. In what is termed the Earthquake Cables, which covers communications on the January 12, 2010 earthquake in Haiti and its aftermath, particularly the flooding of U.S. troops into the country, Hillary Clinton (Herz, 2011) outlined orders for controlling the media message of the event. The unfavorable international media concerned her and she wrote that "it is imperative to get the narrative right" and that embassies must respond "citing specific examples of irresponsible journalism in your host countries, and what action you have taken in response" (Herz, 2011). The effort of state power working to create a narrative for a pliant media to disseminate, illustrates the application of a neoliberal ideology that maintains the pretense of an independent media, a well-intentioned state and hides the process through which those in power are able to influence information consumed by the public.

In addition, WikiLeaks is instrumental in discovering stories that have been blacked out by corporate media, including struggles for social justice. For example, support was growing in Haiti to raise the minimum wage in textiles factories to keep up with inflation and help poor working families. President Préval hoped to raise minimum wage for all workers to $5.00 per day. However, after pressure from U.S. diplomats and contractors for Fruit of the Loom, Hanes and Levi's, Préval approved a tiered wage increase in which the textile sector was approved to pay its workers $3.00 a day while all other industries must pay its workers $5.00 per day (Jilani, 2011; Coughlin & Ives, 2011). This struggle of a nation's working people to alleviate poverty was strangely silent in the U.S. mainstream media until the release of cables by WikiLeaks. It is unfortunate that U.S. media outlets black out, either deliberately or not, the influence of U.S. corporations on social justice struggles in other countries. Durrani (2008) explains the situation quite well, in that

> it is an aspect of globalization that information about resistance itself has also been marginalized and banished from the mass media controlled

by the same global controllers. Thus begins people's resistance at the
level of information and communication. The struggle then is not only
to end poverty and exclusion but also to end the embargo on progressive information about the struggle of people around the world to end
their exclusion. (p. 148)

News media acts as a catalyst to spread a corporate, or neoliberal,
ideology to the masses. This state of the media oligopoly affirms Freire's
concern that technology advances "with great efficiency the ideological
support of material power" (Freire, 1998, p. 36). It is important that we
should remember, in relation to the motives of corporate media, that "no
work is ever disassociated from whom it serves" (Freire, 2004, pg. 17).

A State of Awareness and Beyond

One quality of critical consciousness is to be aware of how power is
organized and exercised in society (Shor, 1993). Developing awareness is
a crucial first step after which all other qualities of a critical consciousness
may follow, including action and struggle for progressive change. We at-
tempted to develop awareness in our first-year students, with the activity
discussed in the previous section, on the structure of media power and
how this may affect information creation and production in the societal
landscape. Students worked as a group to identify how oligopolistic structures affected the quality of news media available. However, it felt like
quite a leap to bring our students from awareness to a place where they
felt comfortable to enter into conversations as agents for social change.

Imagination and Transformation

How do we begin to transform society? One teaching strategy we used,
discussed by both Ira Shor and Paulo Freire in *A Pedagogy for Liberation:
Dialogues on Transforming Education* (1987), is to dream the future by integrating imagination and intuition into dialogue. Since mass media and
dominant culture "shape the way people think about the past, present,
and future" we are at risk of being unable to think outside the box, or in
other words, to break out of either a state of false consciousness or as op-

pressor or oppressed. Shor and Freire suggest a pedagogy that embraces alternative thinking through the use of one's imagination "can be exercised as a resource to expel dominant ideology and to open up some space in consciousness for transcendent thinking" (p. 185).

Diane J. Goodman (2000) in her book *Promoting Diversity and Social Justice: Educating People from Privileged Groups* also makes use of this exercise, specifically while encouraging students to imagine the shared benefits of social justice and equality. Students identified psychological, social, moral, intellectual, material, and physical benefits from a socially just society. Goodman's participants admitted that

> it wasn't simply that there would be less fear, better relationships, or improved quality of life. There also would be more joy and fun. This is a wonderful example of how health is not simply the absence of illness, that wellness transcends just the removal of the sickness. [...] people could more fully experience life and truly enjoy themselves and others. There is a freedom and exuberance that is captured by the word *joy* that more accurately reflects the liberation that a just and caring world could offer us. (p. 202)

After a background in the history of power struggles involving censorship, discussions on current events that shape free speech in the United States, and a learned awareness of corporate power and media control, students were asked to imagine a world outside of these structures, and what that world would look like. Our students wrestled together over the various censorship and free speech issues they found most difficult: especially the limits of free speech in relation to national security and the rights of corporations. Neither consensus nor immediate action ensued, but through dialogue and negotiation our students began to imagine other possibilities. Freire (1987) affirms the power of this exercise, for one can use imagination by dreaming beyond tomorrow and by posing the question, "Is the dream a possible one or not? If it is less possible, the question for us is how to make it more possible" (p. 187).

References

American Library Association, Intellectual Freedom Committee Subcommittee on the Impact of Media Concentration on Libraries. (2007, June). Fostering media diversity in libraries: Strategies and actions. Retrieved from http://www.ala.org/offices/sites/ala.org.offices/files/content/oif/ifissues/fostering_media_dive1.pdf

Berman, S., & Danky, J. P. (Eds.). *Alternative library literature: A biennial anthology.* (1982-2001). Jefferson, NC: McFarland & Company.

Bradley Manning Support Network. (n. d.). Collateral murder video. Retrieved from http://www.bradleymanning.org/learn-more/collateral-murder-video

Cope, J. (2010). Information literacy and social power. In E. Drabinski, A. Kumbier & M. Accardi (Eds.), *Critical library instruction: Theories and methods* (pp. 13-27). Duluth, MN: Library Juice Press.

Coughlin, D., & Ives, K. (2011, June 1). WikiLeaks Haiti: Let them live on $3 a day. *The Nation.* Retrieved from http://www.thenation.com/article/161057/wikileaks-haiti-let-them-live-3-day#

Cudd, A. E. (2006). *Analyzing oppression.* New York, NY: Oxford University Press.

Dilevko, J., & Grewal, K. (1997). A new approach to collection bias in academic libraries: The extent of corporate control in journal holdings. *Library and Information Science Research, 19*(4), 359-385.

Durrani, S. (2008). *Information and liberation: Writings on the politics of information and librarianship.* Duluth, MN: Library Juice Press.

Elmborg, J. (2012). Critical information literacy: Definitions and challenges. In C. W. Wilkinson & C. Bruch (Eds.), *Transforming information literacy programs: Intersecting frontiers of self, library culture, and campus community* (pp. 75-95). Chicago, IL: Association of College and Research Libraries.

Elmborg, J. (2006). Critical information literacy: Implications for instructional practice. *The Journal of Academic Librarianship, 32*(2), 192-199.

First Amendment Center. (2012). The state of the First Amendment: 2012. Retrieved from http://www.firstamendmentcenter.org/madison/wp-content/uploads/2012/07/SOFA-2012.pdf

Freire, P., & Macedo, D. (1999). *Ideology matters.* Lanham, MD: Rowman & Littlefield.

Freire, P. (2004). *Pedagogy of indignation.* Boulder, CO: Paradigm Publishers.

Freire, P. (1997). *Pedagogy of the heart.* (D. Macedo & A. Oliveira, Trans.). New York, NY: Continuum.

Freire, P. (2000). *Pedagogy of the oppressed* (30th ed.). (M. B. Ramos, Trans.). New York, NY: Continuum.

Frye, M. (1983). *The politics of reality: Essays in feminist theory.* Trumansburg, NY: Crossing Press.

Giroux, H. A. (2012). *Education and the crisis of public values: Challenging the assault on teachers, students, and public education.* New York, NY: Peter Lang.

Giroux, H. A. (2010). *Politics after hope: Obama and the crisis of youth, race, and democracy.* Boulder, CO: Paradigm Publishers.

Giroux, H. A., & Giroux, S. S. (2004). *Take back higher education: Race, youth, and the crisis of democracy in the post-civil rights era.* New York, NY: Palgrave MacMillan.

Giroux, H. A. (2004). *The terror of neoliberalism: Authoritarianism and the eclipse of democracy.* Boulder, CO: Paradigm Publishers.

Gisonny, K., & Freedman, J. (2006). Zines in libraries: How, what, and why? *Collection Building, 25*(1), 26-30.

Goodman, D. J. (2000). *Promoting diversity and social justice: Educating people from privileged groups.* Thousand Oaks, CA: Sage Publications.

Harvey, D. (2005). *A brief history of neoliberalism.* Oxford: Oxford University Press.

Herman, E. S., & Chomsky, N. (1988). *Manufacturing consent: The political economy of the mass media.* New York, NY: Pantheon Books.

Herz, A. (2011, June 15). WikiLeaks Haiti: The earthquake cables. *The Nation.* Retrieved from http://www.thenation.com/article/161459/wikileaks-haiti-earthquake-cables#

Ideology. (2000). In *The Blackwell Dictionary of Sociology.* Retrieved from http://0-www.credoreference.com.books.redlands.edu/entry/bksoc/ideology

Jacobs, H. L. M. (2008). Information literacy and reflective pedagogical praxis. *The Journal of Academic Librarianship, 34*(3), 256-262.

Jensen, M. (2007, June 15). The new metrics of scholarly authority. *The Chronicle Review, 53*(41), B6.

Jilani, Z. (2011, June 8). WikiLeaks cables: U.S. companies, diplomats fought to prevent minimum wage increase in Haiti's textiles factories. *Think Progress.* Retrieved from http://thinkprogress.org/security/2011/06/08/239144/wikileaks-cables-haiti-wage/

Jost, J. T. (1995). Negative illusions: Conceptual clarification and psychological evidence concerning false consciousness. *Political Psychology, 16*(2), 397-424.

Kapitzke, C. (2003). Information literacy: A review and poststructural critique. *Australian Journal of Language and Literacy, 26*(1), 53-66.

Kaščák O., & Pupala, B. (2011). Governmentality – neoliberalism – education: The risk perspective. *Journal of Pedagogy, 2*(2), 145-160.

Lilburn, J. (2007). Challenging the conditions that make alternatives necessary: Librarians, the news media and the information literate citizen. *Progressive Librarian, 30*, 3-17.

McDonald, P. (2008). Corporate inroads and librarianship: The fight for the soul of the profession in the new millennium. In A. Lewis (Ed.), *Questioning neutrality: Essays from Progressive Librarian* (pp. 9-23). Duluth, MN: Library Juice Press.

McLaren, P. (2000). *Che Guevara, Paulo Freire, and the pedagogy of revolution.* Lanham, MD: Rowman & Littlefield.

McLaren, P. (2011). Critical pedagogy in stark opposition to western neoliberalism and the corporatization of schools: A conversation with Peter McLaren. In P. W. Orelus (Ed.), *Rethinking race, class, language, and gender: A dialogue with Noam Chomsky and other leading scholars* (pp. 97-110). Lanham, MD: Rowman & Littlefield.

Nappo, C. M. (2009). Resisting abridgement librarianship as media reform.

Journal of Communication Inquiry, 33, 413-422.

Oakleaf, M. (2010). *Value of academic libraries: A comprehensive research review and report*. Chicago, IL: Association of College and Research Libraries.

Olson-Kopp, K., & Kopp, B. M. (2010). Depositories of knowledge: Library instruction and the development of critical consciousness. In E. Drabinski, A. Kumbier & M. Accardi (Eds.), *Critical library instruction: Theories and methods* (pp. 55-67). Duluth, MN: Library Juice Press.

Sanders, B. (2012, December 6). Media monopolies [Video file]. Retrieved from http://youtu.be/t-SztlLxgAE

Sensoy, Ö., & DiAngelo, R. J. (2012). *Is everyone really equal? An introduction to key concepts in social justice education*. New York, NY: Teachers College Press.

Shor, I. (1993). Education is politics: Paulo Freire's critical pedagogy. In P. McLaren & P. Leonard (Eds.), *Paulo Freire: A critical encounter* (pp. 24-35). New York, NY: Routledge.

Shor, I., & Freire, P. (1987). *A pedagogy for liberation: Dialogues on transforming education*. Westport, CT: Bergin & Garvey.

Sleeter, C. E. (2011). Reexamining social inequality in schools and beyond: A conversation with Christine E. Sleeter. In P. W. Orelus (Ed.), *Rethinking race, class, language, and gender: A dialogue with Noam Chomsky and other leading scholars* (pp. 67-74). Lanham, MD: Rowman & Littlefield.

Seale, M. (2010). Information literacy standards and the politics of knowledge production: Using user-generated content to incorporate critical pedagogy. In E. Drabinski, A. Kumbier & M. Accardi (Eds.), *Critical library instruction: Theories and methods* (pp. 221-235). Duluth, MN: Library Juice Press.

Swanson, T. A. (2004). A radical step: Implementing a critical information literacy model. *portal: Libraries and the Academy, 4*(2), 259-273.

University of Redlands. (2012). The first year seminar experience. Retrieved from www.redlands.edu/docs/StudentLife/First_Year_Seminar_Experience.pdf

Critical Legal Information Literacy:
Legal Information as a Social Construct

Yasmin Sokkar Harker
City University of New York, School of Law

While many librarians have explored the social justice dimensions of information literacy, (Jacobs, 2008; Swanson, 2005) a similar body of literature has only recently begun to develop with regards to *legal* information literacy. In her article "Leveraging Legal Research," Sarah Valentine (2011) discusses the link between legal social justice education and information literacy. She identifies the development of information literacy as one of three criteria for structuring a legal research curriculum within a social justice framework. Valentine argues that information literacy development is especially critical to law students who intend to work in public interest and social justice institutions, not only because they will likely be working with organizations that have less access to resources than traditional law firms, but because they may work with marginalized populations who are on the disadvantaged side of the digital divide.

Legal information literacy education is crucial to teaching toward a social justice and public interest mission and will further support this mission if it has a critical dimension. The goals for this chapter are: to begin a dialogue on how to add a critical dimension to legal information literacy education, both in the classroom and at the reference desk, and to demonstrate the application of critical information literacy concepts to legal information. This discussion is rooted in and informed by concepts from critical pedagogy, as well as the literature on critical information literacy. Part I of this chapter provides background on critical information literacy and legal information literacy, and proposes merging these two concepts into a holistic approach for legal research education. Part II gives an example of how legal information may be described as a social construct, and examines the power structures that create, organize and provide access to legal information. This example is then used to demonstrate strategies for critical legal research education.

Critical legal information literacy education will encourage law students to develop a critical consciousness about legal information and to perceive information as a social construct. This will in turn help them to understand legal information beyond its uses in client representation, and to appreciate legal information as a broader tool for promoting social justice, empowering people and redressing disadvantage. Law students who are critical information literate will also understand their own potential to develop and change the law itself.

Towards Critical Legal Information Literacy

Critical Information Literacy

Since the 1970 publication of Paulo Freire's seminal work, *Pedagogy of the Oppressed*, Freire and other educational theorists have developed a philosophy of education called critical pedagogy. Critical pedagogy seeks to use education as a tool for overcoming social injustice by promoting critical thinking and change in the world. In *Pedagogy of the Oppressed* (1970), Freire critiques prevailing models of education, particularly what he terms the "banking concept," and argues that instead of encouraging passivity by depositing information into the minds of students via the "banking concept" model of education, educators should engage in "problem-posing education." "Problem-posing education" presents material for student consideration, and encourages them to critically perceive how they themselves exist in relation to it (pp. 79-85). Students are then able perceive the world as continuously in transformation and understand their own potential to participate in its transformation.

For the past few decades, librarians have increasingly taken on instructional and pedagogical work (Swanson, 2005). Although librarians have developed several approaches and standards for teaching information literacy, most of them, such as the ACRL standards, are what K. Strege (1996) terms as "functional" in nature. This means that information is often presented as value-neutral, and information literacy is taught so that students can become productive workers and informed citizens.

Troy Swanson (2005) posited the limitation of a "functional" approach to information literacy and advocated for the inclusion of a critical information literacy approach in which information is taught as a social construct. As a social construct, information is something that is not just true or false but is created by people for specific purposes (p. 72). In order to teach information as a social construct, educators must move beyond a functional understanding of information literacy and work to engage students with questions about how information is created, how it is published, and the power structures that exist within the information world.

James Elmborg (2006) asks educators to use Freire's "problem-posing education" concept when teaching information literacy and to develop a critical consciousness about the library. Building on Elmborg's work, Heidi L.M. Jacobs (2008) urges critical information literacy educators to use praxis–"the interplay of theory and practice"–to engage in a process of critical self-reflection about what information literacy means (p. 260). Educators must constantly reflect on the meaning of information literacy and bring those reflections into the classroom where they can encourage their students to develop a critical awareness about information. Jacobs (2008) further encourages educators to resist the urge to situate critical information literacy in rigid definitions or standards. Instead, she suggests that educators situate critical information literacy in a process of dialogue and problem-posing about information, both with students and with themselves.

Information Literacy in Legal Education

Historically, law students have been taught to view legal information as a tool for advocating the interests of their clients. They are expected to be information literate to the extent that they can accomplish legal research for the purpose of predicting and solving client problems, planning transactions, and advancing client interests. For example, they are expected to understand the legal authority of documents and the government institutions, (such as the judiciary and the legislature) which create authority.

In recent years, information literacy in law schools has become a subject of great interest to law librarians. Recognizing that competent, efficient and ethical attorneys need to be information literate, law librarians have called for the explicit instruction of information literacy skills in the classroom (Valentine, 2010). Law librarians and legal research educators have studied the information literacy of incoming law students (Gallacher, 2007), discussed techniques for teaching information literacy in the classroom (Kaplan & Darvil, 2011), and offered strategies for bringing information literacy to the legal curriculum as a whole (Kauffman, 2010).

Despite the importance of information literacy for law students, standards for legal information literacy have only recently been developed (Kim-Prieto, 2011). Early discussions about information literacy training tended to focus on specific legal research techniques, rather than broad standards for assessing literacy (Bird, 2011).H. Kumar Percy Jayasuriya and Frances Brillantine (2007) recognized the applicability of the ACRL standards to legal information, and identified the need for additional standards specific to legal information. In addition to the top-level ACRL standards describing specific skills—know, access, evaluate, use, and ethical/legal use—Jayasuriya and Brillantine suggest incorporating knowledge of legal authority and its hierarchy. For example, students should know the legal authorities given to different law-making bodies.

In 2009-2010, a joint special interest section committee of the American Association of Law Libraries drafted Law Student Information Literacy standards (LSIL). The LSIL standards were approved in July 2012. The standards use the framework expressed by the ACRL information literacy standards, but link them to legal sources, problems and analysis. Thus, although the top-levels of the LSIL standards are based on the five ACRL standards, the skills and examples identified under each standard are specific to legal research. For example, under the "knowing" standard, the standard states that the student should be able to "identify whether the issue at hand requires application of statute, case law, regulation or other relevant information", based on the jurisdiction and whether the facts are subject to statutory, regulatory or common law rule (or all of the above) (American Association of Law Libraries).

Critical Legal Information Literacy

Ira Shor (1992) remarked that "education is a socializing process that 'helps make the people who make society'" (p. 15). Similarly, legal education is a socializing process that helps make lawyers. From the very beginning of their education, law students are immersed in specialized legal information, such as court cases, statutes and regulations, and scholarly commentary about the law. To the extent that they are taught legal research, they are generally taught about legal information as a tool for problem solving, predicting and planning.

Recently, legal research educators have begun to articulate what information literacy means for law students. Standards such as the LSIL standards have the potential to transform legal research education and address the deficiencies in law student and lawyer legal research skills (Kim-Prieto, 2011). A critical dimension will be a complementary addition to current legal information literacy approaches and standards.

What does critical legal information literacy look like? Drawing from the work of Elmborg, Jacobs and Swanson, critical legal information literacy:

• Describes legal information as a social construct;
• Connects legal information to the people and institutions that produce and publish it; and
• Engages students in a process of problem-posing about who produces legal information, and who benefits from it.

This enables students to develop a critical consciousness about legal information, which will in turn move them beyond a paradigm of lawyers working within current legal systems to realize their potential as advocates for social justice.

Legal Information as a Social Construct:
Access Providers, Organizers, Creators

Rather than trying to create standards, the goal of this section is to initiate a dialogue on how instructors can add a critical approach to legal information literacy. Teaching legal information as a social construct produced and published by people is one such way a critical pedagogy can be adopted by instructors.

The approach presented here divides the producers of legal information into three categories:

- Those who provide access to legal information;
- Those who organize legal information; and
- Those who create legal information.

It should be clear that this is not the only way to categorize legal information. These categories are simply meant to provide one possible framework in which to generate ideas.

For each category I present two examples, each of which includes a background discussion for context and sample questions for encouraging dialogue, reflection and problem-posing. The ideas presented are not comprehensive: they are meant to represent a sample of the potential multitude of ideas. Above all, the ideas presented are meant to initiate a reflective practice for educators from which more ideas can be generated.

Access Providers

Many legal research classes cover cost awareness and cost efficiency. Students are taught to be aware of how much legal information costs, how to control costs through efficient use of databases, and where to find free sources of legal information.

Educators can add a critical dimension to this discussion by encouraging students to critique who profits from the current legal information industry and who is disadvantaged by it and discuss alternatives to commercial legal information.

Tiered pricing models: Westlaw/Lexis duopoly. In 1834, the Supreme Court established that written court opinions are not protectable by copyright (Wheaton v. Peters). Despite this, the legal information industry is extremely profitable, with Thomson Reuters Legal ("Westlaw") and LexisNexis evolving into legal information duopoly over the past several decades (Arewa, 2006, p. 821). In 2010, LexisNexis had operating profits of $922 million (Reed Elsevier, 2010), while Westlaw had operating profits of $1.06 billion (Thomson Reuters, 2010).

Both Westlaw and Lexis employ a tiered pricing model where law schools are charged relatively small fees, government institutions are charged moderately higher fees, and law firms and other commercial users are charged significantly higher fees. These prices are set by contracts negotiated between the parties. Unaffiliated individuals who want to purchase single session access to a database may pay well over a hundred dollars for a simple research transaction or a few minutes of searching (Arewa, 2006).

This pricing model may privilege some while disadvantaging others. For example law students and professors enjoy low cost access to huge amounts of legal information, and those same students find themselves more hirable because of their experience with Lexis and Westlaw. However, many are disadvantaged by this system. Among them are *pro se* litigants, lawyers who represent clients who cannot pay, and libraries that want to offer legal databases to the public, but cannot afford access to these expensive yet indispensable tools.

Because many law firms bill Westlaw and Lexis charges directly to clients, this reduces their incentive to demand changes to the *status quo* (Nina Platt Consulting, 2011).

To promote critical analysis of legal information pricing, educators might ask students such questions as:

- How does the price of legal information affect access to justice?
- Is it fair that private companies profit from the dissemination of public information?
- How might the pricing of legal information advantage some individuals over others?

Dissemination of information to the public: Government legal information websites. Free alternatives to Westlaw and Lexis do exist, but are inadequate. Coverage is often incomplete. Many court websites publish recent decisions only, while Westlaw and Lexis offers coverage from the late 1800's onward. Moreover, each court website publishes its own decisions so researchers cannot search combined jurisdictions. (Gallacher, 2007). The searching mechanisms offered by court websites are very limited, and even if a researcher finds a case in a court website, she will not have the ability to validate the case with the citator services offered by Westlaw and Lexis (Mills, 2003).

Besides the inadequacy of the websites, free legal information is fraught with other problems. Many states give the exclusive right to publish "official" codes and regulations to commercial publishers (Martin, 2000). For example, New York's "official" administrative regulations are published in print and in a Westlaw database. A free version of the administrative rules is available online, but comes with the warning:

> The information contained in the on-line version of the NYCRR is not the official version of the NYCRR. No representation is made as to its accuracy, nor may it be read into evidence in New York State courts. To ensure accuracy and for evidentiary purposes, reference should be made to the official NYCRR which is available from Thomson West.
> (New York Department of State – Division of Administrative Rules, n.d.)

To promote critical analysis of government provided legal information, educators might ask students such questions as:

• Do governments have an obligation to provide comprehensive, searchable legal information websites? If so, who will pay for it?
• Do they have an obligation to provide citator services?
• Should governments be able to sell the rights to the official versions of their codes?

Organizers

The organizational structure of legal information substantially impacts how individuals understand the information (Kuh, 2008). Educators can add a critical dimension to this discussion by encouraging dialogue on who organizes legal information, how the organizational scheme might change the meaning and content of legal information and how that can impact its use.

Taxonomies: West Digest system. Since 1879, the West Digest system has provided the dominant organizational paradigm for case law (Jarvis, 2010). The West Digest system summarizes points of law from legal cases and places each one under a topic and subtopic in West's extensive legal taxonomy. Every point of law distilled from the cases is placed into the taxonomy. To find case law, a researcher selects a topic and subtopic and is presented a list of relevant case summaries. Practically speaking, the West Digest System *can be described as a legal research tool, an index to case law or a finding aid.*

However, many commentators have argued that the Digest has been powerful enough to shape the understanding and development of the law, at least until the advent of online keyword searching. Bob Berring (2000) credits it for having defined the "universe of thinkable thoughts" (p. 311) and others have critiqued it for inhibiting progressive thinking about the law and reproducing dominant legal traditions (Stefanic, 1989).

To promote critical analysis of legal taxonomies educators might ask students such questions as:

• How important has the Digest system been in the development of American law and how will online searching affect its importance?
• How might legal information develop in its absence?

Relevancy rankings: Crowdsourced legal search tools. New online legal research systems such as WestlawNext use "crowdsourcing" technology to return and rank search results. WestlawNext purportedly helps legal researchers by offering "ranked, relevant results, with one plain language query" (Thomson Reuters, 2012). It does this by incorporating crowdsourcing as one aspect of the search. In other words, WestlawNext analyzes which documents have been previously viewed, downloaded and printed, and uses those statistics to inform future searches. As a result, the more popular documents will rise in the relevancy rankings.

Ron Wheeler (2011) has suggested that although this type of search will, in most cases, produce more useful, desirable results, it will be a problem for researchers who are looking for less popular or alternative legal theories. Ideas that are less popular will be buried at the bottom of the results, and potentially lost to the researcher, while mainstream ideas are promoted to the top.

To promote critical analysis of crowdsourced legal information databases educators might ask students such questions as:

• What are the implications for using crowdsourcing technology to return results?

• Will the technology shape the future of legal information? If it does, what problems could this create?

Creators

Legal information is a social construct created by people and institutions. Legal information creators, such as judges, legislators, editors and scholars, are human beings who exist within their own culture and society. Law students are generally quite knowledgeable about and interested in legal information creators. For example, the political leanings of judges and legislators are often a topic of dialogue and debate. Thus, law students often already have a burgeoning critical consciousness about this aspect of legal information.

Educators can help develop this critical consciousness by encouraging a critical analysis of the people who create legal information, particularly the people who may be less discussed or less understood, but nonetheless participate in the creation of legal information.

Selective reporting: Case law. One area for reflection and dialogue is the reporting and publishing of case law. Students often perceive case law as a body of information that represents every decision made by the judiciary and assume that all judicial decisions set precedents. While this is true for the United States Supreme Court and other state supreme courts, it is not true for lower court decisions.

Lower courts practice selective publication, which means that the judges decide whether or not they want to submit a decision for publication. Moreover, a state reporter often has the final say in whether or not a decision will be published, even after a judge submits it for publication. In New York, for example, only lower court decisions that the "state reporter, with the approval of the court of appeals, considers worthy of being reported because of its usefulness as a precedent or its importance as a matter of public interest" are published and currently less than 6% of decisions submitted by trial court judges appear in the official Reporter (New York State Law Reporting Bureau, 2012).

To promote critical analysis of case law reporting, educators might ask students such questions as:

• What is the impact of this selective practice of publication?
• Does it restrict a diversity of ideas and deprive lawyers of alternative arguments, or does it help streamline and make legal information more accessible?
• Who decides what is worthy of being reported?

Authoritative vs. popular sources: Judicial citation to blogs. Elie Margolis (2011) has pointed out that traditional print-based research kept legal information and non-legal information very separate and distinct. However, the arrival of online research has blurred that distinction, because physical boundaries between information sources have been erased and "everything looks the same on the internet" (p. 929). In the past, a researcher would locate an official code or a case reporter in the library and know that it had the force of law. Now, one Google search may retrieve primary sources of law, such as cases and codes from both official and unofficial sources, along with newspaper articles, blog essays, and commentary from scholarly and non-scholarly sources.

Lee Peoples (2010) has studied judicial citation to blog posts and has found a sharp increase in judicial citation to blog posts to support their legal reasoning and authority. This is not to say that the judiciary has been indiscriminate in choosing sources for authority–judicial citation to blogs is often to those written by well-known scholars and practitioners (Peoples, 2012). The bloggers are often law professors who have already published treatises and articles on the subject, or practitioners who are well-known for their legal work. However, this practice is self-perpetuating: the more a source is used as an authority, the more authoritative they become (Peoples, 2010, 51).

To promote critical analysis of this judicial citation to blogs, educators might ask students such questions as:

• Does judicial citation to blogs matter?
• Does this phenomenon increase the diversity of legal authority?
• Does judicial citation to blogs increase the available points of view

found in legal information?

Conclusion

Legal research educators who want to support a social justice and public interest mission should teach *critical* legal information literacy. A critical pedagogical dimension will encourage students to develop a critical consciousness about legal information and help them realize their potential to advocate for justice and change current legal systems.

Critical legal information literacy urges educators to present legal information as a social construct through a process of dialogue and problem-posing. This chapter presented a framework for teaching legal information as a social construct, with ideas for discussion in order to inspire educators to engage in a process of critical inquiry about legal information with students and with themselves.

Note

Thanks to Meg Butler, Doug Cox, Raquel Gabriel, Mary Godfrey-Rickards, Babe Howell, Allie Robbins, Sarah Shik Lamdan, Jonathan Saxon and the participants of the CUNY Law Junior Faculty Workshop for comments and encouragement. Thanks to Prathiba Desai and Moira Meltzer-Cohen for research assistance. Thanks to Julie Lim for her advice and support. Thanks to my parents, Ellen and Samir, and my sister Leila Sokkar Narvid for support and encouragement. Thanks to Jace Harker for providing advice, comments, and inspiration. Finally, thanks to Morgan Metzner for the "spark" that became this chapter.

References

American Association of Law Libraries. (2012). AALL research competencies and standards for law student information literacy. Retrieved from http://www.aallnet.org/main-menu/Leadership-Governance/policies/PublicPolicies/policy-lawstu.html
Arewa, O. B. (2006). Open access in a closed universe: Lexis, Westlaw, law schools, and the legal information market. *Lewis and Clark Law Review, 10*(4),

797-839.

Association of College and Research Libraries. (2000). Information literacy competency standards for higher education. Retrieved from http://www.ala.org/acrl/standards/informationliteracycompetency

Berring, R. C. (2000). Legal research and the world of thinkable thoughts. *Journal of Appellate Practice and Process, 2*(2), 305-318.

Bird, R. (2011). Legal information literacy. In D. Danner & J. Winterton (Eds.), *IALL handbook of legal information management* (pp. 115-134). Burlington, VT: Ashgate Publishing Company.

Delgado, R., & Stephanic, J. (1989). Why do we tell the same stories? Law reform, critical librarianship and the triple helix dilemma. *Stanford Law Review, 42*(1), 207-225.

Elmborg, J. (2006). Critical information literacy: Implications for instructional practice. *The Journal of Academic Librarianship, 32*(2), 192-199.

Freire, P. (2000). *Pedagogy of the oppressed* (30th ed.). New York: Continuum Publishing.

Gallacher, I. (2007). "Who are those guys?" The results of a survey studying the information literacy of incoming law students. *California Western Law Review, 44*, 151-206.

Jacobs, H. L. M. (2008). Information literacy and reflexive pedagogical praxis. *The Journal of Academic Librarianship, 34*(3), 256-262.

Jayasuriya, H. K. P., & Brillantine, F. M. (2007). Student services in the 21st century: Evolution and innovation in discovering student needs, teaching information literacy, and designing library, 2.0-based student services. *Legal Reference Services Quarterly, 26*(1-2), 135-170.

Jarvis, R. M. (2010). John B. West, founder of the West Publishing Company. *American Journal of Legal History, 50*(1), 1-22.

Kauffman, B. (2010). Information literacy in law: Starting points for improving legal research competencies. *International Journal of Legal Information, 38*(3), 339-351.

Kaplan, A. L., & Darvil, K. (2011). Think [and practice] like a lawyer: Legal research for the new millennials. *Legal Communication & Rhetoric: JALWD, 8*, 153-190.

Kim-Prieto, D. (2011). The road not yet taken: How law student information literacy standards address identified issues in legal research education and training. *Law Library Journal, 103*, 605-630.

Kuh, K. F. (2008). Electronically manufactured law. *Harvard Journal of Law and Technology, 22*, 223-271.

Margolis, E. (2011). Authority without borders: The world wide web and the delegalization of law. *Seton Hall Law Review, 41*, 909-945.

Martin, P. W. (2000). Legal information – a strong case for free content, an illustration of how difficult "free" may be to define, realize, and sustain. *Cornell University Law School Legal Information Institute*. Retrieved from http://www.law.

cornell.edu/working-papers/open/martin/free.html

Mills, W. R. (2003). The shape of the universe: The impact of unpublished opinions on the process of legal research. *New York Law School Journal of International and Comparative Law, 22,* 59-76.

New York Department of State – Division of Administrative Rules. (n.d.). Welcome to the online source for New York codes, rules and regulations. Retrieved from http://government.westlaw.com/linkedslice/default.asp?SP=nycrr-1000

New York State Law Reporting Bureau. (2012). New York official reports: Frequently asked questions. Retrieved from http://www.courts.state.ny.us/reporter/Faq.htm

New York State Law Reporting Bureau. (2012). New York official reports: Selection of opinions for publication. Retrieved from http://www.courts.state.ny.us/reporter/Selection.htm

Nina Platt Consulting. (2011, April 22). Legal research one of leading irritants says new survey on cost recovery. [Web log post]. Retrieved from http://strategiclibrarian.com/2011/04/22/legal-research-one-of-leading-irritants-says-new-survey-on-cost-recovery/

Peoples, L. F. (2010). The citation of blogs in judicial opinions. *Tulane Journal of Technology and Intellectual Property, 13,* 39-80.

Reed Elsevier. (2010). Financial report. Retrieved from www.reedelsevier.com/ar10

Shor, I. (1992). *Empowering education: Critical teaching for social change.* Chicago: University of Chicago Press.

Strege, K. (1996). *Using critical literacy to improve library instruction.* (Doctoral dissertation). Retrieved from Dissertation Abstracts International, *58*(01A), 0014.

Swanson, T.A. (2005). Applying a critical pedagogical perspective to information literacy standards. *Community Junior College Libraries, 12*(4), 65-77.

Thomson Reuters. (2012). Leverage the power of WestSearch. In *WestlawNext.* Retrieved from http://store.westlaw.com/westlawnext/about/west-search/default.aspx

Thomson Reuters. (2010). 2010 financial report. Retrieved from http://ar.thomsonreuters.com

Valentine, S. (2010). Legal research as a fundamental skill: A lifeboat for students and law schools. *University of Baltimore Law Review, 39*(2), 173-226.

Valentine, S. (2011). Leveraging legal research. In Society of American Law Teachers & Golden Gate University School of Law (Eds.), *Vulnerable populations and transformative law teaching: A critical reader* (pp. 145-162). Durham, NC: Carolina Academic Press.

Wheaton v. Peters, 33 U.S. 591 (1834).

Wheeler, R. E. (2011). Does WestlawNext really change everything? The implications of WestlawNext on legal research. *Law Library Journal, 103*(3), 359-377.

Information – Power to the People:
Students and Librarians Dialoguing about Power, Social Justice, and Information

Amanda J. Swygart-Hobaugh
Georgia State University

"The biggest and most generalized takeaway that I got from this course is that information is indeed power." From a student's final course reflection

Pushing the Boundaries of the ACRL Information Literacy Standards

When dialoguing about power, social justice, and information, Standard Five of the Association of College and Research Libraries (ACRL) *Information Literacy Competency Standards for Higher Education,* "The information literate student understands many of the economic, legal, and social issues surrounding the use of information and accesses and uses information ethically and legally" (ACRL, 2000, Standard Five, para. 2), is especially compelling because of its potential for examining critical theory and social justice as it applies to information access. But, as Seale (2010, p. 229) attests, Standard Five's Performance Indicators and Outcomes largely focus on the "procedural" aspects of information literacy, thus obscuring relevant issues ripe for critical analyses. Namely, as Luke and Kapitzke (1999) observe, the language of the ACRL Standards neglects broader critiques steeped in critical theory, such as discussions of "social construction and cultural authority of knowledge; the political economies of knowledge ownership and control; [and] the development of local communities' and cultures' capacities to critique and construct knowledge" (p. 483-484). For example, Outcomes A, B, and C delineated under Standard Five, Performance Indicator One specify that the information literate student "identifies and discusses issues related to privacy and security in both the print and electronic environments...to free vs. fee-based access to information...[and] to censorship and freedom of speech" (ACRL, 2000, Standard Five, para. 2). However, as written, a discussion of the listed "issues" could exclude critiques of the societal power structures that often play a key role in these arenas. For instance, would discussion of issues related to free vs. fee-based access to information be merely "the library's databases are not free like on the open web," or would it delve into critical dialogues regarding why some information is free and other information is not, who controls access to fee-based as well as so-called free information, and how ownership/control disempowers some while empowering others? Moreover, the language of Standard Five, Performance Indicator One, Outcome D is even more problematic: the information literate student "demonstrates an understanding of intellectual property, copyright, and fair use of copyrighted material" (ACRL, 2000, Standard Five, para. 2). "Demonstrating understanding" implies uncritical acceptance of the present laws governing intellectual property, copyright, and fair use—which does not bode well for critical information literacy. As illustrated by the recent court case *Cambridge University Press et al. v. Becker et al.* (2012), the academic community—including students—cannot afford to uncritically accept the present legal conditions regarding intellectual property, copyright, and fair use. Similarly, Standard Five, Performance Indicator Two—"The information literate student *follows* [emphasis added] laws, regulations, institutional policies, and etiquette related to the access and use of information resources" (ACRL, 2000, Standard Five, para. 2), implies that there is no space for critiquing the validity of the laws, regulations, and policies that surround information access/use and how these may act as agents of disempowerment.

Thus, while Standard Five is admirable in its attempt to address issues surrounding access and use of information, it falls short of challenging librarians to integrate critical-theoretical and social-justice frameworks into their approach to information literacy pedagogy. As Jacobs (2008) argues, librarians need to engage in a pedagogical praxis of information literacy, wherein we "emphasiz[e] the democratizing and social justice elements inherent in information literacy" and bring to the forefront of our teaching that "information literacy...also encompasses...empowering people, promoting social inclusion, redressing disadvantage, and advancing the well-being of all in a global context" (Jacobs, 2008, p. 257). However, as

Peterson (2010) notes, librarians' ability to engage in critical information literacy pedagogy is often stymied by the one-shot, "cram-it-all-in approach" (p. 71) to library instruction.

The semester-long honors freshman seminar discussed in this chapter offered a unique opportunity to take up the charge to integrate critical information literacy into my pedagogy. By exposing students to the various disparities of information access and how these are intertwined with racial, socioeconomic, age, and other power-laden statuses, the issues alluded to abstractly in Standard Five can be contextualized and therefore more readily critiqued as social-justice issues. And, just as "critical pedagogues and multicultural scholars [aim] to create educational environments that empower historically marginalized people, that challenge inequitable social arrangements and institutions, and that offer strategies and visions for creating a more just world" (Hytten & Bettez, 2011, p. 8), librarians, too, can strive to further social-justice aims via critical information literacy pedagogy. While the typical one-shot instruction session may prove challenging to integrate critical information literacy into the curriculum, a semester-long course provided an ideal situation to examine social justice and information access.

Engaging Students in Dialogic, Problem-Posing Learning

Products of No-Child-Left-Behind educational policies, today's incoming college students have been indoctrinated in what Freire (2000) coined the "banking concept" of education, wherein "teachers make daily deposits of knowledge in students' heads which they bank for future use...and [students] subsequently approach their education as consumers and passive receivers of knowledge rather than active agents shaping their own lives" (Elmborg, 2006, p. 193). In juxtaposition to the banking model is a problem-posing, dialogic learning process:

Banking education...attempts, by mythicizing reality, to conceal certain facts which explain the way human beings exist in the world; problem-posing education sets itself the task of demythologizing. Banking education resists dialogue; problem-posing education regards dialogue as indispensable to the act of cognition which unveils reality. Banking education treats students as objects of assistance; problem-posing education makes them critical thinkers. (Freire, 2000, p. 83-84)

Embracing Freire's (2000) pedagogy, I structured my class to enable a problem-posing, dialogic learning process. As a seminar-style course, free of lecturing and rote exams, the students, the guest speakers, and I engaged in dialogues about the session topics. Each topic was a problem posed for dialogue and aimed at exposing why it was a problem. Students and teacher debated the nature of the problem, explored our own experiences in relation to the problem, and discussed possible solutions.

The following excerpts from a student's Final Course Reflection aptly illustrate the empowering nature and effectiveness of the problem-posing, dialogic process. He stated that, "In these class discussions I learned that not only do other people have dissenting opinions that I ought to respect, but I am not always right," thus recognizing that the dialogic learning process enabled him to see his fellow students as "respected sources of knowledge" (Takacs, 2002, p. 177). Similarly, his reflection resonates with McArthur's (2010) declaration that "critical pedagogy needs to be a movement that welcomes disagreement; in which people engage with the disagreement rather than rant or retreat" (p. 497). The same student also observed the following:

In high school, I was not often asked to apply my knowledge. I would simply learn the material that the state required me [to] memorize and regurgitate for the exam. This course gave me a chance to learn about a topic, see examples of it in society, and then use what I had learned to discover something new. The process of applying the knowledge I had learned in a class to a situation in real life has been a very thought provoking experience and seems to be a very effective way to approach material in my other classes. This course taught me a lot about information imbalances, my interactions with other people, and how to approach learning more effectively through thought and discussion.

The student's reflection illustrates his growing understanding that the "banking" (Freire, 2000) approach to education that he experienced in high school had stifled his learning, and that the dialogic, problem-posing process had empowered him to exercise more agency in his own learning and to apply new knowledge. His comments resonate with Takacs (2002) observation regarding the value of a dialogic learning process:

> When we ask students to learn to think for themselves and to understand themselves as thinkers—rather than telling them what to think and have them recite it back—we help foster habits of introspection, analysis, and open, joyous communication... (p. 169)

In addition to Freire's (2000) problem-posing, dialogic process of learning, his goals of liberating the oppressed fit the overarching critical-theoretical and social-justice themes of this course. As McArther (2010) in her discussion of social justice in higher education states, "critical pedagogy also needs to be reminded of Freire's essential point regarding the oppressed and oppressor: freedom does not involve swapping roles, but can only come when the oppressed help the oppressors to also be free" (p. 497). Accordingly, a goal of this course was to dialogue about whether existing power structures serve to disempower certain individuals (and, concomitantly, empower others) in terms of information access, and whether a duty to social justice necessarily compels those with power as well as the powerless to pursue efforts to ameliorate the inequalities of information access.

Expanding Students' Perceptions of Librarians

As noted in previous research (Seale, 2008; Fagan, 2003), the general public as well as undergraduate students have very little understanding of librarians' professional and knowledge backgrounds, let alone the ethical and professional principles that librarians commonly espouse regarding access to information. Moreover, because academic librarians are often solicited by faculty members to do instruction that is solely skill-and resource-focused, and are seldom (if ever) asked to lead critical discussions about the broader social issues of information literacy and access, students are exposed to a limited view of our professional lives and principles. As Budd (2003) reflected, librarians' ability to engage in praxis that involves "action that carries social and ethical implications" is hindered by the typical reduction of our instruction to "technical performance of tasks" (p. 20).

Consequently, this seminar aimed to expand and challenge the students' perceptions of librarianship by elucidating the role librarians play in social justice and democratizing efforts related to information access. While some more clearly than others, all of the session topics for this course overlapped with many interests and principles found in librarianship. By dialoguing with librarians about these issues, students learn that librarians not only have unique knowledge to bring to the table, but that they are passionate, principle-driven agents for social justice pertaining to the use of and access to information.

An Honors Freshman Seminar: What Did Students Learn?

This chapter provides a case study of teaching an Honors Freshman Seminar at Georgia State University. The pedagogical goals for this course were: (1) to push the boundaries of the Association of College & Research Libraries (ACRL) *Information Literacy Competency Standards for Higher Education*; (2) to engage students in applying critical-theoretical and social-justice frameworks to the course topics via dialogic, problem-posing learning; and (3) to expand and challenge the students' perceptions of librarianship by elucidating the role librarians play in social justice and democratizing efforts related to information access.

Topics for the seminar were chosen in order to: (1) examine various power structures influencing information access; (2) capitalize on the knowledge and interests of library colleagues; and (3) explore topics that students might be able to readily relate to personally, as well as challenge them to consider issues that they might be exempt from due to their own privileged statuses (i.e., race, socioeconomic status, ability, gender, etc.). For example health literacy, open access and scholarly communication, access to the legal system, etc. A full list of course topics is available in Appendix A, and the course syllabus is online (Swygart-Hobaugh, Fall 2011).

Readings for each session in the seminar typically included a combination of scholarly articles, popular press articles, statistical tables, organizational or governmental reports, and video clips. With each topic, guiding questions provided a framework for students to glean information from the readings. For example, the readings for the session on information poverty and the digital divide included: (1) a scholarly article deconstructing the many moral and ethical issues of information poverty (Britz, 2004); (2) a media clip and brochure by the now-defunct *InternetForEveryone.org* (2009; n.d.) including statistics on disparities in Internet access; (3) statistics reporting Internet usage within the U.S., broken down by state and by various social demographics (U.S. Census Bureau, 2011); and (4) statistics reporting Internet users worldwide by country (Central Intelligence Agency, 2009; World Bank Group, 2011). I provided the following to guide the students' reading/viewing of this session's materials:

• How does Britz's (2004) social justice framework reinforce, expand, and sometimes contradict the critical theory/social justice frameworks we've been discussing?
• How do you see the "contested territories" (e.g., race, age, income level, education, etc.) presented in Miller's (2008) social justice framework playing out in terms of information poverty and the digital divide?
• What underlying factors do you see contributing to information poverty and the digital divide in the U.S. and worldwide?
• When looking at the statistics re: differences of Internet access between different groups, states, and countries, was there anything that surprised you? Do you see similar or different trends as when we examined literacy?
• How do the InternetForEveryone.org organization's goals resonate with the social justice frameworks?

Before each class session, students were required to post Discussion Points to the university's course management system, which they drew from their reactions to the readings and from the guiding questions provided. From these, specific points were selected to jumpstart dialogue in class; with teacher mediation and prompting, class discussion would evolve from there. After the course session, students were required to post Reflections to the course management system, in which they offered further insights from engaging in dialogue with their classmates and teacher(s).

The Discussion Points and Reflections actively engaged students in steering the dialogic learning process and validated the students' personal experiences and opinions as they connected with the session topics. For example, for the information poverty and digital divide topic, rather than presenting students with the statistics and providing interpretations, I posed a question to them – thus necessitating their evaluation and interpretation of the statistics as well as their application of the critical frameworks we were learning in class. One student concluded the following from the statistics provided in the *InternetforEveryone.org* brochure:

> We see a disturbing correlation between race, particularly non-white races, and lack of access to information, in this case the World Wide Web. As well as race, there is a correlation between this lack of information and income levels, which can probably be linked very easily to the same correlation in literacy. This recurring theme in this course begs for a conversation regarding social justice.

Prompted by a guiding question asking how she saw the role of "contested territories" (Miller, 2008) playing out in the issues of information poverty and the digital divide, the student recognized the correlative disparity in Internet access that people of color and of lower-income levels experience and patterns of inequality evident in our previous week's examination of literacy, and deduced that these "disturbing" correlations revealed the situation as a social injustice in need of addressing.

The Final Project required students to organize a lesson plan on a topic related to the course theme.[1] Students proposed a topic, developed learning outcomes, selected and annotated reading and visual materials, provided guiding questions for the materials, and developed learning activities. Via the course management system, we brainstormed topic ideas, with guidance from the instructor, who also provided a framework by suggesting topics that intersected with their academic interests (e.g., computer science majors might have interest in human-computer interaction as an information-access issue). An example lesson plan was provided to aid the students (Swygart-Hobaugh, 2011).

The Final Project topics illustrated their interests and creativity in approaching the assignment. For example, a student majoring in computer

---

1 Students also had the option to do a mini Thesis Project plan; however, no student chose this option.

science proposed a lesson plan entitled, "Human Computer Interaction: Increasing Access to Information," which explored "how physical impairments can reduce access to information" and "how we can increase that access to information through better human computer interfaces." A student whose parents were lawyers proposed a lesson plan entitled "Right to Information…For a Price–Copyright Law in the United States," which examined how U.S. copyright law "limits access to information and disadvantages certain groups of people." An African-American student, who had found "intriguing" the racial discrepancies in U.S. literacy rates, proposed a lesson plan entitled, "Race and Literacy: How do Literacy Rates Vary by Race?" Another student, inspired by Neil Postman's (1985) *Amusing Ourselves to Death: Public Discourse in the Age of Show Business,* critiqued how television "primarily concerned with entertainment…affects the information we have access to and how that has profound consequences on the world." Many students chose topics that resonated with current hot-button topics. One group of students explored the use of new technologies such as YouTube and Facebook as empowering "constituents to voice their opinions against politics," while another student explored the potential exploitation by Facebook of "user's shared information in order to provide better and more lucrative data for its advertisers." Another student, in his lesson plan entitled "Google, Number 1 Search Machine? Censorship in China, The Great Firewall," examined whether Chinese governmental control of the Internet was "necessary or just plain tyrannical." Conclusively, the chosen topics demonstrated the students' ability to creatively apply the critical-theoretical/social-justice frameworks to contemporary societal issues.

Lastly, the students submitted a Final Course Reflection, for which they articulated what they learned from the course and how they would take that knowledge forward in their continued studies, service learning opportunities, and personal life. Apparent in the Final Course Reflections was the concept of praxis–how the students intended to take what they learned forward in embodied actions. For example, the student majoring in computer science declared, "Once I have my computer science degree, I also hope to help increase the availability of Internet with public computers in low-income areas, either by donating to public libraries or volunteering to help install them." Another student similarly saw the connection between knowledge and action:

> A topic that truly affected me this semester included the low literacy levels that many Americans possess... This realization spurred me to further my research and look into potential volunteer programs. I stumbled upon the Literacy Volunteers of Atlanta (thanks to [the] reading you provided us with) and realized that offering my services could potentially help quite a few adults with this problem. I prospectively plan on volunteering there during the spring semester.

In addition to manifestations of praxis, the above reflections resonate with another underlying aim of social-justice education: a duty to social justice compels those with power to pursue efforts to ameliorate inequalities, in this case, inequalities in access to information. The above students recognized their ability to assist those disempowered by various societal factors, and identified practical ways of fulfilling a sense of duty to less-fortunate others.

Similarly, two other students reflected on how the course topics had enlightened them to their relative privileged status. For example, one student stated, "This class has taught me that access to information should not be taken for granted. It is a controversial issue that we in the United States have less trouble with, which makes it less obvious that we still have to be cautious because of censorship," thus he recognized his place of relative global privilege by being a U.S. citizen. He continued, saying that he must "actively fight against any sort of privilege concerning the access of information," and "be conscientious about [his] own personal access to information," and that he also had a duty in this regard "for those who are less fortunate" than himself. Correspondingly, the following student described his illumination to his privileged status:

> I was enlightened to many information imbalances that I was not aware of before this course, such as literacy among adults in America and the navigation of legal documents. As a suburban-grown American, I am literate and by chance also have attorneys for parents, so neither of these issues ever crossed my mind.

This student's words closely resonate with a central aim of privilege theory pedagogy: to challenge those in socially-privileged statuses, who are "rarely explicitly self-conscious of the nature of their privilege" (Johnson, 2009, p. 798) and whose privilege "is granted, not earned or brought into being by one's individual effort or talent" (Black & Stone, 2005, p. 244), to examine their position of privilege in relation to social issues. While I did not overtly incorporate privilege theory into this course, witnessing its workings illustrates the entwined nature of social justice and privilege pedagogies.

Analyses of Students' Assignment Texts

Twelve students consented to content analyses of their assignment texts, which included the Discussion Points, Reflections, and the Final Course Reflection.[2] The content analyses were conducted using Strauss and Corbin's (1998) grounded theory methodology primarily, but also drew from Krippendorff's (2010) content analysis framework. The analyses were facilitated by QSR International's (2011) *NVivo9* qualitative research software. The assignment texts were compiled separately for each student and then imported into *NVivo9* as discrete sources, using a naming convention of S1=Student 1, S2=Student 2, etc., to represent the 12 different student source texts. The source texts were coded according to several themes that emerged from reading the texts. Upon coding all the source texts, features of *NVivo9* were used as well as the instructor's analytical interpretation to infer discursive patterns in the texts. The content analyses were primarily focused on gauging: (1) students' affirmation and/or challenging of the critical-theoretical and social-justice frameworks; and (2) whether and how students discussed librarians and libraries as social justice and/or democratizing agents.

Critical Theory and Social Justice Discourses in Student Texts

NVivo9's word frequency query feature extracted counts of the top 50 words in the texts. The top five occurring words in descending order were

2 I excluded the Final Project assignment from my content analyses because I wished to focus on students' responses to the course readings and class discussion.

as follows: "information," 400 instances; "people," 313 instances; "access," 233 instances; "more," 193 instances; and "should," 167 instances. Fittingly, these words combine into sentences that capture the essence of the course: *People should [have] more access [to] information,* and *more people should [have] access [to] information.*

Of course, frequency of occurrence does not necessarily indicate these words were used in combination with each other; thus, I investigated further. Intrigued by "people" being the second most-frequently occurring word, individual occurrences were examined in the texts. Largely, it was used as a catch-all term to describe groups of people. However, there were various instances where it was paired as "the people" to refer to a populace or citizenship and to facilitate critical-theoretical/social-justice claims. For example, a student's statement that "it is a fundamental right of the people to be well informed" draws on the social-justice discourse of rights. Another student, in stating "the lack of transparency is ignoring the government's first duty to the people, which is to serve the people," and "the legal system is an extension of the government, whose duty is to serve the people. This cannot be done while the people are kept in ignorance," invokes a social-justice discourse by appealing to notions of social duty/responsibility. Moreover, one might interpret his statement about the government "ignoring" its "duty to the people" and keeping "the people…in ignorance" invokes a critical-theoretical discourse, as it implies that the government exercises power/control by withholding of information. Similarly, another student critiqued the U.S. government's control of government information, noting that "[T]he State is still censoring certain information before it becomes fully available to the public, thus putting the power of information in the hands of the government and not the people," again resonating with a central tenet of critical theory we discussed in class: "critique of domination" (McKinnon, 2009, p. 238).

A proximity text search query in *NVivo9* returned 90 instances of the terms "information" and "access" occurring within 5 words of each other. From these search results, *NVivo9* was used to generate a word tree that depicted when "access" and "information" appeared in conjunction with each other, paired with the ten words preceding and following their use.

These terms were often combined with critical-theoretical/social-justice discourses advocating access to information as a basic right, and calling for reforms to address the disparities in information access experienced by different groups. For example, after watching the SPARKY Award winners assigned for our discussion of the Open Access Movement, a student remarked that the winners "did a good job of showing how opening people's access to information could really have a positive effect on how that information is used to change the world"–aligning with social-justice discourse of affecting social change for the betterment of society. Another student similarly reflected that in the course "we learned how access to information is often a stepping stone for social change and restriction of information is a tool for social control," his words resonate not only with social-justice discourse but also incorporate critical-theoretical discourses in relation to information control as a device of social domination and thus disempowerment. A "most memorable" concept another student drew from the course was "that those economically disadvantaged are also at a disadvantage when it comes to their access to information. The two correlate in a shocking way," her words illustrated her awareness of the way social inequalities compound each other and perpetuate the disempowerment of "disadvantaged" groups, which again aligns with critical-theoretical discourses. Similarly, another student proclaimed the following:

> [S]ociety, as a whole, must agree that informational imbalances are unjust and that all possible efforts should be made to eliminate them. The illiterate must be taught to read, the uninformed must be given access to information, and the impoverished must seek out ways to become equal with their economic antithesis.

This student's words capture the spirit of social-justice discourse: he admonished "informational imbalances" as "unjust and expounded on specific steps that should be taken to "eliminate them"–his repetition of the word "must" places imperative emphasis on the gravity of the situation but also appeals to a sense of duty to take action.

The word frequency and proximity analysis alone proved fruitful for teasing out the students' use of critical-theoretical and social-justice discourses. Additionally, coding the texts allowed further exploration of how the students employed and/or challenged the critical-theoretical and social-justice discourses. In reading the texts, recurring themes were identified and constructed as codes (or "nodes" as labeled in *NVivo9*), which were then linked to various excerpts of texts (or "references" as labeled in *NVivo9*). Initially, 45 codes were constructed and applied to the texts. Multiple codes were attached to the same excerpt if that excerpt evoked the nuanced themes differentiated by the discrete codes. For example, an excerpt of text could be coded with the broader "social justice" code, but also with the "domination/disempowerment" code if it involved that rhetoric within the appeal, and with "access to information—no limits" if it declared as such in the text. After coding *NVivo9*'s cluster analysis was used to combine codes that had significant similarity in theme and in application, and codes that had not been applied across more than six student source texts were deleted. There were 439 total excerpts coded with the 10 finalized codes.

Of the 10 final codes, Table 1 below contains those that were applied when students affirmed various nuances of the social-justice and critical-theoretical discourses.

Table 1: Thematic Codes, Affirming Critical-Theoretical/Social-Justice Discourses

Thematic Code	Coded Sources	Coded Excerpts (% of Total Coded Excerpts)
social justice	12	117 (27.8%)
access to information – no limits	11	75 (17.8%)
domination/disempowerment	12	60 (14.3%)
critiques of U.S./democracy	11	36 (8.6%)
accessibility of information	10	26 (6.2%)

As indicated by the number of coded excerpts listed in Table 1, the students largely affirmed critical-theoretical and social-justice discourses in their assignment texts. At 117 instances occurring across all 12 sources, "social justice" themes permeated the student texts. Similarly, the "domination/disempowerment" code, applied when students offered explicit critiques of power and its resultant disempowerment, was applied in 60 instances across all 12 sources. Moreover, students frequently affirmed critical-theoretical discourses by specifically critiquing the failures of the United States to live up to democratic ideals, as is indicated by the 36 instances of my applying the code "critiques of U.S./democracy." And, applying the "access to information—no limits" code when students' words advocated as such, 75 instances emerged in all but one of the 12 sources. Lastly, the code of "accessibility to information," applied primarily when students discussed the understandability of legal information by laypersons, resonating with critical-theoretical and social-justice discourses, emerged in 26 instances across 10 of the 12 sources.

Students were particularly likely to affirm social-justice and critical-theoretical discourses when addressing Internet access and the digital divide. For example, one student declared that "the social justice theory applies here in a very fundamental manner, as I believe it is a basic human right for people to be able to access the Internet and all the knowledge that comes with it" and another stated "a common basic right is the right to information, and in this age that means having access to the Internet more than anything else"—both students specifically appealed to social-justice and rights discourse. Another similarly employed social-justice rhetoric, proclaiming loudly that "poorer people cannot access Internet thus THE JUSTICE OF SOCIETY IS NOT YET SERVED." While not explicitly using social-justice or rights rhetoric per se, other students recognized that lack of Internet access severely disadvantages groups and thus disempowers them in an information society. For example, in examining the statistics that indicate many countries have severely limited Internet access, one student observed that, "without it, it seems to keep them behind the rest of the world because everyone else in the world is always updated," thus he recognized the disempowering effect. Another student declared that "we live in the technology era, and anyone not connected to this movement will be left behind and socially degraded for years to come," similarly observing the disempowering effect of disparities in Internet access.

Students' reactions to our collective dialogues regarding open access to scholarly communication resonated with critical-theoretical discourses. In learning from our Dean of Libraries the relevance of the Open Access movement to Georgia State University's involvement in *Cambridge*

University Press et al. v. Becker et al. (2012), some students were outraged at the perceived abuse of power that publishers exercise over the academic community. The following statement by one student cut to the core of the critical-theoretical critique:

> The publishing industry is one of the most capitalistic entities [in] today's society...The academic publishers are the worst kind of criminals...Information should not be used as goods, with which one may raise the price due to demand, because information is not a good. Information is a vital part of intellectual growth, scientific discoveries, and societal growth.

This student's critique of the publishing industry as "one of the most capitalistic entities [in] today's society" and his equation of them with "the worst kind of criminals" strongly invokes a critical-theoretical critique of the political economy of capitalism. Likewise, his reproach that "information is not a good" to be bought and sold deftly resonates with Luke and Kapitzke's (1999) call for critical information literacy to critique "the political economies of knowledge ownership and control" (pp. 484).

In approaching the topics of youth rights, book challenges, access to LGBTQ information, transparency of government information, and legal literacy, students often critiqued traditional authority structures (parents, schools, government, legal system) by applying critical-theoretical concepts. Most students readily denounced the ACLU-alleged incidences of schools filtering positive LGBTQ information but allowing anti-gay websites through the filters. One student reflected:

> The act of censoring material in public schools, such as an informational LGBT website, effectively forces a child into a specific ideology if they encounter this censorship at an impressionable age. Children are taught that the school is a safe place full of authority figures who want to help them and will make the best decisions for them. If a child is browsing the Internet at school and sees that the LGBT Community Center website is blocked (especially after seeing that other websites are blocked for having violent or sexually explicit material) then the child may make the assumption that "LGBT" is something bad and will grow up with that prejudice because in their mind, why would the school censor it if it wasn't bad?

This student's comments illustrate a critique of the "social construction and cultural authority of knowledge" (Luke & Kapitzke, 1999, pp. 483-484). He recognized that the school "authority figures" wield particular influence over "impressionable" children, and that by filtering LGBTQ content they are abusing their "cultural authority" (Luke & Kapitzke, 1999) by, in effect, socially constructing the LGBTQ community as "something bad."

Likewise, other students were quick to challenge the government's practice of withholding information from the public and to challenge parents and schools exercising too much control over information access–their rhetoric often appealed to democratic ideals and empowerment. For example, one student stated that "it is amazing how the government can create a mirage of openness to the American eye" and that "this also makes me wonder who exactly determines whether something is classified and a threat to national security, and what are the standards to be called so." His nuanced critique revealed his understanding of how the government capitalizes on national security fears to limit information access while simultaneously creating a "mirage of openness." Another student argued that "democracy demands an informed public, and without accessible information the public cannot be informed," appealing to information as a democratizing agent for citizen empowerment. Regarding "youth access to information" as a "fundamental right," another student criticized the United States for its failure to ratify the United Nations *Convention on the Rights of the Child* (1989), saying it was "quite telling of how a child is seen in this country. Is the view of children as property a correct way to go in relation to empowering them in the future?" This quote invokes social-justice discourses of empowerment/rights to express dismay at the United States' eschewing of youth rights.

When discussing legal literacy, the students often critiqued accessibility of legal information as disempowering to laypersons and concomitantly reinforcing the power-laden structure of the legal system. For example, one student recognized the disempowering function of "legalese" as "a major problem for the common person," as "lawyers are able to structure agreements in ways that could bring harm to one of the parties in the deal," thus "creating a power imbalance between the educated and the non-educated, or between the rich and the poor." Another student applied critical-theoretical discourses to argue that the legal system has a vested interested in disempowering laypeople by suggesting "the legal system is designed to keep the layman out of touch and the lawyer in a job," and "to preserve the informational advantage it enjoys over the general public."

While students predominantly affirmed the critical-theoretical and social-justice discourses within their assignment texts, there were instances in which they challenged or expressed conflicted beliefs about them, as the coded sources and excerpts in Table 2 below indicate.

Table 2: Thematic Codes, Challenging or Conflicted
about Critical-Theoretical/Social-Justice Discourses

Thematic Code	Coded Sources	Coded Excerpts (% of Total Coded Excerpts)
parent vs. child rights	11	36 (8.6%)
access to information – need for limits	12	29 (6.9%)
access to information – conflicted re: limits	9	23 (5.5%)

The codes contained in Table 2 were largely applied to texts in which students weighed youth rights to information against parental rights to control the information their children accessed, and citizens' rights to government information against the government's need to protect national security. Regarding these topics, some students seemed torn while others held fairly strong beliefs in opposition to a typical critical-theoretical stance. In the texts, this often emerged as a conflict between rhetoric of rights and freedoms versus protection and security as well as a respect for, or trust in, authority. For example, one student argued "censorship is often for good reasons. These reasons are usually age limits; this is not violat[ing] any of the 1st amendment because children are not truly equal because of their status as minors," thus he illustrated a belief that censorship of materials in the name of protecting children was morally and legally justifiable. Another student stated that he believed that "children are not ready for many ideas being presented in books" and that he believed "that it is up to the discretion of the librarian to place appropriate books in children's libraries" and that parents as well must also "monitor what their children are reading." In contrast, another student revealed her conflicted feelings regarding youth rights and access to information, stating that "certainly parents have a say in what their child is exposed to...but when does that start becoming an infringement on the child's rights?" The same student was hesitant to take a strong critical-theoretical stance regarding government transparency; she understood that although "absolute transparency in the government would probably result in a paranoid country, allowing citizens to have access to government information is what makes a democratic society."

Student Reflections about Libraries and Librarians

The final code of "libraries/librarians" was applied when students explicitly used the word(s) in their texts, with 19 instances occurring across 10 of the 12 sources (see Table 3).

Table 3: Sources and Excerpts mentioning Libraries/Librarians

Thematic Code	# of Coded Source Texts (% of Total Sources)	# of Coded Excerpts (% of Total Coded Excerpts)
libraries/librarians	10	19 (4.3%)

Students primarily commented on libraries/librarians in their responses on book challenges and Internet filtering. A daring couple of students turned a critical eye toward libraries/librarians. For instance, one student offered the following critique:

> The assertion that all information should be presented in all points of view is a fundamental point of the ALA's Bill of Rights. Assuming that the standard is followed uniformly by librarians, is every effort made to collect literature on as many different viewpoints on a subject that exist? Banning a book from libraries is the most prominent form of censorship, but omission of information is a more subtle form of the same practice that must not be overlooked.

This student astutely employed a critical-theoretical stance toward the power librarians can wield regarding access to information. Likewise, he brought into question whether there exists a uniform commitment to the Library Bill of Rights (ALA, 2012) principle of neutrality, and whether,

as Lewis (2008) decries, "the word 'all' in the Library Bill of Rights statement is an impossible goal, dooming librarians to failure in following
its dictates" (p. 1). "Since there is a Library Bill of Rights, why can the
Library still ban books?" and "How can librarians in America 'inculcate
values' if every parent may want to teach their children separate values?"
asked another student who recognized possible discontinuities between
professional principles and actions.

However most students expressed positive opinions about the role librarians play in social justice and democratizing efforts. For instance, one
student discussed librarians' role in advocating against book banning and
deemed them "champions of the 1st Amendment," and "major players in
today's youth and the country's future." Another student, after reading
the Library Bill of Rights (ALA, 2012) was pleased to learn that librarians strive to be "unbiased and neutral" in their collecting. Still another
student reflected on the class discussion of "the mindset of librarians" and
recognized their social justice efforts by noting that "most people working with libraries are striving to bring information to people who would
otherwise not have access to it" and that "librarians are doing a good job
of providing information to the people without censoring them." One
student's reflections were particularly heartening:

> Even in high school, I didn't really comprehend the full purpose of librar-
> ies or librarians. Sadly, the extent of their usefulness to me was a way
> of getting the newest novel I wanted to read and help finding it. Since
> coming to college and going through this course, I have come to deeply
> appreciate and admire the devotion that libraries and their librarians
> have towards knowledge and the sharing of it. This devotion towards
> organizing information and making it accessible may seem boring, but
> I think I kind of understand why librarians do it. It is hard to explain
> but, for me, there is something very comforting about knowing that this
> diverse mass of information is there in case I or the rest of humanity
> ever need it.

Conclusion

Collectively the students, the guest teachers, and I pushed the boundaries of the Association of College & Research Libraries (ACRL) *Information Literacy Competency Standards for Higher Education*. We delved beyond the "procedural" (Seale, 2010, p. 229) aspects of information literacy into the various social, legal, and ethical issues alluded to in the ACRL standards that rarely get addressed adequately in the one-shot library instruction sessions to which librarians are oft relegated. Moreover, the dialogic, problem-posing class structure successfully engaged students in applying critical-theoretical and social-justice frameworks to the course topics. As illustrated in the content analysis of the students' assignment texts, the students adeptly gleaned that critical information literacy indeed "encompasses...empowering people, promoting social inclusion, redressing disadvantage, and advancing the well-being of all in a global context" (Jacobs, 2008, p. 257). The students passionately declared that they and others had a duty to ameliorate inequalities stemming from access to information and began to understand the role librarians play in social justice and democratizing efforts related to information access. In our explorations of librarians' central involvement in anti-censorship and open-access movements as well as in our examination of the American Library Association's Library Bill of Rights (2012) students learned of the everyday, principle-driven actions that librarians take to democratize access to information. Throughout this seminar, students and instructors alike experienced Freire's (2000) "liberating education," in which "the teacher is no longer merely the-one-who-teaches, but one who is himself taught in dialogue with the students...They become jointly responsible for a process in which all grow" (p. 80).

Appendix A: Course Topics

INFORMATON–POWER TO THE PEOPLE

"Knowledge is power. Information is liberating...." Kofi Annan

Guided by this notion and the sociological frameworks of "critical theory" and "social justice," we will address specific situations in which access to, control of, and use of information is unequal, impeded, manipulated, and/or abused and thus can result in people's disempowerment. We will also explore efforts aimed at empowering those within these situations. Course session topics include the following:

"Knowledge is Power; Information is Liberating" – An Analytical Framework. We'll discuss what this phrase means to us, and how it, and the sociological frameworks of "critical theory" and "social justice," will guide our examining the course topics.

First Things First – Literacy in the U.S. and Worldwide. We'll look at literacy rates in the U.S. and beyond and examine what groups are disproportionately placed at a disadvantage due to low literacy.

Internet a "Basic Human Right"? – Information Poverty and the Digital Divide. We'll examine the existence of "information poverty" and a "digital divide" within the U.S. and globally.

You Can't Read That? - The 1st Amendment and Your Librarian. We'll explore the role librarians play in supporting the 1st Amendment Right of freedom of speech, focusing on challenges to books in library collections.

The Kids are All Right? – Youth Rights and Access to Information. We will explore youth rights in relation to access to information, focusing on sexuality information. Amy Elliott, a GSU Librarian who researches Information Access & Services for LGBTQ people, will lead our discussion.

In the Spirit of Thomas Jefferson – Access to Government Information. Joe Hurley, the GSU Government Information Librarian, will lead our discussion of the transparency movement to make government information accessible to the masses.

No More Ivory Towers – Open Access to Scholarly Communication. Nan Seamans, the Dean of the University Library, will lead us in examining the movement to provide Open Access to scholarly information as challenging the power structures of traditional publishing.

This Might Be Shocking – Research Ethics and the "Informed" Research Subject. Ida Martinez, the GSU Psychology Librarian, will lead us in examining landmark cases in which (among other transgressions) withholding or manipulating information given to research subjects resulted in shocking abuses, and subsequently paved the way for establishing research ethics guidelines.

The Doctor's Always Right? – Health Literacy. Sharon Leslie, the GSU Public Health Librarian, will lead us in examining (1) factors that impede access to health information, and (2) patient advocacy for their health.

Legalese and Attorney Fees – Access to the Justice System. We'll consider how legal language and economic inequalities hinder access to legal information and counsel and consequently to the judicial system. Attorneys Beth Stephens and Karen Moskowitz from the Atlanta Legal Aid Society will discuss how their organization addresses these issues.

References

American Library Association. (2012). Library bill of rights. Retrieved from http://www.ala.org/ala/issuesadvocacy/intfreedom/librarybill/index.cfm

Association of College and Research Libraries (ACRL). (2000). Information literacy competency standards for higher education. Retrieved from http://www.ala.org/ala/mgrps/divs/acrl/standards/informationliteracycompetency.cfm

Black, L. L., & Stone, D. (2005). Expanding the definition of privilege: The concept of social privilege. *Journal of Multicultural Counseling and Development, 33*(4), 243–255.

Britz, J. J. (2004). To know or not to know: A moral reflection on information poverty. *Journal of Information Science, 30*(3), 192 -204.

Budd, J. M. (2003). The library, praxis, and symbolic power. *Library Quarterly, 73*(1), 19-32.

Cambridge University Press et al. v. Becker et al. 2012 U.S. Dist. LEXIS 123154 (2012).

Central Intelligence Agency. (2009). Country comparison: Internet users. Retrieved from https://www.cia.gov/library/publications/the-world-factbook/rankorder/2153rank.html

Convention on the Rights of the Child, G.A. res. 44/25, annex, 44 U.N. GAOR Supp. (No. 49) at 167, U.N. Doc. A/44/49 (1989).

Elmborg, J. (2006). Critical information literacy: Implications for instructional practice. *The Journal of Academic Librarianship, 32*(2), 192–199.

Fagan, J. (2003). Students' perceptions of academic librarians. *The Reference Librarian, 37*(78), 131–148.

Freire, P. (2000). *Pedagogy of the oppressed* (30th anniversary ed.). New York: Continuum.

Georgia State University, The Honors College. (2012). Faculty – The Honors College – Georgia State University. Retrieved from http://www.gsu.edu/honors/faculty.html

Hytten, K., & Bettez, S. (2011). Understanding education for social justice. *The*

Journal of Educational Foundations, 25(1/2), 7-24.

Internet for Everyone. (2009). What does digital divide mean to you? Retrieved from http://www.youtube.com/watch?v=fCIB_vXUptY

Internet for Everyone. (n.d.). One nation online. Retrieved from http://www.freepress.net/files/IFE_Brochure.pdf

Jacobs, H. L. M. (2008). Information literacy and reflective pedagogical praxis. *The Journal of Academic Librarianship, 34*(3), 256–262.

Johnson, F. L. (2009). Privilege. In S. W. Littlejohn & K. A. Foss (Eds.), *Encyclopedia of Communication Theory*. Thousand Oaks, CA: Sage Publications Inc.

Kapitzke, C. (2001). Information literacy: The changing library. *Journal of Adolescent & Adult Literacy, 44*(5), 450–456.

Krippendorff, K. (2010). Content analysis. In N. J. Salkind (Ed.), *Encyclopedia of Research Design*. Thousand Oaks, CA: Sage Publications Inc.

Lewis, A. M. (2008). Questioning neutrality: An introduction. In A. M. Lewis (Ed.), *Questioning library neutrality: Essays from Progressive Librarian* (pp. 1-4). Duluth, MN: Library Juice Press.

Luke, A., & Kapitzke, C. (1999). Literacies and libraries: Archives and cybraries. *Pedagogy, Culture & Society, 7*(3), 467–491.

McArthur, J. (2010). Achieving social justice within and through higher education: The challenge for critical pedagogy. *Teaching in Higher Education, 15*(5), 493-504.

McKinnon, S. L. (2009). Critical theory. In S. W. Littlejohn & K. A. Foss (Eds.), *Encyclopedia of communication theory*. Thousand Oaks, CA: Sage Publications Inc.

Miller, P. (2008). Social justice. In L. M. Given (Ed.), *The SAGE encyclopedia of qualitative research methods*. Thousand Oaks, CA: Sage Publications Inc.

Peterson, E. (2010). Problem-based learning as teaching strategy. In M. T. Accardi, E. Drabinski, & A. Kumbier (Eds.), *Critical library instruction: Theories and methods* (pp. 71–80). Duluth, MN: Library Juice Press.

Postman, N. (1985). *Amusing ourselves to death: Public discourse in the age of show business*. New York: Viking.

QSR International. (2011). NVivo9 [computer software]. Doncaster, Victoria, Australia: QSR International.

Seale, M. (2008). Old maids, policeman, and social rejects: Mass media representations and public perceptions of librarians. *Electronic Journal of Academic and Special Librarianship, 9*(1). Retrieved from http://southernlibrarianship.icaap.org/content/v09n01/seale_m01.html

Seale, M. (2010). Information literacy standards and the politics of knowledge production: Using user-generated content to incorporate critical pedagogy. In M. T. Accardi, E. Drabinski, & A. Kumbier (Eds.), *Critical library instruction: Theories and methods* (pp. 221–236). Duluth, MN: Library Juice Press.

Strauss, A. L., & Corbin, J. M. (1998). *Basics of qualitative research: Techniques and procedures for developing grounded theory* (2nd ed.). Thousand Oaks, CA: Sage Publications Inc.

Swygart-Hobaugh, A. J. (Fall 2011). Syllabus - "Information - Power to the People,"

(Georgia State University, Honors Freshman Seminar). Retrieved from http://
works.bepress.com/amanda_swygart-hobaugh/11
Takacs, D. (2002). Positionality, epistemology, and social justice in the classroom.
Social Justice, 29(4), 168–181.
U. S. Census Bureau. (2011). Table 1155. Household internet usage by type of
internet connection and state: 2009; Table 1156. Internet access and usage: 2009.
Statistical Abstract of the United States. Washington, D.C.: U.S. Census Bureau. Retrieved from http://www.census.gov/compendia/statab/2011/tables/11s1155.pdf
World Bank Group. (2011). Internet users (per 100 people). Retrieved from http://
data.worldbank.org/indicator/IT.NET.USER.P2/countries/1W?order=wbapi_
data_value_2009%20wbapi_data_value%20wbapi_data_value-
last&sort=desc&display=default

Community Engagement as Social Change

Information Literacy and Service-Learning: Creating Powerful Synergies

Christopher A. Sweet
Illinois Wesleyan University

> For the first two-thirds of the twentieth century a powerful tide bore Americans into ever deeper engagement in the life of their communities, but a few decades ago–silently, without warning–that tide reversed and we were overtaken by a treacherous rip current. Without at first noticing, we have been pulled apart from one another and from our communities over the last third of the century. (Putnam, 2001, p. 27)
>
> -*Bowling Alone: The Collapse and Revival of American Community.*

Bowling Alone is the highly-influential essay (and later book) by American political scientist Robert Putnam. The title refers to one of Putnam's findings that while more people in the U. S. were bowling, significantly fewer than in the past were participating together in bowling leagues. It's not just declining participation in bowling leagues that should worry us. Putnam gathers a preponderance of evidence that includes shrinking voter turnout, apathy towards participation in community organizations, and decrease in volunteerism. He even found that fewer people were entertaining groups of friends in their homes when compared with earlier generations. Taken together, these trends document an alarming decline in American civic life and "social capital." Putnam (2000) defines social capital as simply: "connections among individuals –social networking and the norm of reciprocity and trustworthiness that arise from them" (p. 19).

Higher education has been largely complicit, and at times, an active contributor to this erosion of social capital and civic engagement. Our nation's earliest institutions of higher education were founded on the concept of educating students to become active, democratic citizens. Service-learning scholar M.W. Smith points out that "Since the founding of Harvard College in 1636, the goals of American higher education have included the preparation of citizens for active involvement in community life" (1994, p.

55). This democratic and civically-minded conception of higher education was still the prevailing philosophy at the beginning of the 20th century. Woodrow Wilson, who was president of Princeton University before he became president of the United States, said in an 1896 commemorative address: "It is not learning, but the spirit of service that will give a college a place in the public annals of history" (Wilson, "Princeton in the Nation's Service"). Our great land-grant institutions as conceived by John Morrill and Abraham Lincoln were based on a "Public University" model that would teach a more practical curriculum in service of the nation. Teaching students to recognize and redress social injustices was for a long time implicit in this educational model.

During much of the same period (second half of the 20th century) in which Putnam traced the decline of American's civic involvement, higher education underwent a sea change in relation to its primary mission. Large research universities in particular were first called upon to support two World Wars by strongly emphasizing the research component of their mission. At the same time there was a trend within disciplines to focus on ever narrower fields of study thereby preserving the expertise and autonomy of a given field of study. In 2000 the Kellogg Commission on the Future of State and Land-Grant Universities declared: "If this nation is to succeed in a new century, the covenant between our institutions and the public they serve must be renewed again and made binding" (2000, "Renewing the Covenant"). As will be discussed later in this chapter, many calls for higher education reform in the last two decades have called for a similar return to civic engagement and experiential education.

Service-learning has been championed by many as one way for higher education to reverse course and engage students with the learning process and for universities to reconnect with their local communities and public service roots. Similarly, information literacy has been called an essential 21st skill and the foundation for lifelong learning. Thoughtfully combining service-learning and information literacy can create a powerful pedagogical foundation to help students connect classroom learning with real-world problems. The purpose of this chapter is to explore the synergies between service-learning and information literacy. In the article, "Where's the

Library in Service Learning?" John Riddle (2003) points out that:

> It would seem that opportunities exist, and have existed for some time, for scholars in both service learning and information literacy to recognize a common ground, perhaps join their efforts to demonstrate the efficacy of these pedagogies. Yet, one can examine separately the library and information science and the service learning scholarly literature and barely find a mention...of the impact of service learning on library services, information literacy, information-seeking behavior, or critical thinking. (p. 71)

To better establish the "common ground" that Riddle mentions, this chapter will first seek to define service-learning and information literacy. Each of these concepts is then situated within contemporary higher education and academic librarianship. Next, the educational and pedagogical theories that undergird service-learning are summarized. The chapter grounds the discussion of combining service-learning and information literacy with a case-study of an Environmental Studies course which the author co-taught. In way of summary, the synergies created by combining service-learning and information literacy are discussed and a list of emerging best practices for combining service-learning and information literacy is provided.

Defining Service-Learning and Information Literacy

Service-Learning

As with any term that seeks to encompass a broad range of practices there has been a good deal of dissension when attempting to define service-learning. A 1990 review of the service-learning literature found 147 different terms and definitions related to service-learning (Kendall, 1990). Since that time, the creation of a few large, national organizations dedicated to service-learning has helped to establish some consensus regarding basic definitions of service-learning. The *National Service-Learning Clearinghouse* defines service-learning as follows: "Service-Learning is a teaching and learning strategy that integrates meaningful community service with instruction and reflection to enrich the learning experience, teach civic responsibility, and strengthen communities" (National Service-Learning Clearinghouse). *Learn and Serve America*[1] offers a similar definition: "Service-learning engages students in the educational process, using what they learn in the classroom to solve real-life problems. Students not only learn about democracy and citizenship, they become actively contributing citizens and community members through the service they perform" (Learn and Serve America). The most basic principle of service-learning has been stated as: "Service, combined with learning, adds value to each and transforms both" (Honnet & Poulsen, 1996, p. 1). Complicating the matter somewhat, is the fact that the terms "action research" and "community-based education" are often used interchangeably with "service-learning." Service-learning, action research, and community-based education are all forms of experiential learning that engage students with problems in their local communities. Determining whether or not a given course has all the characteristics of a service-learning course almost has to be done on a case-by-case basis. For example, sometimes action research courses place more emphasis on the doing (the action) and less on the critical reflection that is a key component of service-learning.

The greatest struggle in defining service-learning has arisen from the need to differentiate it from simple community service or volunteerism on one end of the spectrum and internships on the other end. Part of the difficulty lies in the fact that community service is a critical component of service-learning. At issue is whether or not the service is grounded in the academic curriculum and whether or not opportunities are provided for critical reflection upon the service. Isolated community service still has some benefits to both students and the community, but it can't accomplish curricular learning outcomes in and of itself. On the other end of the spectrum internships are also a common form of experiential education that is often conflated with service-learning. Similar to isolated community service, many internships are just focused on the experience without specific grounding in the curriculum or critical reflection. Depending on

---

1 The National Service-Learning Clearinghouse (est. 1997) and Learn and Serve America (est. 2001) are both national service-learning organizations funded by the federal Corporation for National and Community Service. Taken together, these two organizations have been quite influential in promoting service-learning in the U.S.

the structure and requirements of the internship, though, it could be made into a genuine service-learning experience.

The following example and diagram attempt to clarify service-learning. The *National Youth Leadership Council* provides this succinct distinction between service, learning, and service-learning.

* Cleaning up a riverbank is SERVICE
* Sitting in a science classroom looking at water samples under a microscope is LEARNING
* Science students taking samples from local water sources, then analyzing the samples, documenting the results and presenting the scientific information to a pollution control agency is SERVICE-LEARNING (National Youth Leadership Council, 2012)

Prominent service-learning scholar Andrew Furco developed the diagram below to help illustrate the differences between community service, service-learning, internships and other forms of experiential education.

SERVICE ENGAGEMENT
(Service Learning)

| RECIPIENT | ← | BENEFICIARY | → | PROVIDER |

| SERVICE | ← | FOCUS | → | LEARNING |

SERVICE LEARNING

COMMUNITY SERVICE | FIELD EDUCATION

VOLUNTEERISM | INTERNSHIP

(Furco, 1996)

Information Literacy

The terms information literacy and service-learning are roughly contemporary in their origins. Service-learning was first used as a distinct term in the mid-sixties while the term information literacy was coined in the mid-seventies (Zurkowski, 1974). Both terms were created to better codify a group of practices that had been occurring in both fields for a long period of time. In education the idea of experiential education was popularized by John Dewey in the early 20th century and then faded from prominence only to re-emerge during the social unrest of the 1960s. In academic librarianship "bibliographic instruction" sessions led by librarians had been used to teach students the fundamentals of academic research for decades. Similar to service-learning the most oft-cited definition of information literacy comes from a prominent national organization, in this case the *Association of College and Research Libraries* (ACRL): "Information literacy is a set of abilities requiring individuals to recognize when information is needed and have the ability to locate, evaluate, and use effectively the needed information" (Presidential Committee on Information Literacy, 1989). In the years since this definition became the standard one for the profession, many have criticized it as far too narrow and limiting. The detractors point out that the inherent civic and political aspects of information literacy are largely absent in the ACRL definition and the related Information Literacy Competency Standards. In 2005, the *International Federation of Library Associations and Federations* crafted *The Alexandria Proclamation* which highlights the sociopolitical aspects of information literacy:

> Information Literacy lies at the core of lifelong learning. It empowers people in all walks of life to seek, evaluate, use and create information effectively to achieve their personal, social, occupational and educational goals. It is a basic human right in a digital world and promotes social inclusion of all nations. Lifelong learning enables individuals, communities and nations to attain their goals and to take advantage of emerging opportunities in the evolving global environment for shared benefit. It assists them and their institutions to meet technological, economic and social challenges, to redress disadvantage and to advance the well being of all. (Alexandria Proclamation, 2005)

Within the expanded definition of information literacy provided by the *Alexandria Proclamation* one can begin to see some of the potential synergies of combining service-learning and information literacy as both are concerned with empowerment, social justice, and civic engagement. Some scholars have argued that the library profession shouldn't get hung up in debates over the definition of information literacy, but rather move towards a "critical practice of librarianship" (Elmborg, 2006). In an 2006 article entitled "Critical Information Literacy: Implications for Instructional Practice," James Elmborg asserts that "The real challenge for libraries in treating information literacy seriously lies not in defining it or describing it, but in developing a critical practice of librarianship- a theoretically informed praxis" (p. 198). Praxis is the recursive process whereby theory informs practice and practice informs theory. This chapter makes a small contribution towards the goal of developing a critical practice of librarianship through documenting the synergies between service-learning and information literacy and grounding both in sound educational theory.

Situating Service-Learning within Higher Education

To fully understand the role of service-learning in modern higher education, it is important to recognize recent national calls for education reform and increased civic engagement. The National Service-Learning Clearinghouse maintains an annotated history of service-learning that begins with the 1862 Morrill Act that established land grant institutions. For the purposes of this chapter, only the more recent history of significant events that shaped the service-learning movement within higher education will be considered.

The turmoil and activism of the 1960's created the foundation for a return to service marked by the civil rights movement, the formation of the Peace Corps, and Lyndon Johnson's Volunteers in Service to America (VISTA) program. Educational philosopher Paulo Freire published his highly influential *Pedagogy of the Oppressed* in 1970. In this work Freire repositioned education as an inherently political act that could actually bring about revolution and liberation.

The early to mid 1980s saw a resurgence of interest in campus service and service-learning, with multiple high-profile critiques of higher education. Probably the most well known of these was *A Nation at Risk* published in 1983 by the *National Commission on Excellence in Education*. The commission's report took great pains to make it clear that American higher education was foundering:

> Our Nation is at risk... the educational foundations of our society are presently being eroded by a rising tide of mediocrity that threatens our very future as a Nation and a people...Our concern, however, goes well beyond matters such as industry and commerce. It also includes

the intellectual, moral, and spiritual strengths of our people which knit together the very fabric of our society... A high level of shared education is essential to a free, democratic society and to the fostering of a common culture, especially in a country that prides itself on pluralism and individual freedom. (p. 5)

A Nation at Risk was in many ways a wake-up call for public higher education which in previous decades had cultivated a great deal of autonomy and had grown used to very little outside oversight or assessment. In 1985, shortly after the publication of *A Nation at Risk*, the presidents of Brown, Georgetown and Stanford came together to create *Campus Compact*. The mission of *Campus Compact* is to "advance the public purposes of colleges and universities by deepening their ability to improve community life and to educate students for civic and social responsibility." Today *Campus Compact* includes more than 1,100 colleges and universities, representing 6 million students (Campus Compact, "Who We Are").

Following in the footsteps of the great educational reformers John Dewey and Paulo Freire, Ernest Boyer became known as one of the late 20th century's most influential critics of education. He was commissioner of education under President Jimmy Carter and then served for 16 years as president of the *Carnegie Foundation for the Advancement of Teaching*. While working for *Carnegie Foundation*, he authored a number of important reports including *College: The Undergraduate Experience in America* (1987). A call for experiential education and a return to service were the core components of Boyer's philosophy:

> Boyer believed strongly in a broad concept of service at every level of education as a way of connecting schools to the world beyond the campus, while simultaneously creating an ethical base for learning. He felt that students, from the first-grader to the doctoral candidate, should understand that they have something to offer their communities. Serving was for him a critical part of the human experience, one of the ways in which we understand and fulfill life's purposes. (Coye, 1997, p. 22)

One of the next major milestones in the service-learning movement was the *Wingspread Declaration of Renewing the Civic Mission of the American Research University* written in 1999. This document is the final product of Wingspread conferences held in 1998 and 1999. These conferences involved a veritable who's who in American higher education including university presidents, provosts, deans, and faculty members as well as representatives of professional associations, private foundations, and civic organizations. The *Wingspread Declaration* concludes as follows:

> Research universities and leaders from all levels of our institutions need to rise to the occasion of our challenge as a democracy on the edge of a new millennium. We need to help catalyze and lead a national campaign or movement that reinvigorates the public purposes and civic mission of our great research universities and higher education broadly. We need to renew for the next century the idea that our institutions of higher education are, in a vital sense, both agents and architects of a flourishing democracy, bridges between individuals' work and the larger world. (Boyte and Hollander, p. 14)

Two more examples will serve to document the continued momentum of the service-learning movement in the 21st century. The *Carnegie Commission on Higher Education* first began the Carnegie Classification system in 1970 to help distinguish between the wide array of colleges and universities that make up the American education system. Some of the characteristics that the system uses to rank institutions include curricula, degrees offered, student enrollment, etc. In an acknowledgement of the growing importance of a return to civic engagement and the service-learning movement, the *Carnegie Classification on Community Engagement* was created in 2006. According to Carnegie, the Community Engagement Classification, "describes the collaboration between institutions of higher education and their larger communities (local, regional/state, national, global) for the mutually beneficial exchange of knowledge and resources in a context of partnership and reciprocity" (Carnegie Foundation, online). Elective classifications are voluntary and require substantially more evidence from an institution and are therefore more difficult to achieve. As of 2010, 115 institutions had been awarded this prestigious classification.

A final example demonstrates support for service-learning in higher education. In 2008, the influential Association of American Colleges and Universities (AACU) released a report on *High-Impact Educational Practices: What They Are, Who Has Access to Them, and Why They Matter.* The introduction to the report notes that high-impact educational practices speak, "...

directly to what is arguably our most important national challenge in higher education: helping America's extraordinarily diverse students reap the full benefits –economic, civic, and personal- of their studies in college" (Kuh, 2008, p. 1). These practices are derived from recent research on student engagement. The report's author, George Kuh, identifies ten high-impact educational practices. While all ten high-impact practices could be applied to service-learning courses, the two that are most relevant to the subject matter of this chapter are Service Learning / Community-Based Learning and Undergraduate Research. In his description of service-learning experiences Kuh explicitly distinguishes authentic service-learning from community service:

> The idea is to give students direct experience with issues they are studying in the curriculum and with ongoing efforts to analyze and solve problems in the community. A key element in these programs is the opportunity students have to both apply what they are learning in real-world settings and reflect in a classroom setting on their service experiences. (2008, p. 11)

The point of recounting this brief history of higher education reform and the service-learning movement is to enable the reader to better understand how service-learning can be used to fulfill the missions of many institutions and re-engage students in the learning process. The success and integration of service-learning into the undergraduate curriculum requires continued advocacy. To be an effective advocate for service-learning it is essential to understand contemporary calls for higher education reform and how service-learning can enable some of those reforms.

Situating Service-Learning and Information Literacy within Academic Libraries

As mentioned above, undergraduate research was one of the high-impact educational practices identified by the AACU in 2008. The potential synergies between information literacy and service-learning become more apparent in relation to undergraduate research. Intensive undergraduate research, whether in the sciences or the humanities, requires information literacy skills at every stage, from forming a hypothesis through synthesizing results. Service-learning and research are high-impact educational practices that can easily be combined in a single course. Before exploring those synergies more fully, the following section situates both service-learning and information literacy within the contemporary academic library environment.

The earliest American conception of the "Free Public Library" was based on the idea that citizens in a democracy require equal access to information to fulfill their civic duties. In the preface to *Libraries and Democracy: the Cornerstones of Liberty*, Nancy Kranich (2001) writes:

> Democracies need libraries. An informed public constitutes the very foundation of a democracy; after all, democracies are about discourse – discourse among the people. If a free society is to survive, it must ensure the preservation of its records and provide free and open access to this information to its citizens. It must ensure that citizens have the resources to develop the information literacy skills necessary to participate in the democratic process. It must allow unfettered dialogue and guarantee freedom of expression. Libraries deepen the foundation of democracy in our communities. (p. *v*)

As noted above, information literacy is a relatively new term, but its' key components: accessing, evaluating, synthesizing and ethically using information pervade the historical foundations of American libraries.

In the last 30 years, higher education as a whole has generally focused more on the essential concepts and processes that are critical to learning. Library instruction has followed suit with an increased focus on "big picture" learning goals in addition to teaching basic research tools and skills. This marked the beginning of a transition from focusing on academic libraries as more than just passive repositories of information to the concept of "Teaching Libraries." A teaching library "is characterized by its commitment to instruction as a core library service and by robust instructional service program that reflects not only the teaching and learning that goes on in the classroom, but also that which goes on in the co-curriculum, the extra-curriculum, and the surrounding community" (Scott, 2007 p. 2).

As mentioned earlier, information literacy was introduced as a distinct term in the 1970s, but it didn't gain universal recognition as a core component of the modern academic library until the *American Library Association* (ALA) formed the *Presidential Committee on Information Literacy* in 1987. The committee was formed with three specific purposes:

• to define Information Literacy within the higher literacies and its importance to student performance, lifelong learning, and active citizenship;
• to design one or more models for information literacy development appropriate to formal and informal learning environments throughout people's lifetimes; and
• to determine implications for the continuing education and development for teachers. (American Library Association's Presidential Committee on Information Literacy, 1989, online)

It took more than ten years for the library profession to create an agreed upon set of *Information Literacy Competency Standards for Higher Education* (2000). The five standards and twenty-two performance indicators were designed as a framework for assessing the information literacy abilities of students. The information literate student:

• defines and articulates the need for information;
• accesses needed information effectively and efficiently;
• evaluates information and its sources critically and incorporates selected information into his or her knowledge base and value system;
• uses information effectively to accomplish a specific purpose; and
• understands many of the economic, legal, and social issues surrounding the use of information and accesses and uses information ethically and legally
    (ACRL, 2000, online)

These standards were successful in creating a standardized framework for assessing information literacy, but some have criticized the standards as sterilizing information literacy and diminishing the larger sociopolitical contexts of information literacy. Jacobs (2008) elaborated on this point when she wrote: "This is not to say that we should not use the ACRL standards… we need to use them judiciously so that information literacy's tremendous potential for creative, critical and visionary thinking does not become –literally and figuratively- boxed in and compartmentalized"

(Jacobs, 2008, p. 258).

It should be noted that the existence of these standards has contributed greatly to legitimizing information literacy within higher education. It should also be noted that the *Information Literacy Competency Standards* listed above are currently (2012) being revised. An important question for the library profession, and the arguments put forth in this chapter, is whether or not these standards work for assessing information literacy within service-learning contexts? Are the core goals of service-learning courses which include fostering civic engagement and using classroom knowledge to solve real-world problems adequately covered by the standards? One could argue that these pedagogical goals are implicit in the Information Literacy Competency Standards, but a direct correlation is not there.

In their seminal work *Where's the Learning in Service-Learning?*, Eyler and Giles (1999) recount the results of a national survey of over 1500 students in service-learning classes. Although none of the survey questions asked students directly about information literacy or the research process, some of the conclusions the authors reached demonstrate the need to better integrate information literacy and service-learning. For example, the survey found that "Service Learning students talked more about the need to gather information and define issues regarding community problem solving" (Riddle, 2003, p. 73). This finding aligns quite closely with the Information Literacy Competency Standards, #1 and #2. The authors also concluded that "Service learning students are better able to apply subject concepts, authorities, and information to new problems" (p. 73). Applying concepts and information to new problems shows that students in service-learning courses are meeting standards #3 and #4. These survey findings demonstrate some of the synergies that can be created when service-learning and information literacy are combined. Combining information literacy and service-learning makes sense not only from the perspective of meeting standards, but it also ties into important trends within the library profession. The ACRL *Research Planning and Review Committee* regularly reviews the recent library science literature and administers a broad-based survey to determine "Top Trends in Academic Libraries." The 2010 report included ten trends, one of them especially relevant to the subject matter of this chapter: "Increased collaboration will expand the role of the library within the institution and beyond. Collaboration efforts will continue to diversify: collaborating with faculty to integrate library resources into the curriculum and to seek out information literacy instruction, and as an embedded librarian" (2010 Top Trends, p. 287-288).

Embedded librarianship is an important trend within academic libraries and was the model used in the case study discussed later in the chapter. The term was first applied to journalists who were "embedded" on the frontlines of the Iraq War. The embedded librarian model is, of course, far less dangerous than the embedded journalist model, but both involve close, extended interactions. In a final report to the Special Libraries Association, titled "Models of Embedded Librarianship" Shumaker and Talley (2010) specify that embedded librarianship involves: "focusing on the needs of one or more specific groups, building relationships with these groups, developing a deep understanding of their work, and providing information services that are highly customized and targeted to their greatest needs. It involves shifting the model from transactional to high trust, close collaboration, and shared responsibility of outcomes" (p. 9). This discussion of embedded librarianship as an important trend is significant because it is one of the best models for integrating information literacy into service-learning courses. There is certainly value in offering traditional "one-shot" research instruction sessions to students in service-learning courses, but to maximize the synergies between service-learning and information literacy a more intimate, extended relationship is required.

One final example will serve to further situate information literacy with service-learning in the modern academic library environment. In 2011, ACRL released an updated strategic plan (*ACRL Plan for Excellence*). This plan begins with a "Vivid Description of a Desired Future" for academic libraries that includes: "Librarians drive and enable transformation of libraries, student learning, and scholarly research by building powerful coalitions and collaborations, setting standards, exploring innovative methods and approaches, modeling behavior, and embedding their results in dynamic user environments" (ACRL, 2011). Beneath the heading of "Student Learning" is the following goal: "Librarians transform student learning, pedagogy, and instructional practices through creative and innovative collaborations" (ACRL, 2011). One method to meet these challenges is through library integration with service-learning courses.

To best advocate for integration of information literacy into the academic curriculum it is important for librarians to be able to demonstrate that information literacy is not just part of the academic library agenda, but is increasingly recognized by educational associations, government organizations and corporate America as an essential 21st century skill. As our country continues its conversion to an information economy, businesses are demanding that educational institutions produce information literate graduates. In 2002, the U.S. Department of Education in conjunction with major businesses including Apple, Dell, Microsoft and Cisco, formed the *Partnership for 21st Century Skills*. This group identified information literacy as a key 21st century skill students need "to succeed as effective citizens, workers and leaders" ("Partnership," n.d.).

In addition to *AACU*'s "High Impact Educational Practices" another important initiative called "Liberal Education and America's Promise" has specifically recognized information literacy as one of the "Essential Learning Outcomes." Beyond academia, the importance of information literacy in the 21st Century was acknowledged through a Presidential Proclamation when Barack Obama designated October 2009, *National Information Literacy Awareness Month*. The Proclamation notes, "In addition to the basic skills of reading, writing, and arithmetic, it is equally important that our students are given the tools required to take advantage of the information available to them. The ability to seek, find, and decipher information can be applied to countless life decisions, whether financial, medical, educational, or technical" (Obama, 2009).

Situating service-learning and information literacy within higher education and the academic library environment was a necessary exercise in understanding how both have evolved and how they meet modern educational challenges. As Fowler and Walter pointed out in a 2003 article, library "instruction programs are becoming increasingly complex, and ever more closely tied to initiatives of import across the campus because of broader trends both in the profession and in higher education" (p. 466).

The next step in developing a praxis of service-learning and information literacy is grounding both in educational theory and philosophy. Without this theoretical grounding it is all too easy to discount service-learning as mere community service lacking in academic rigor.

Towards a Philosophy of Service-Learning Wedded to Information Literacy

According to James Elmborg, "instructional librarianship requires extensive knowledge of pedagogies and of the cultures and discourse communities of higher education" (2006, p. 198). Without this theoretical background it is difficult to effectively argue for integration of information literacy into the academic curriculum, yet very little attention is given to educational theory and pedagogy in most library and information science degree programs. In regards to promotion and tenure for librarians it is quite useful to be able to explain the theoretical underpinnings of time-intensive activities such as teaching in service-learning courses and embedded librarianship.

Dewey

Service-learning most often looks to constructivist educational theories for support. Constructivist theorists say that people construct their own understanding and knowledge of the world, through experiencing things and reflecting on those experiences. As such experiential and active learning are common constructivist pedagogies. John Dewey (1859-1952) is generally recognized as the founding father of constructivism.

Dewey's educational philosophy is based on three principles:

• Education must lead to personal growth.
• Education must contribute to humane conditions.
• Education must engage citizens in association with one another (Hatcher, 1997)

Given these three core principles, it is easy to see why Dewey's constructivist theories are so often cited in support of service-learning. Any well-designed service-learning course will lead to personal growth, contribute to humane conditions, and engage citizens in association with one another. Also central to Dewey's theories was the need to reconcile naturally arising dualisms in the educational process. For example he states that the classic knowledge versus action dualism can be resolved through a process of experience and reflection. This same dualism when encountered in service-learning courses is also resolved through critical reflection upon the service experiences. Another dualism that was important to Dewey was individual versus society. Dewey argued that this particular dualism could be resolved by combining education with civic participation, another cornerstone of service-learning. For Dewey, service was inextricably linked to education: "When the school introduces and trains each child of society into membership within such a little community, saturating him with the spirit of service, and providing him with the instruments of effective self-direction, we shall have the deepest and best guarantee of a larger society which is worthy, lovely, and harmonious" (1900, p. 44).

Freire

Paulo Freire (1921-1997) was a Brazilian professor and educational theorist. In some ways Freire was responsible for a re-popularizing of a constructivist approach similar to that advocated by Dewey. Freire's theories as exemplified in his well-known *Pedagogy of the Oppressed* (1970) diverged from Dewey in their radical foundations. Freire believed that education was an inherently political act and could be used to overcome oppression and could even lead to revolution. Ira Shor lists the basic descriptors of Freirean pedagogy as "participatory, situated (in student thought and language), critical, democratic, dialogic, desocializing, multi-cultural, research-oriented, activist and affective" (Deans, 1999, p. 21). Another key component of Freirean pedagogy is the development of critical consciousness. Critical consciousness is the ability to perceive social, political, and economic oppression and to take action against the oppressive elements of society. Critical consciousness consisted of four primary components: "power awareness (understanding social history), critical literacy (analytically reading, writing and discussing social matters), desocialization (examining the internalized myths and values of mass culture), and self-organization/self-education (taking initiative in ongoing social change) (Deans, 1999, p. 22). Service-learning advocates cite Freire's theories to support both the educational and social goals of service-learning. Service-learning courses can develop critical consciousness in students by opening their eyes to oppressive structures in society and education. In *Service-Learning and Social Justice* (2010), Susan Benigni Cipolle does an excellent job documenting service-learning's ability to develop critical consciousness in students. In this work, Cipolle provides many direct quotations from students in service-learning courses that show their awakening to social justice issues. For example, one student commented:

> My experiences helped me realize that there are so many disenfran-chised people in this country for whatever reasons. You learn that it is not fair or appropriate to blame individuals for their poverty or other problems. Somewhere along the line the community or government has failed them. (p. 24)

Praxis is also an important component of Freire's theories. He defines praxis in *Pedagogy of the Oppressed* as "reflection and action upon the world in order to transform it" (1986, p. 36). Here again the Freirean roots of service-learning are apparent. Service-learning courses require both action and critical reflection before any meaningful transformations can occur. Thomas Deans (1999) compares Dewey and Freire in regards to service-learning and concludes:

> Both offer sound theoretical frameworks for service-learning. They overlap on several key characteristics essential to any philosophy of service-learning: an anti-foundationalist epistemology; an affirmation of the centrality of experience in learning; an articulation of the intimate relationship between action, reflection, and learning; an emphasis on dialogue; and an abiding hope for social change through education combined with community action. (p. 26)

Dewey and Freire are probably the best known theorists whose work is often cited as the basis for service-learning. Contemporary theorists such as David Kolb (1981) and recent developments in cognitive psychology also support service-learning as a viable pedagogy. This brief overview lays the groundwork for the following case study, as well as further discussions on information literacy and service learning in higher education.

Case Study: Creating a Sustainable Society: Illinois Wesleyan University's Environmental Studies Senior Seminar

In the spring of 2010, a call for proposals went out to Illinois Wesleyan University faculty that sought ideas for incorporating some of the above-mentioned AACU "High-Impact Educational Practices" into our campus curriculum. Funded by a grant from the Teagle Foundation, the call was for "teams of faculty (two or more participants), to submit proposals for curricular initiatives that would focus upon developing, implementing and assessing the consequences on faculty work of a variety of 'high-impact' pedagogical practices that reflect progressively more radical approaches to changing faculty work through engaging in a collaborative effort." I serve as the library liaison to the Environmental Studies Program and had in the past successfully worked with a variety of faculty and courses. The senior seminar capstone course is titled "Creating a Sustainable Society" and is designed around a service-learning model. This seminar also met the criteria for "Writing-Intensive Courses, Focus on Undergraduate Research and Capstone Courses." In short, the course was a perfect candidate for exploring how collaborative faculty efforts could help to promote these practices on our campus.

Because of its integration of research, writing, and service learning, the Environmental Studies Senior Seminar exemplifies the service-learning model and engagement with local communities. Students enrolled in this course each "identify a specific environmental project, find a community partner interested in the project, design [a] project in consultation with the community partner, conduct the research, and offer policy proposals" (course syllabus). According to the department chair, Dr. Abby Jahiel, who designed this course, it also serves another pedagogical goal. Jahiel explains that the very nature of Environmental Studies can be depressing. Over the course of four years students learn about the vast array of environmental problems facing our society. Some of these problems exist on a worldwide scale such as global warming, ocean pollution and deforestation. At the end of their studies Jahiel wanted to show students that they could make a contribution towards sustainability and social justice in their own communities. Like any well-designed service-learning course the service is contextualized through classroom learning and critical reflection. Students have to complete a thorough literature review to demonstrate an intimate understanding of the issues surrounding their topic; they must conduct focused, detailed, research to produce successful projects; and they must use this research to demonstrate to their community partners the feasibility of their proposals. Information literacy was always a critical component of this course, but after the approval of this new collaboration, I became embedded in the course by becoming a co-teacher who was actively involved in every class session.

At 13 students, this was Illinois Wesleyan's largest-ever Environmental Studies Senior Seminar. This may seem like an enviably small number, but given the additional demands of service-learning courses, it would have been incredibly difficult to teach the course in the same manner as in previous semesters with one instructor. Preparatory work for this class always begins many months before the class begins. Students are actually brought together the semester before the seminar begins so that we can communicate expectations and encourage students to think about projects they may want to pursue. There is also a great deal of communication that needs to occur between faculty members and representatives of various community organizations before, during, and after the class. Rather than teaching specific content such as international environmental politics, this course focuses primarily on social science research methods. In addition to learning how to do comprehensive research for their literature review, students also learn how to conduct interviews, focus groups, and surveys.

The majority of the student projects included environmental or social justice elements in addition to sustainability goals. One successful project involved a student who researched ways to alleviate "food deserts"[2] and to provide access to healthy foods in an economically depressed area near

---

2 Food deserts occur anywhere in industrialized countries where access to healthy, affordable foods is either difficult or non-existent.

the Wesleyan campus. His project eventually led to creating a system for area residents on the Supplemental Nutrition Assistance Plan (formerly food stamps) to use their cards at the local farmers market. This concept has now been applied to other farmers markets in Illinois and around the country (Hatch, 2009). During the semester that I co-taught the course, students were working on projects such as: improving the inclusion of minorities in local environmental work, bringing back endangered barn owls, establishing a campus eco-house, and documenting the environmental benefits of roadside prairies.

Embedding in this course was the single most meaningful teaching experience in my career as an academic librarian. I observed students apply research to solve local sustainability problems. I also built rapport with students far beyond the normal one- or two- shot library instruction sessions. This sentiment was echoed by other librarians who have either taught, or been embedded in service-learning courses. Maureen Barry, regarding her experiences embedded in a composition course at Wright State University writes, "It was, without a doubt, the most positive and extensive interaction I have experienced with undergraduates aside from those in my own IL courses" (2011, p. 9). Nancy Herther, on her work with service-learning classes at the University of Minnesota, said they have "allowed for deeper, more personal, ongoing contact with students... Long after the course is over, I often get e-mails asking for assistance with other classes, advice on job hunting, etc. Making this type of connection with undergraduates is rare in academic libraries" (2008, p. 387). I would add to this that librarians experience many of the hardships of teaching, but miss out on some of these fundamental rewards. As a whole librarians care about enabling lifelong learning and educating our students so that they have the opportunity to become effective citizens, employees, and parents. This type of education happens over time and the results can't be seen within the confines of visiting a class once or twice.

After teaching this course it is my belief that service-learning is one of the most effective methods for teaching students information literacy skills and concepts. Service-learning courses are such an effective model for teaching information literacy because students begin to understand how research is used in the "real world." Most academic research is done in a sort of vacuum; as part of a course assignment that ends when the professor grades the final product. In this service-learning model, students were held accountable to the community partner and conducted research to find the feasibility of their project, established best practices, similar projects, potential problems, etc. Information literacy and the ability to evaluate information are certainly essential life skills, but many undergraduates only experience research as means for meeting the bibliography quota on a term paper. On the final course evaluation when asked, *What did your experience conducting research and working on a real world problem teach you?*, one student responded: "I learned that it is quite enjoyable researching a topic you're passionate about. This was my first opportunity to do so in such depth. I also learned what a difference one person can make in making something happen." Another student when asked, *What is the most significant outcome you've gained from this course?*, responded: "I am proud that I actually did something meaningful instead of another seemingly pointless class project." These student comments highlight the synergies that can be created when service-learning is combined with information literacy.

Service-Learning and Information Literacy Synergies

As stated earlier, the most basic principle of service-learning can be summarized as: "Service, combined with learning, adds value to each and transforms both" (Honnet & Poulsen, 1989). This statement could be modified to capture the synergies between service-learning and information literacy: "Service-learning, combined with information literacy adds value to each and transforms both." The integration assists students with understanding the "why" and "how" behind a service-learning project. Service-learning that is not properly situated within the appropriate sociopolitical contexts is simple volunteerism. Information literacy requires students to seek, evaluate and synthesize information. Most well-designed service-learning courses require this sort of background research from students to better understand the problems at hand and the organizations/communities that students will be working with. This type of contextual research may not be referred to as information literacy by either the instructor or students, but it is quite commonplace in most authentic service-learning courses. As Hernandez and Knight point out, "The learning goals of SL [service-learning] can be enhanced by intentional inclusion of information literacy in the curriculum to foster a broader understanding of the relationship between agencies and the communities that they serve based on the social, political and historical issues at play" (2010, p. 10). To improve involvement with service-learning efforts, academic libraries could identify information literacy elements that are already part of service-learning courses on campus and suggest ways to strengthen and improve those components.

Reflection upon service activities is another essential component of service-learning courses and another place where information literacy can play a strong supporting role. Basic reflection activities might include student journaling about service experiences or follow-up classroom discussions. Many service-learning advocates, in particular those who ground service-learning in Paulo Freire's theories, call for much more rigorous reflection: "While there are many worthwhile service projects that meet real needs in the community, for service-learning to be critical, students and teachers need to examine issues of power, privilege, and oppression; question the hidden bias and assumptions of race, class and gender; and to work to change the social and economic system for equity and justice" (Cipolle, 2010, p. 5). This sort of thoughtful, nuanced reflection is impossible to achieve without the application of information literacy skills. Providing students with information literacy instruction can greatly strengthen and enhance the reflection component of service-learning courses.

Combining service-learning and information literacy also strengthens the information literacy side of the equation. At the beginning of this chapter I recounted the challenge made by James Elmborg for libraries to develop a praxis of "Critical Information Literacy" (2006). Strategic collaboration with service-learning courses is one method to meet this challenge. In her article, "Information Literacy and Reflective Pedagogical Praxis" Heidi Jacobs notes "What I am suggesting is that the dialogues we have surrounding information literacy instruction strive to find a balance in the daily and the visionary, the local and the global, the practices and the theories, the ideal and the possible" (2008, p. 258). Combining service-learning and information literacy is one way to resolve the dualisms mentioned by Jacobs. Within the service-learning environment many of the lofty, abstract goals, such as increasing civic engagement and promoting social justice, of information literacy are made concrete through application to very real-world problems. Instead of conducting research for yet another academic paper which will only be read by the professor, students do research to solve an actual problem in their local community. Furthermore, the results are often shared with partnering organizations and their local communities. This outside audience often motivates students to go above and beyond in their research and writing for service-learning courses.

Outside of the direct pedagogical benefits in the classroom, combining service-learning and information literacy can lead to powerful synergies for accomplishing institutional and library missions. Many institutional mission statements or strategic plans include something about increasing students' civic engagement. Service-learning courses, in particular service-learning courses with a strong information literacy component, are one way to advance these goals.

Emerging Best Practices for Library Support of Service-Learning Courses

As discussed above, the scholarly literature that examines combining service-learning and information literacy is scant, at best. This list of emerging best practices is a first attempt at providing some guidelines to libraries wanting to support and enhance service-learning on their campuses.

• Be able to situate both service-learning and information literacy within pedagogical theory and higher education reform movements.
• When appropriate be able to tie service-learning to institutional and library mission statements and/or strategic plans.
• Identify existing information literacy elements in service-learning courses and explain how they could be strengthened through collaboration with the library.
• Focus on information literacy's ability to strengthen the contextual-

izing and reflection portions of service-learning courses.
• Know your campus organizations and faculty that are involved in service-learning
• Know your local social service organizations and their needs.
• Monitor listservs that focus on service-learning such as those maintained by Campus Compact and the National Service-Learning Clearinghouse.
• Collaborative, embedded librarian models are one of the best ways to support service-learning, but one-shot research instruction sessions can also be of benefit to service-learning courses.
• Librarian-led courses, particularly information literacy courses, can also benefit when structured around a service-learning model.

Final Thoughts

This chapter began with a quote that summarized the main theme of Robert Putnam's *Bowling Alone*. Taken out of context, that quote would seem to indicate a doom and gloom vision of civic engagement that peaked mid-20th century and has been in decline ever since. While documenting that decline is the primary focus of *Bowling Alone*, Putnam makes it clear that he believes American civic engagement is cyclical:

> It is emphatically not my view that community bonds in America have weakened steadily throughout our history- or even throughout the last hundred years. On the contrary, American history carefully examined is a story of ups and downs in civic engagement, *not just downs* –a story of collapse *and* of renewal...it is within our power to reverse the decline of the last several decades. (p. 25)

In a follow-up work to *Bowling Alone*, called *Better Together: Restoring the American Community*, Putnam and co-author Lewis Felstein document individuals and groups that are actively promoting social activism and civic renewal. Interestingly, one of the examples of civic renewal that this book cites is the revival of the Chicago Public Library system. The authors note

> The CPL [Chicago Public Library] thrives today because it embodies a new idea of how a library functions. No longer a passive repository of books and information or an outpost of culture, quiet and decorum in a noisy world, the new library is an active and responsive part of the

community and an agent of change. (2004, p. 35)

In the same manner, enthusiastic academic library support of service-learning can also lead to increases in social capital and civic engagement. Powerful synergies are created when information literacy and service-learning are combined. These courses teach students to apply classroom knowledge to become "agents of change" and to address real social justice issues in their local communities. Recent calls for the reform of the American system of higher education and a return to its civic roots have been broad-based and influential. If American civic engagement comes and goes in waves as Putnam suggests, then embracing the service-learning movement may be one of the best ways for higher education, to turn the tide in the 21st century.

References

ACRL Research Planning and Review Committee. (2010). 2010 top ten trends in academic libraries: A review of the current literature. *College & Research Libraries News, 71*(6), 286-292.

American Library Association's Presidential Committee on Information Literacy. (1989). *Presidential committee on information literacy: Final report.* American Library Association. Retrieved from http://www.ala.org/acrl/publications/whitepapers/presidential

Association of College and Research Libraries. (2011). *ACRL plan for excellence.* Retrieved from http://www.ala.org/acrl/aboutacrl/strategicplan/stratplan

Association of College and Research Libraries. *Information literacy competency standards for higher education.* Retrieved from http://www.ala.org/acrl/standards/informationliteracycompetency

Barry, M. (2011). Research for the greater good: Incorporating service learning in an information literacy course at Wright State University. *College & Research Libraries News, 72*(6), 345-348.

Boyte, H., & Hollander, E. (1999). Wingspread declaration on renewing the civic mission of the American research university. Retrieved from http://www.compact.org/initiatives/trucen/wingspread-declaration-on-the-civic-responsibilities-of-research-universities/

Campus Compact. Who we are. Retrieved from http://www.compact.org/about/history-mission-vision/

Carnegie Foundation. Community engagement elective classification. Retrieved from http://classifications.carnegiefoundation.org/descriptions/community_engagement.php

Cipolle, S. B. (2010). *Service-learning and social justice: Engaging students in social change.* Lanham, MD: Rowman & Littlefield Publishers, Inc.

Coye, D. (1997). Ernest Boyer and the new American college: Connecting the disconnects. *Change, 29*(3), 21-29.

Deans, T. (1999). Service-learning in two keys: Paulo Freire's critical pedagogy in relation to John Dewey's pragmatism. *Michigan Journal of Community Service Learning, 6,* 15-29.

Dewey, J. (1900). *The school and society: being three lectures* (3rd. ed.). Chicago: The University of Chicago Press.

Elmborg, J. (2006). Critical information literacy: Implications for instructional practice. *The Journal of Academic Librarianship, 32*(2), 192-199.

Eyler, J., & Giles, D. E., Jr. (1999). *Where's the learning in service-learning?* San Francisco: Jossey-Bass.

Fowler, C. S., & Walter, S. (2003). Instructional leadership: New responsibilities for a new reality. *College & Research Libraries News, 64*(7), 465-468.

Freire, P. (1986). *Pedagogy of the oppressed.* New York: Continuum.

Furco, A. (1996). Service-learning and school-to-work: Making the connections. *Journal of Cooperative Education, 32*(1), 7-14.

Gibson, C. (Ed.). (2006). *Student engagement and information literacy.* Chicago: American Library Association.

Hatch, R. (2009). Pioneering work by alumnus helps low-income access to fresh food. Retrieved from http://digitalcommons.iwu.edu/news/358/

Hatcher, J. A. (1997). The moral dimensions of John Dewey's philosophy: Implications for undergraduate education. *Michigan Journal of Community Service Learning, 4,* 22-29.

Hernandez, M., & Knight, L. (2010). Reinventing the box: Faculty-librarian collaborative efforts to foster service learning for political engagement. *Journal for Civic Commitment, XVI*(1), 1-15.

Herther, N. K. (2008). Service learning and engagement in the academic library: Operating out of the box. *College & Research Libraries News, 69*(7), 386-389.

Honnet, E. P., & Poulsen, S. J. (1996). Principles of good practice for combining service and learning. Retrieved from http://www.nationalserviceresources. org/files/Principles-of-Good-Practice-for-Combining-Service-and-Learning.pdf

Jacobs, H. L. M. (2008). Information literacy and reflective pedagogical praxis. *The Journal of Academic Librarianship, 34*(3), 256-262.

Kendall, J. C. (1990). *Combining service and learning: A resource book for community and public service.* Raleigh, NC: National Society for Internships and Experiential Education.

Kolb, D. (1981). Learning styles and disciplinary differences. In A. W. Chickering (Ed.), *The modern American college: Responding to the new realities of diverse students and a changing society* (pp. 232-255). San Francisco: Jossey-Bass.

Kranich, N. C. (2001). *Libraries and democracy: The cornerstones of liberty.* Chicago, IL: American Library Association.

Kuh, G. D., & Schneider, C. G. (2008). *High-impact educational practices: What they are, who has access to them, and why they matter.* Washington, DC: Association of American Colleges and Universities.

Kvenild, C., & Calkins, K. (2011). *Embedded librarians: Moving beyond one-shot instruction.* Chicago: Association of College and Research Libraries.

Learn and Serve America. (n.d.). What is service-learning? Retrieved from http://www.learnandserve.gov/about/service_learning/index.asp

National Commission on Excellence in Education. (1983). *A nation at risk: The imperative for educational reform.* Washington, D.C.: U.S. Government Printing Office.

National Forum on Information Literacy. (2005). The Alexandria proclamation on information literacy and lifelong learning. Retrieved from http://portal.unesco.org/ci/en/ev.php- URL_ID=20891&URL_DO=DO_TOPIC&URL_SEC-TION=201.html

National Service-Learning Clearinghouse. (n.d.). What is service-learning? Retrieved from http://www.servicelearning.org/what-is-service-learning

National Youth Leadership Council. (n.d.). What is service-learning? Retrieved from http://www.nylc.org/

Obama, B. (2009). National information literacy awareness month. Retrieved from http://www.whitehouse.gov/assets/documents/2009literacy_prc_rel.pdf

Partnership for 21st Century Skills. Framework for 21st century learning. Retrieved from http://www.p21.org/overview/skills-framework

Putnam, R. D. (2000). *Bowling alone: The collapse and revival of American community.* New York: Simon & Schuster.

Putnam, R. D., Feldstein, L. M., & Cohen, D. (2003). *Better together: Restoring the American community.* New York, NY: Simon & Schuster.

Kellogg Commission on the Future of State and Land-Grant Universities. (2000). Renewing the covenant: Learning discovery and engagement in a new age and different world (No. 6). Retrieved from http://www.aplu.org/NetCommunity/Document.Doc?id=186

Riddle, J. S. (2003). Where's the library in service learning? Models for engaged library instruction. *The Journal of Academic Librarianship, 29*(2), 71-81.

Shumaker, D., & Talley, M. (2010). Models of embedded librarianship: A research summary. *Information Outlook, 14*(1), 26-28, 33-35.

Smith, M. W. (1994). Issues in integrating service-learning in the higher-education curriculum. *Effective learning, effective teaching, effective service.* Washington, D.C.: Youth Serve America.

Walter, S. (2007). *The teaching library: Approaches to assessing information literacy instruction.* Binghamton, NY: Haworth Information Press.

Wilson, W. (n.d.) Princeton in the nation's service. Retrieved from http://www.princeton.edu/~mudd/exhibits/wilsonline/indn8nsvc.html

Zurkowski, P. G. (1974). *The information service environment relationships and priorities.* Washington, D.C.: National Program for Library and Information Services.

The Public Academic Library: Friction in the Teflon Funnel

Patti Ryan
York University

Lisa Sloniowski[1]
York University

How does one engage in a radical pedagogical praxis when constrained by a growing awareness of the ways in which academic libraries and librarians have become institutions of hegemonic order and often serve the imperatives of neoliberal capitalism that have dominated political and social discourse for the last thirty years? How might we develop an alternate vision of libraries as imaginative and conceptual spaces of resistance? This chapter explores these questions, and considers both the challenges and opportunities that arise when working towards a theoretically-informed praxis that gives primacy to cultivating an engaged and empowered citizenry,[2] and moves issues of social justice and social responsibility to the forefront of information literacy work.

Of particular concern is how academic librarians can resist what Henry Giroux (2010) describes as the "scourge of neoliberalism"; an interconnected system of political, social and economic practices that values the production of competent servants of the state, and the supremacy of the free market. This essay draws heavily from Giroux's (2005, 2010) work on critical pedagogy and its potential for cultivating democratic citizenship, and on the role of public institutions and public intellectuals in this process. While Giroux does not give direct attention to libraries, Gage (2004) notes that his work is highly relevant for librarians because it offers "trenchant critiques that draw out and illuminate the ways in which the

---

1 These authors contributed equally to this paper.
2 In this paper, the concept of citizenship refers to the classical republican tradition of active participation in governing and in being governed, rather than to more modern conceptions of contractualism between individuals and the state.

production, circulation, and consumption of information, knowledge, and meaning are never innocent but instead sutured to issues of power, political economy, and specific subject positions" (p. 67). While Giroux's work has been used in recent years to explore a range of issues in librarianship (Eryaman, 2010; Lilburn, 2007), we focus specifically on his thoughts about "the vital role that critical pedagogy might play as both a language of critique and possibility by addressing the growing threat of free market fundamentalism" (Giroux, 2005, p. 210). We intersect critically with his clarion call to retake the University, acknowledging it as both "an ethical referent and a call to action" (2010, p. 190), and view the cultivation of a radical information literacy praxis as a meaningful response to this call.

Pawley (2003) and Elmborg (2006) note that librarians have historically been reluctant to critically interrogate the concept of information literacy. Indeed, much of the practitioner scholarship on information literacy is reflective of, rather than resistant to, the core values of neoliberalism. Swanson (2004) reminds us that the ACRL standards themselves were adopted primarily as a strategic response to broad economic shifts in which knowledge has come to replace capital as the basis of the economy, and information itself has become commodified. Countering the scholarship of neoliberal accommodation is a growing body of more progressive work that addresses the importance of incorporating critical perspectives into research and practice in librarianship (Accardi, Drabinski & Kumbier, 2010; Leckie, Given & Buschman, 2010). A number of scholars have argued for more critical engagement with assumptions about information literacy, and with the standards and practices which guide our work in this area, and have advocated for the adoption of a theoretically-informed approach to teaching that recognizes that education is not itself apolitical (Elmborg, 2006; Lilburn, 2007; Jacobs, 2008; Jacobs and Berg, 2011; Luke and Kapitze, 1999).

Recognizing the value of connecting theory and practice, the authors combine a theoretical rationale for adopting a radical praxis with self-reflective accounts of the specific ways in which we have, haltingly, begun to move towards it in our own work. We examine ways that neoliberal ideology has impacted our work as academic librarians, and provide an argument for resisting the current political climate of higher education. We offer practical examples of ways for librarians to create opportunities for citizen engagement and empowerment, and explore how drop-in programming might be re-conceptualized to focus on the development of vocabularies of resistance, global information justice, and civic responsibility. We argue that such work provides a bridge by which we can connect our day-to-day work directly to the core democratizing values of the profession, and that such acts can, and should, move us closer to the tradition and practice of progressive librarianship that has been powerfully articulated by Toni Samek (2001; 2004).

We will also argue that a turn towards a radical praxis is not only important because of its potential to empower and engage citizenry, but also because it encourages an important shift in public perception of the academic library by reminding students, faculty and librarians of the public-ness of their institutions, and the social contributions of librarians to democracy. This reminder is a critically important form of advocacy and solidarity-building for librarians at a time when the profession is undeniably in crisis (Sloniowski, 2012), and when the public spheres from which to launch a moral vision or to engage in a viable struggle against the hegemonic order are under constant threat from the corporate bottom line (Giroux, 2005). As Naomi Klein insists, librarianship is a revolutionary choice (2004).

The Scourge of Neoliberalism: The Crisis of Higher Education

Giroux (2010) points to a "general consensus among academics around the world that higher education is in a state of crisis" (p. 185), and describes the ways in which the discourse of neoliberalism has transformed social life. Giroux is among the most vociferous in his assessment of neoliberalism, noting that it has become "one of the most pervasive and dangerous ideologies of the twenty-first century" (2005, p. 210), but many others have contributed to what is now a robust critique of the global consequences of the neoliberal agenda (Chomsky, 1999; Harvey, 2005, Stiglitz, 2002).

It is difficult to offer a purely theoretical definition of neoliberalism, as

INFORMATION LITERACY AND SOCIAL JUSTICE

the term is used to refer to a broad range of social, economic, and political practices which have been historically associated with the supply-side economic policies of the Thatcher and Reagan eras. Moreover, there is significant disagreement as to the nature and effects of neoliberalism (Auerbach, 2007). However, Harvey (2005) offers a useful summary of the essential characteristics of neoliberalism as an economic doctrine:

> Neoliberalism is in the first instance a theory of political economic practices that proposes that human well-being can best be advanced by liberating individual entrepreneurial freedoms and skills within an institutional framework characterized by strong private property rights, free markets, and free trade. The role of the state is to create and preserve an institutional framework appropriate to such practices. (p. 2)

Using Harvey's definition as a conceptual starting point, the ideological imperatives of neoliberalism can be broadly characterized as that which values the centrality and effectiveness of the free market, the accumulation of capital, deregulation, privatization, individualism and the private over public good.

Giroux (2010) argues that neoliberalism has had dramatic consequences for higher education, and illustrates the ways in which the University has been "conscripted to serve as corporate power's apprentice" (p. 186). He argues that institutions of higher education are no longer being understood as a public good, but rather, are being refashioned by and for corporate interests to meet the needs of a changing marketplace. A full discussion of the corporatization of university campuses is beyond the scope of this paper, but has been substantively addressed by others[3]. However, the most troubling elements in Giroux's analysis include: the shift towards standardized, market-driven curricula and programs, the downsizing of permanent faculty positions in favor of contract faculty and other forms of precarious academic labor, the erosion of shared governance between faculty and administrators, diminished understandings of academic freedom, and a weakened conception of higher education as a political and civic institution that is committed to addressing, or at least considering,

---

3 See for instance James Turk's anthology on the corporate campus compiled in 2000, or the bibliography at the "Living in Interesting Times" blog. https://livingininterestingtimes.wordpress.com/resources/corporatization/

critical social problems. Borrowing from the work of Agamben (1998), Giroux (2010) argues that universities have adopted a form of "bare pedagogy" that "strips education of its public values, critical contents and civic responsibilities as part of its broader goal of creating new subjects wedded to the logic of privatization, efficiency, flexibility, the accumulation of capital, and the destruction of the social state" (p. 185). Or, as Eisenhower and Smith (2010) argue, the University has become a sort of Teflon funnel into which students are poured, homogenized, and then shot out the other end, ready to assume their places in the knowledge economy.

The Academic Library Context

As libraries are inextricably linked to their institutions, they are not impervious to the creeping tentacles of neoliberalism. Fister (2010a) observes that "the neoliberal turn that has led to the commodification of what scholars do - teach and create knowledge - has had a profound effect on the academic library" (p. 83). There are myriad ways in which neoliberal impulses have impacted our professional culture, our collections, our physical spaces, and our labor as professional librarians. While these issues are not easily disentangled from one another, this paper will focus upon the ways in which our pedagogical work has been affected.

In relation to the teaching practices of librarians, Giroux's adaptation of the concept of "bare pedagogy" is useful in thinking about the ways in which the current political climate of knowledge production has impacted our work. For instance, the increase in precariously employed contract faculty impinges upon our ability to permanently embed information literacy in departmental curriculum. When undergraduate programs are largely taught by a revolving door of contract faculty, how can librarians successfully build relationships, develop new material and assess information literacy goals in meaningful ways?

Another example of neoliberalist logic at work in libraries lies in the eager embrace of online learning as a more flexible, efficient and innovative way to provide library instruction. Narrowly conceived in the library context as the transmission of fungible skills - online learning initiatives typically package information literacy as a general commodity to be acquired. We describe them as "learning objects," emphasizing their instrumentality. Sometimes, online tutorials are "monetized" - turning our expertise and pedagogical labor into a commodity form for commercial transaction. In this model, ownership and intellectual control often reside with institutions rather than with the person or people who write and design the tutorial. Even where librarians are able to hold copyright over their work, the technologies of online learning so far lend themselves primarily to a transactional, banking model of education that offers little in the way of relationship building (Noble, 2000), or much emphasis on information literacy as a situated process and habit of mind leading to critical thinking and an empowered citizenry.

This emphasis on information literacy pedagogy as skill-based training is prevalent in our physical classrooms as well where we often operate as extensions of the database vendors whose products we rent and encourage our students to consume for the brief time that they are with us. Many faculty seem to expect little more of us than to ensure that students know which databases to use and the mechanics of searching them. Problematically, these are not tools we have built ourselves and we are often unaware of the proprietary search algorithms that govern search and retrieval functions. We also have little control over which journals are indexed or dropped from within these tools, or which ones are given priority in large federated search tools or discovery layers. Rather than deciding for ourselves how best to organize and provide access to our collections, we let vendors define our users' research experiences and outcomes and instead "willingly serve as the corrections officers for corporate information prisons" (Fister, 2010b, para 11). In other words, in not building our own open source, open access, and vendor agnostic research tools, we risk becoming taxpayer-subsidized training instruments for commercial entities at worst, and marketing outreach programs for the library at best.

Time is another issue. Increasingly librarians complain about lack of time as the primary obstacle to developing innovative content for their workshops and lectures. Rising student enrolments and a shrinking public sector workforce have led to poor librarian-to-student ratios at many institutions. With fewer people juggling more work, it becomes easy to fall back on database training as the sum total of our teaching efforts, rather than working towards higher level information literacy competencies. It also makes it easier to justify our unwillingness to engage in more nuanced questions about how information is used, collected, packaged, and marketed (Lilburn, 2007). Who has the time to think carefully through these questions and prepare such challenging material in ways that resonate with students while still teaching them the basic skills needed for their assignments? The neoliberal emphasis on a downsized public sector has a significant impact on our classroom content.

Lastly, the emergence of an audit culture in the 21st century university (Shore, 2008) has ramifications for librarians. Increasingly, we are asked to spend our limited time gathering data to assess our value and justify our existence and we often, perhaps unconsciously, adapt our work to be quantified accordingly. How can we be comfortable taking risks in such an environment? What is the incentive for expanding our pedagogical frame to offer, for instance, a series of new workshops which might be poorly attended or risk alienating a faculty member by insisting on critical content for one of our guest lectures? We continue to look to the number of classes and students taught as a key measure of "success" for an IL program, and rely on available summative measures of learning outcomes like SAILS, undergraduate degree level expectations documents, and/or key performance indicators in colleges as the barometers of student achievement and public accountability. We engage in these practices despite knowing that they do little more than assess a range of skills rather than indicate that any actual education has occurred. As Noble (2000) insists,

> Training involves the honing of a person's mind so that that mind can be used for the purposes of someone other than that person....knowledge is usually defined as a set of skills or body of information designed to be put to use, to become operational, only in a context defined by someone other than the trained person. Training thus typically entails a radical divorce between knowledge and the self. (p. 101)

The multiple neoliberal encroachments upon the work of professional librarians described above have the impact of re-framing our teaching as training and foreclose upon the possibility of education as a process of transformational self-awareness and empowerment. Neoliberal logic has implications in the construction of academic subjectivities (Shore, 2008). In this environment, librarian-as-trainer becomes complicit in the formation of the student-as-commodity for the market.

So What Can Be Done?

Notwithstanding these significant problems, there are always spaces of resistance that allow academic librarians to make critical interventions at key moments. Eisenhower and Smith (2010) suggest, somewhat cryptically, that librarians might be able to create some friction in the Teflon funnel, and slow down that otherwise smooth and seamless passage through the edu-factory. Indeed, librarians are unusual agents within institutions, marginal in many respects. However, because we work across disciplines, in and out of the curriculum, we are also reasonably autonomous as a result of our marginality. How might we use our unique position within the academy to effect change? How can we resist the current climate in our professional practice and move towards, as Giroux suggests, both the promise and the possibilities of critical positioning? In particular, how can instruction librarians incorporate a radical praxis when, as Lilburn (2007) reminds us, we are largely constrained by widely-adopted professional standards that claim the cultivation of an informed citizenry but give no attention to political issues or how citizens can use information in a socially responsible manner? These standards run the risk, as Jacobs (2008) suggests, of reinforcing a banking model of education and compartmentalizing "information literacy's tremendous potential for creative, critical, and visionary thinking" (p. 258).

We argue the answer is two-fold. First, we take as absolutely necessary the need, as summarized convincingly by Elmborg (2006), to ground our information literacy work in a theoretically-informed, critical practice of progressive librarianship that shouldn't, and can't be, neutral. We reject positivism and explicitly acknowledge the situated and shifting subjectivities in our work. Such grounding also helps us understand the ways in which our work inevitably supports the status quo and is at times complicit in the neoliberal agenda. No one is neutral. Resistance is impossible without such awareness. Second, we take action and those of us with academic freedom work to define alternative visions for our information literacy programs in our policies and programs.

Theory becomes Policy: Creating the Environment for Critical Pedagogy

An important first step in moving towards a pedagogical praxis focused on social justice lies not in the classroom but in thinking programmatically about a library's information literacy efforts. Rather than thinking about our teaching as purely a reaction to faculty and student demand, it is important for librarians to work together as a group and set the stage for what they would like to do with their teaching, both individually and institutionally. At the individual level this might mean developing a teaching philosophy mindful of social justice, critical thinking, global information justice and which explores pedagogical methods that interrogate power and authority in the library and in the classroom. At an institutional level, a policy document for the library's IL program would reflect the overarching goals and climate of the University and the library itself and would simultaneously contain the seeds that allow radical praxis to bloom. In setting our sights beyond academic success and faculty support and inserting language which gestures towards citizenship in our policy documents, we send a message to administrators, faculty and our librarian colleagues about the democratic imperatives of information literacy. In short, careful policy development can provide a spur to action. For example, in 2003 librarians at the University of Windsor in Ontario decided to define information literacy in their first policy document in accordance with the ACRL standards—with an important deviation—a sixth standard was added which focused on students' understanding of the socio-political context of information, scholarly communication and technology.[4] Where the fifth ACRL standard seems to be largely about

---

4 "The information literate person understands cultural, economic, ethical, legal, and social issues surrounding the production of information." Leddy Library IL policy, 2003: http://web4.uwindsor.

understanding and abiding by the laws surrounding use of information, the Windsor definition opened the door to critical information literacy which considers the production of information within a social context.

Another example is at York University, where teaching librarians largely ignored the ACRL standards and developed an Information Literacy Manifesto (2005) which states,

> Our overarching purpose in developing an Information Literacy program is to graduate critically engaged, information literate citizens able to fully participate in the information society across all levels – scholarly, personal, vocational and political. Our program, therefore, will focus on enabling students to develop information-seeking behaviours that transcend specific finding tools, to recognize the societal context of information, to think critically about the information they find and to let that information transform them.[5]

Admittedly, both policies accommodate neoliberal imperatives as was necessary in order to gain administrative support, and neither policy mapped out a specific way forward to student empowerment and citizenship. In hindsight, such accommodations may have gone too far. It is worth noting that most of the librarians involved in crafting these policies were pre-tenure and perhaps somewhat tentative in the face of authority. Jacobs and Berg's (2011) suggestion that ALA Core Values be included in information literacy policies would certainly offer a more historically grounded and generative place from which to frame our efforts. However, at the very least, these policy examples offer a touchstone for librarians to use, should they wish to move towards a more radical praxis. Such efforts can also help to develop a culture whereby thinking programmatically about what we teach includes attention to critical thinking, citizenship, and social justice. Even if an individual librarian rejects such a framing, s/he is asked to consider a radical praxis, and this consideration might offer a useful epistemological rupture in and of itself. When faculty approach the library for assistance with their courses or curriculum design, the policy document can be deployed as a way of deepening the conversation about

---

ca/units/leddy/leddy.nsf/ILpolicy.pdf
5 York University Libraries IL Manifesto, 2005. http://www.library.yorku.ca/binaries/Home/ILManifesto.pdf

what librarians might do in and out of the classroom. When the program is advertised and the policy is made public, it also attracts progressive allies and activists. Such policies should not dictate how or what a librarian should teach, and do not by themselves enable radical praxis, but they create a space where resistance is not only possible but encouraged.

From Policy to Praxis

Another step in developing a theoretically informed praxis involves shifting towards a model in which drop-in workshops, lecture series and library-hosted events are valued as much as our efforts to become embedded in disciplinary curriculum. Developing our own programming is key to moving social justice and social responsibility to the center of our information literacy work. In thinking through the types of extra-curricular programming we might offer in libraries, we should consider compelling ways to engage our community in relevant and timely civic dialogues that we believe, along with Giroux, are conducive to a substantive and flourishing democracy. We must recognize that our pedagogical work is not supplemental, but vital to the so-called "information age."

In this, we stand with Paulo Freire and other theorists in the critical pedagogy tradition who view education as a profoundly political activity and argue for an alternative pedagogy in which, "rather than focus on knowledge acquisition, students identify and engage significant problems in the world" (Elmborg, 2006, p. 193). However, as Jacobs (2008), adapting from the work of the New London Group on literacy reminds us, one of our most difficult tasks is to make information literacy "embodied, situated and social" for our diverse student body (p. 259). Speaking pragmatically, re-focusing on extracurricular programming as civic dialogue may increase the appeal of the workshops, resulting in higher levels of interest and attendance. It also creates opportunities for academic librarians to become a vital ingredient in the public sphere. In her "Liberation Bibliography" Fister calls for us to recognize that the world is "not separated into the scholarly and the ordinary. If knowledge matters, it must matter beyond the boundaries of our campuses, and beyond the conference halls of our scholarly societies" (2010b, para. 6). Our extra-curricular programming may offer a key bridge between academic work and civic activity.

While we do not foreclose upon the possibility of a radical praxis in curriculum-integrated environments, we argue that extra-curricular programming can mitigate the significant challenges that instruction librarians face in working with curriculum that is designed by other people for other ends. Such efforts can also help to address the peculiar complexities of the relationship that academic librarians have with disciplinary faculty, even in institutions such as ours where librarians are granted full academic status, and the ways in which the dynamics of this relationship can impact, and often constrain, our own teaching practices (Eisenhower & Smith, 2010). Bearing these challenges in mind, one of the guiding philosophies of drop-in programming should be, in at least some instances, to remove the locus of control of curriculum from faculty to librarian hands and provide an alternative safe space for thinking, debating and learning on campus. We normally wait for invitations from faculty, or we elbow our way into their curriculum, making a case for our value in terms we believe they will appreciate and to which they will be responsive. Yet, these efforts ultimately reinforce the problematic and ultimately limiting dynamics of the power relationship. In our own programming, we have the opportunity to autonomously design and deliver our own material in such a way as to offer students an opportunity to integrate the ideas and learning taking place in their multiple classrooms. Such material may well be re-used in our curriculum-integrated initiatives in ways both overt and covert.

Also, it is important that in hosting workshops, panels and lectures about contemporary issues, we must maintain a constant connection, however tenuous, with the research and information literacy issues raised by the event. In so doing, we reinforce the importance of research, knowledge, and information literacy across all aspects of one's life and begin to work towards a new pedagogical model for library instruction, as will be demonstrated by the two following case studies. These events were not research workshops per se, but offered a sort of stealth information literacy instruction packaged inside a broader context. Or, in keeping with Noble's (2000) view of education, the information literacy instruction is not divorced from content and hence new knowledge is not divorced from the self. In other words, the boundaries between the subject matter of the event and the information literacy skills being encouraged were porous and seamless, fostering an understanding of research as a socially necessary and situated act central not only to one's academic activities and future role in the marketplace, but to one's whole engagement with society.

Case Study #1: Can You Trust the Media?
The Leddy Library Iraq War Teach-In

In March 2003 during the immediate lead up to the American invasion of Iraq, I (Lisa Sloniowski) and a colleague, Mita Williams, were employed at the Leddy Library at the University of Windsor and attended several anti-war demonstrations. The war was particularly resonant for the citizens of Windsor, partly because of a large population of Middle Eastern communities on both sides of the Windsor/Detroit border, but also because, perhaps more than many places in Canada, the specter of U.S. militarism confronted us daily due to our immediate proximity to the border and our regular crossings back and forth over the Ambassador bridge or through the Detroit/Windsor tunnel. At these border checkpoints, signs of ever higher alert were manifested daily. Amidst this charged environment, Mita and I began to wonder if we should be organizing something in the library, particularly after overhearing a group of concerned professors talking at a demonstration about the need to hold teach-ins on campus once the U.S. declared war. We very quickly organized a teach-in that brought together a panel of media scholars, philosophers and librarians who spoke about the relatively uncritical acceptance of the war in the North American mainstream press as well as the rhetorical strategies deployed by the supporters of the war—in essence, the ways in which support for the war was discursively produced. From an information literacy perspective, the librarians' role in organizing the panel was to draw attention not only to these discursive practices, but also to the research implications emanating from the silencing of dissent in the mainstream press for people trying to get current and accurate information. To assist people in gathering a wider range of viewpoints, we built a subject guide to both alternative and mainstream news sources and presented it at the event.[6] We saw this guide as a tool for library instruction but also as a form of collection development not usually performed in libraries, and tried to make this collection activity transparent to our teach-in attendees. We made the point that by not providing space for the voices of dissent in the present, the mainstream media made it very difficult for a record of such resistance to be preserved for scholars in the future. We made it clear that this erasure was in fact why we were hosting this event in the library. It served to remind them that librarians have a praxis and agenda of our own that embraces cultural stewardship and access to information. We were not apolitical; in fact we were outraged.

We were particularly surprised by the turnout. We were just heading into exam period, we held the event in the evening, and in a room at the top of the library not visible from the front entrance. For advertising, we had postered the campus a few days in advance of the event and flyered at another campus demonstration the day before. Despite little marketing and the awkward time and location, we had approximately 100 students and faculty show up. When we saw how heavily the subject guide was used in the days that followed, we knew we were on to something.

There was also great feedback from attendees. We heard from a graduate student who said she had been very troubled by the media coverage but didn't know how to get other opinions until our event. She also mentioned that she had been lacking a vocabulary to explain her concerns and this event helped her articulate her resistance... There were other benefits for us personally as well. In building our subject guide, we discovered many alternative press sources, learned about political rhetorical strategies, and sharpened our own analysis of mainstream media. In other words, this form of critical pedagogy positions librarians as learners and citizens as well as teachers. It made me think differently about my responsibilities for collection development, questions with which I still wrestle. Over time it became evident that there were not many portals collecting both the voices of mainstream media and those of dissent, and subsequently we were linked to by a number of news sites and public library sites. We

---

6 Iraq 2003: sources of news. Available online at: https://ospace.scholarsportal.info/handle/1873/45

were told that public librarians appreciated our site as they did not have the academic freedom to create such guides in their own workplaces.

Faculty who spoke at or attended the teach-in were universally grateful to us for hosting the event, and began to see librarians in a new light. We were invited to speak at conferences about the event; librarian conferences and non-academic conferences. We became visible to other activists on campus. I eventually left the university for a job at another, but Mita Williams continued thinking about citizenship and information literacy and has subsequently hosted the Windsor Essex Change Camp at the Windsor Public library (WPL), an unconference dedicated to rethinking government in the age of participation, with some of the WPL public librarians and Dr. Nicole Noel from the University's Centre for Social Justice. Williams cites the teach-in as the inspiration for this next event. For me, it was the precursor to both the Information Literacy Manifesto at York University, and our next case study, the "Occupy your Mind" knowledge sharing circle.

Case Study #2: Occupy your Mind at Scott Library, York University

In August 2011, Lisa Sloniowski and I (Patti Ryan) were both returning to work after year-long leaves, and began to talk about the ways in which our reading and thinking over the previous year had impacted our intentions for information literacy work. Years earlier, the Information Literacy Manifesto had provided a blueprint for grounding our teaching practices in a framework of social responsibility, and we were interested in revisiting those principles as a way to engage our community in social justice issues. By mid-September, we had mapped out provisional plans for a series of drop-in workshops that would focus on current events and would, we hoped, create opportunities for our students to connect their classroom learning to what was happening in the world around them. We came up with a working title, the "Research for Citizenship" series, and set up a blog[7] to keep track of ideas and as a way to keep thinking

---

7 http://researchforcitizenship.wordpress.com/

and writing about the role of libraries and librarians in creating spaces of resistance.

As those early conversations took place, the Occupy Movement was unfolding around us, and it soon became clear that we had the topic for an inaugural event. By mid-October, the Occupy Wall Street protest had spread to over 150 cities, and Toronto's Occupy site had been set up in a downtown park, and was gaining momentum. As we started to think through the information literacy issues related to the movement and about the questions we might explore in a public forum, we were continuously struck by the close connections between the emerging values of the Occupy Movement and those that have traditionally animated librarianship—specifically, sharing, education, openness, and the importance of public spaces. The role of the People's Library in various Occupy sites reinforced these connections for us and led us to think more deeply about the role of the libraries in the movement. We visited the Toronto occupation and came away inspired by the commitment of the people involved and noted that some of our students and faculty were amongst their ranks. With these ideas swirling around and in the face of increasing curiosity about Occupy from our community, our first event began to take shape.

Taking our pedagogical cues from the Occupy protests, we organized a knowledge sharing circle in the atrium of the Scott Library, the largest and busiest library in the York University Library system. We promoted the "Occupy your Mind" event for less than a week, advertising it as an opportunity for community members to come together for a participatory and informal discussion about Occupy. Although we were intent on preserving the non-hierarchical and leaderless format of Occupy, we did invite David McNally, a well-known activist and scholar of social movements, with the hope that his presence would generate interest. We quickly produced flyers and papered the library and parts of the campus, and advertised the event on all the relevant campus websites and listservs. In the days leading up to the event we had to resist our ingrained impulses to over-prepare, but we did think carefully about the information issues arising from Occupy and its penetration into the public consciousness. After much discussion, we prepared ourselves to explore together with students one question: "What exactly is Occupy?" In framing the event around a problem to be posed, rather than information to be delivered, we aligned our vision of information literacy to that of Jacobs and Berg (2011) who suggest,

> [r]ather than viewing information literacy teaching as a kind of banking where librarians deposit knowledge about how to identify, evaluate, find, and use information, if we position ourselves and our students as critical co-investigators in the problem-posing education of information literacy, we begin to move toward a critical information literacy praxis where we can work toward the ideals of critical literacy such as democracy, equity, shared decision making, empowerment, and transformative action in addition to the ideals articulated in the Alexandria Proclamation. (p. 390)

In our usual workshops and guest lectures we would have approached the event as experts in helping students find the answers to their research questions. In this case, we approached the event as learners ourselves, and recognized that while we had some information we could share, so could others in our community. And in pointing to our need to learn more, we not only foregrounded our own social concerns, but also pointed to an information literacy issue, namely, that amidst all the noise in both the mainstream and alternative press about any historical event, one has to pick and choose very carefully through multiple streams of information from various perspectives before arriving at one's own analysis. In other words, we modeled information literacy as a lifelong and inherently social process, rather than a commodity to be acquired.

After the introduction and our broad-based opening question, a wide-ranging and at times penetrating discussion started to unfold. Lisa and I were both struck by the level of engagement and articulateness of the students, and the self-reflectiveness of their comments. One of the most powerful exchanges occurred when one participant offered a forceful critique of the movement, and drew particular attention to its insularity, lack of openness to marginalized groups, and to the reports of sexual assault and rape at several Occupy sites. As we listened to several other students respond thoughtfully to her astute critique, even though it generated very difficult emotions in the group, we were quietly reminded of the raw power and authenticity of student voices that can emerge when we actively work to create conditions to support them.

The event resulted in unprecedented attendance for a Scott Library drop-in workshop. There were approximately 70 people in the circle at most points during the two hour event, and since it was held in a visible area of the library, we were able to attract passersby who were curious about the gathering. It was serendipitous browsing from our perspective. While we are hopeful that discussion itself helped a few people to think more about Occupy and its significance to their own lives as citizens, we were even more encouraged by developments that followed. We were excited to see a number of students gather immediately after the event to compile an email list to continue the discussion and organize in some way. We were interviewed by a student journalist at another university and our event was covered in our own student newspaper (Perlin, 2011). Two weeks later, we were approached by the president of a student association to participate in a student-run Occupy event. This was the first time in memory that we have been invited to attend a student event in which we were not asked to talk about "the library" or information literacy in particular, but rather, asked to participate as community members with a shared interest in a timely social issue. This lent some weight to our hunch that holding the event in the library would help our community to make deeper intellectual connections between the idea of libraries and the public good, and to the ways in which librarians can work as allies for social change.

The Occupy Research Guide was linked to and shared in the social media by a number of Occupy-related websites and groups and had unexpectedly high traffic.[8] This issue-specific guide disrupted our library's adherence to traditional discipline-based subject guides, and provided a template for thinking about how we might use them to draw attention to other relevant social and political issues. As with the Iraq media coverage subject guide, the creation of the subject guide allowed us to collect and curate alternative press voices and foreground material outside mainstream debate and typical scholarly sources while also serving as a lead-in to various scholarly databases, data sources, and influential authors

---

8 Available online at: http://researchguides.library.yorku.ca/occupy

who had inspired the movement. The guide works on the sidelines to offer students ways into socio-political information which might answer or further complicate their questions about Occupy or social protest in general. We also had a page within the guide about the Occupy Libraries, drawing attention to the role of libraries and librarians in counter-cultural movements. In keeping with the notion that students could be our critical co-investigators in attempting to learn more about the movement, we encouraged suggestions for the guide and were delighted to receive a few links to articles and forums from interested students.

Praxis makes Perfect?

As mentioned above, benefits of both case studies were myriad—heightened student engagement, relationship building, development of new knowledge around political issues, and conference and publication opportunities due to professional interest in the work, just to name a few. Other benefits were simultaneously immeasurable. For example, we'll never know how our work might have led to moments of personal and political resistance or citizenry supported by responsible information-seeking behavior. Perhaps, in the current climate, designing events whose outcomes are immeasurable is an act of radical praxis in and of itself. At any rate, we acknowledge that the acts described are but brief moments of resistance that are often quickly subsumed by the logic of neoliberalism. Our case studies do not represent massive revolution in and of themselves. We remain conscious of the ways in which the success of such work may ultimately reinforce the values of a neoliberal agenda, and the ways in which our efforts might be "subsumed in its Foucauldian way into numbers that scaffold the very discourse we critique" (Eisenhower & Smith, 2010, p. 305). Indeed, in both cases our administration was highly supportive of our efforts. We maintain, however, that no matter how our efforts may be rationalized or used by administrators, our pedagogical efforts may lead to moments of citizen resistance that live well beyond the annual report. They offer hope rather than despair within the daily grinding of the machinery of the edu-factory, create friction in the Teflon funnel, forge connections and inspire us to further acts of political praxis, both in and outside of the university.

Advocacy and Solidarity

Finally, we'd like to emphasize the impact this work has in terms of re-framing librarianship in the public eye. In focusing our programming on our core professional values—knowledge, sharing, common space, cultural stewardship, freedom of expression and freedom of information—we also quietly underscore our societal role and exemplify the many ways in which librarians can and do contribute to the public good. The academic library may be seen as uniquely critical to the public sphere as a community center and town hall in the midst of intellectual communities. By empha-sizing contemporary issues surrounding the socio-political production of information in our information literacy programming, we demonstrate our relevance at a time of rapid technological change. Our relevance lies not in training people how to use new tools, but as thinkers and citizens particularly engaged in questioning the shifting social complexities of the new information landscapes. At a time when some believe technology is set to replace print culture and, by extension, libraries and librarianship, the de-valuing of the work of librarians must be understood as part of the larger scourge of neoliberalism which seeks to shrink the public sector and lock down information as a profit-making commodity. The praxis outlined in this paper suggests we actively seek to build solidarity with our communities, as allies and equals, rather than as servants, informa-tion gatekeepers and/or pedagogues. In so doing, we make common cause with students and faculty, we build grassroots support, and we wear our public-ness like a suit of armor (Klein, 2004). We occasionally destabilize the hegemonic institutions in which we are embedded. In fostering civic engagement in our student body, we develop a wider horizon upon which to gain perspective on our professional and personal struggles, and we immerse ourselves in the wider battles for social and political change. We live inside the ruptures and contradictions of a revolutionary choice.

References

Accardi, M. T., Drabinski, E., & Kumbier, A. (Eds.). (2010). *Critical library instruction: Theories and methods.* Duluth, MN: Library Juice Press.

Auerbach, N. N. (2007). The meanings of neoliberalism. In R. K. Roy, A. T. Denzau, & T. D. Willett (Eds.), *Neoliberalism, national and regional experiments with global ideas* (pp. 26-50). London: Routledge.

Chomsky, N. (1999). *Profit over people: Neoliberalism and global order.* New York: Seven Stories Press.

Eisenhower, C., & Smith, D. (2010). The Library as "stuck place": Critical pedagogy in the corporate university. In M. T. Accardi, E. Drabinkski, & A. Kumbier (Eds.), *Critical library instruction: Theories and methods* (pp. 305-317). Duluth, MN: Library Juice Press.

Elmborg, J. (2006). Critical information literacy: Implications for instructional practice. *The Journal of Academic Librarianship, 32*(2), 192-199.

Eryaman, M. Y. (2010). The public library as a space for democratic empowerment: Henry Giroux, radical democracy, and border pedagogy. In G. J. Leckie, L. M. Given, & J. E. Buschman (Eds.), *Critical theory for library and information science* (pp. 131-142). Santa Barbara, CA: Libraries Unlimited.

Fister, B. (2010a). Liberating knowledge: A librarian's manifesto for change. *Thought & Action* (Fall), 83-90. Retrieved from http://www.nea.org/home/41990. htm

Fister, B. (2010b, April 2). Liberation bibliography: Trumping ownership with access: a manifesto. *Library Journal.* Retrieved from: http://www.libraryjournal. com/article/CA6723666.html

Freire, P. (1970). *Pedagogy of the oppressed.* (M. B. Ramos, Trans.). New York: Herder and Herder (Original work published 1968).

Gage, R. (2004). Henry Giroux's *Abandoned Generation* & critical librarianship: A review article. *Progressive Librarian, 23,* 65-74. Retrieved from: http://libr.org/ pl/contents23.html.

Giroux, H. A. (2005). Border crossings: Cultural workers and the politics of education. (2nd ed). New York: Routledge.

Giroux, H. A. (2010). Bare pedagogy and the scourge of neoliberalism: Rethinking higher education as a democratic public sphere. *Educational Forum, 74*(3), 184-196.

Harvey, D. (2005). *A brief history of neoliberalism.* New York: Oxford University Press.

Jacobs, H. L. M. (2008). Information literacy and reflective pedagogical praxis. *The Journal of Academic Librarianship, 34*(3), 256-262.

Jacobs, H. L. M., & Berg, S. (2011). Reconnecting information literacy policy with the core values of librarianship. *Library Trends, 60*(2), 383-394.

Klein, N. (2004). Librarianship as a radical profession. *Progressive Librarian, 23,* 46-54.

Leckie, G. J., Given, L. M., & Buschman, J. E. (Eds.). (2010). *Critical theory for library and information science: Exploring the social from across the discipline.* Santa Barbara, CA: Libraries Unlimited.

Lilburn, J. (2007). Challenging the conditions that make alternatives necessary: Librarians, the news media and the information literate citizen. *Progressive Librarian, 30,* 3-17. Retrieved from http://libr.org/pl/PL30_2007_08.pdf

Luke, A., & Kapitzke, C. (1999). Literacies and libraries: Archives and cybraries. *Pedagogy, Culture & Society, 7*(3), 467-491.

Noble, D. (2000). Digital diploma mills: Rehearsal for the revolution. In J. L. Turk (Ed.), *The corporate campus: Commercialization and the dangers to Canada's colleges and universities.* Toronto, ON: Lorimer.

Pawley, C. (2003). Information literacy: A contradictory coupling. *The Library Quarterly, 73*(4), 422-452.

Perlin, J. (2011, November 9). Occupy Scott Library. *Excalibur.* Retrieved from: http://www.excal.on.ca/news/occupy-scott-library

Samek, T. (2001). *Intellectual freedom and social responsibility in American librarianship, 1967-1974.* Jefferson, NC: McFarland.

Samek, T. (2004). Internet and intention: An infrastructure for progressive librarianship. *International Journal of Information Ethics, 2*(11), 1-18.

Shore, C. (2008). Audit culture and illiberal governance: Universities and the politics of accountability. *Anthropological Theory 8,* 278-298.

Sloniowski, L. (2012). *Solidarity is a two way street.* Ontario Library Association Superconference Presentation. Retrieved from http://researchforcitizenship. wordpress.com/2012/02/06/137

Stiglitz, J. E. (2002). *Globalization and its discontents.* New York: Norton.

Swanson, T. A. (2004). Applying a critical pedagogical perspective to information literacy standards. *Community and Junior College Libraries, 12*(4), 65-77.

Turk, J. L. (2000). *The corporate campus: Commercialization and the dangers to Canada's colleges and universities.* Toronto, ON: Lorimer.

Contributor's Biographies

Andrea Baer is an Instruction/Reference Librarian at King's College (PA), as well as an Adjunct Lecturer for the University of Tennessee-Knoxville's Master's Program in Information Sciences. Prior to entering the library world, Andrea taught literature and writing while completing a doctoral program in comparative literature at the University of Washington. Andrea received her Master's in Information Sciences from the University of Tennessee-Knoxville. Andrea can be contacted at andreapbaer@gmail.com.

Andrew Battista is an Information Literacy and Reference Librarian at the University of Montevallo, Alabama's public liberal arts university. He received a Ph.D. in English Literature from the University of Kentucky, and he earned his M.L.S from SUNY at Buffalo. His research interests include social media and citizenship, games-based learning, and writing pedagogy. He may be contacted at abattista@montevallo.edu.

Carrie Donovan is Head of Teaching & Learning for the Indiana University Libraries, where she works with students, faculty, and instructors to connect the Libraries to student learning. With 12 years of experience providing information literacy instruction to a diverse university community, Carrie is committed to ensuring the relevance of libraries and librarians through educational initiatives and teaching partnerships. Her research areas of interest include the review and reward of librarians' teaching, active learning for library instruction, and critical information literacy.

Dave Ellenwood joined the University of Washington Bothell and Cascadia Community College as the Research & Instruction / Social Sciences Librarian in August, 2011. He received graduate degrees in Library and

Information Science and African Studies from the University of Illinois at Urbana-Champaign. Dave enjoys his new home in the Puget Sound area where he is exploring and learning about the region's unique hip-hop culture and history. He may be contacted at dellenwood@uwb.edu.

Nathaniel F. Enright is a PhD student at Royal Melbourne Institute of Technology University in the School of Business IT and Logistics. You can reach him at natenright@gmail.com.

Lua Gregory received her M.L.I.S. from University of California, Los Angeles. She worked at Massachusetts College of Pharmacy and Health Sciences before moving back to her hometown of Redlands, CA. Currently she is First Year Experience Librarian at University of Redlands. Her research interests include social justice issues in librarianship and critical information literacy. She may be contacted at lua_gregory@redlands.edu

Yasmin Sokkar Harker received her J.D. from Case Western Reserve University and her M.L.I.S. from SUNY Buffalo. She worked in legal publishing for several years before moving to New York City. She is currently a Legal Reference Librarian and Associate Library Professor at the City University of New York Law School. She may be contacted at yasmin.harker@law.cuny.edu.

Shana Higgins is the Education, and Area & Interdisciplinary Studies Librarian at University of Redlands. She received her MLS and MA in Latin American & Caribbean Studies from Indiana University. Her professional interests include critical information and media literacies, the intersection of information literacy and writing pedagogy, and social justice activism in librarianship. She may be contacted at shana_higgins@redlands.edu.

Anne Leonard is an Instruction/Reference librarian at New York City College of Technology of the City University of New York in downtown Brooklyn. She received her MLS from the University of Texas at Austin and her MS in Urban Affairs from Hunter College. Her professional interests include the intersection of libraries and spatial humanities, place-based approaches to pedagogy in urban settings, and the professional status of academic librarians.

Jeff Lilburn received his M.L.I.S. from McGill University and his M.A. in English Literature from the University of Western Ontario. He is Public Services Librarian at Mount Allison University in Sackville, New Brunswick, and has published in *portal: Libraries and the Academy*, *Progressive Librarian*, and *SIMILE: Studies in Media & Information Literacy Education*. He may be contacted at jlilburn@mta.ca.

Sara O'Donnell received her MLS and MA in Religious Studies from Indiana University. She currently serves as the User Experience Reference Librarian and Webmaster at the University of Northern Colorado. Her professional interests include the philosophy of librarianship, the convergence of technology and public services, and the symbiotic relationship between librarians and cats.

Patti Ryan has been the liaison librarian for political science at York University since 2000. Her research interests focus heavily on feminist and critical pedagogy, and the socio-political dimensions of information literacy. She spends a lot of her spare time thinking about how to find time to implement good ideas. She can be reached at pryan@yorku.ca.

Maura Seale received her M.S.I. from the University of Michigan and her M.A. in American Studies from the University of Minnesota. She began her library career at Grand Valley State University and is currently a Research and Instruction Librarian/Bibliographer at Georgetown University. She welcomes comments and can be contacted at mauraseale@gmail.com.

Lisa Sloniowski received her M.I.St. from the University of Toronto in 1999. She's worked at the University of New Brunswick and the University of Windsor, and is currently the English Literature Librarian at York University. Her research interests surround feminist archives and special collections, literary archives and special collections, information literacy for citizenship and advocacy for librarians. She may be contacted at lisasl@yorku.ca.

Maura A. Smale is Associate Professor/Information Literacy Librarian at New York City College of Technology of the City University of New York in downtown Brooklyn. Her academic interests include critical information literacy, undergraduate scholarly habits, games-based learning, and open access publishing. She has a PhD in Anthropology from New York University and a MLIS from Pratt Institute. Contact Maura at msmale@citytech.cuny.edu.

Christopher Sweet is the Information Literacy Librarian at Illinois Wesleyan University in Bloomington, IL. He graduated with a B.A. from Augustana College (Rock Island, IL) and a MS degree from the Graduate Studies in Library and Information Science program at the University of Illinois (Urbana-Champaign). Christopher's background includes a wide range of experience in archives, public libraries and community colleges. His current research interests include information literacy pedagogy, the impact of new media on information, and service learning. He is also active in campus and community environmental causes. Chris may be contacted at csweet@iwu.edu.

Amanda "Mandy" Swygart-Hobaugh is currently the Librarian for Sociology, Anthropology, and Gerontology at Georgia State University but worked previously at Cornell College and University of Kansas. She hails from Indiana, where she earned her M.L.S. from Indiana University and her Ph.D. in Sociology from Purdue University. She may be contacted at aswygarthobaugh@gsu.edu.

Index

Y

CPSIA information can be obtained at www.ICGtesting.com
Printed in the USA
BVOW02s1832030216

435381BV00004B/105/P